ESTUARY

ESTUARY

Out from London to the Sea

Rachel Lichtenstein

HAMISH HAMILTON
an imprint of
PENGUIN BOOKS

HAMISH HAMILTON

UK | USA | Canada | Ireland | Australia
India | New Zealand | South Africa

Hamish Hamilton is part of the Penguin Random House group of companies
whose addresses can be found at global.penguinrandomhouse.com.

First published 2016
001

Copyright © Rachel Lichtenstein, 2016

The moral right of the author has been asserted

The photograph acknowledgements on pages 323–4 constitute an extension
of this copyright page. Every effort has been made to trace copyright holders and to
obtain their permission for the use of copyright material. The publisher apologizes for
any errors or omissions and would be grateful to be notified of any corrections
that should be incorporated in future editions of this book

Set in 12.25/15 pt Fournier MT Std
Typeset by Jouve (UK), Milton Keynes
Printed in Great Britain by Clays Ltd, St Ives plc

A CIP catalogue record for this book is available from the British Library

ISBN: 978–0–241–14288–2

This book is dedicated to John Dickens (1945–2016)

The fishermen I came into contact with at Leigh were old men with no scholarship. They told me of their thoughts; the things they said within themselves as they sailed with the stars and with the wild waters about and beneath them. For sheer poetry I have never heard more beautiful things than fell from the lips of those unlettered men.

— Nineteenth-century Methodist minister of Leigh

CONTENTS

PART III
THE OUTER REACHES

INTRODUCTION

On the night of the summer solstice 2011, I made my way to Hermitage Moorings, just east of London's Tower Bridge. There were about a dozen vessels in the harbour when I arrived, tugs and Thames barges mainly, which had all been lovingly restored by a community of passionate enthusiasts. The historic boats made an impressive sight with the dark, wooden masts of the barges and their folded, heavy red sails silhouetted against the great royal palace behind.

I found *Ideeal* moored alongside an immaculately refurbished Thames sailing barge which now served as a permanent residence for a young couple and their dog. Skipping over the artfully arranged nets and ropes on the deck of the sailing boat, I hopped on to the fifty-ton Dutch barge. It had originally been built in the 1920s as a working barge to carry freight and has since been converted into a live/work studio by owner Ben Eastop although it remains a seaworthy vessel.

As the light slowly faded on the longest day of the year, I sat on deck with the rest of the crew, drinking bottled beers, sharing stories and watching the cityscape transform. By dusk, a low mist had begun to obscure most of the buildings. The iconic dome of St Paul's temporarily disappeared before re-emerging, floodlit, against the London skyline. Red-flashing beacons began to appear sporadically through the fog, marking the tops of tall cranes and skyscrapers. The skeletal frame of the Shard came suddenly into focus as every floor lit up simultaneously. At the same time, the beautiful Gothic structure of Tower Bridge behind us was illuminated from above and below, throwing a sparkling reflection into the black waters of the Lower Pool of London – a place where so many of the world's most important ships have anchored at different points in time. As night fell, the lights inside all the flats, hotels and offices along the riverside came on. We floated in the dark void of the river, suspended in time.

On the water, the sounds of the city seemed altered. I could hear the distant hum of traffic on the bridge, the clatter of trains rumbling past, the intermittent backdrop of sirens wailing, but it was as if these sounds were coming from another place altogether, not from the great, throbbing metropolis around me. I sat and watched the vast twin bascules of Tower Bridge being raised little by little. When they were fully open a Thames barge sailed silently past and drifted beneath the bridge before quickly disappearing into the shadows on the other side. On the remains of a wooden jetty nearby, I could just make out the shape of a large, black cormorant standing perfectly still, its huge wings outstretched.

The temperature dropped. The rest of the crew went below deck. I sat up top for a while longer, transfixed by the patterns in the dark water, before realizing we were moored somewhere near to where Irongate Stairs used to be – the place where my Polish-Jewish grandparents would have disembarked nearly a century ago after a long, harrowing journey by sea. Their boat, packed full of Yiddish-speaking migrants, would have anchored offshore. Passengers would then have been transferred from the ship by rowing boat to the shore before making their way up the stairs and into the backstreets of Whitechapel and elsewhere to a new life. I remember the legendary East London Jewish playwright Bernard Kops telling me that, when his parents arrived from Eastern Europe by boat, they saw the open arms of the bridge 'as a mother welcoming [them] home'.

There is another story about Jews and the river which haunts me whenever I am on the water. Further upriver, around London Bridge, is the site of a terrible legend from the time of the Plague. Back then, people hired skippers to take them out of the City to avoid contagion.

One time, a group of Jews was rowed out to a sandbank, where London Bridge was later to stand. The skipper demanded extra money to take them to the other side, which they did not have, so he left them there and they all drowned. The white water that swirls around this sandbank is said to be caused by these lost Jewish souls kicking up in torment.

By the time the night sky had grown completely dark, I had joined the others below in the former hold, which now served as the living quarters for the male members of the crew, with a small galley kitchen at one end and a large wooden table and chairs in the centre of the open-plan space. Ben asked us to gather around the table to examine a nautical chart of the Thames Estuary. We spent the next hour or so

deliberating over the definition of 'the Thames Estuary'; all we could agree on was that it encompasses the stretch of water between the River Thames and the North Sea. Defining its outer and inner limits seemed almost impossible; as we talked, the imaginary boundary lines shifted constantly throughout our discussion.

The Greater Thames Estuary encompasses an enormous area, covering over eight hundred nautical square miles, and is roughly defined as a zone that starts around Tower Bridge and stretches all the way up to Clacton in Essex and down to Whitstable in Kent, and includes multiple creeks, islands and tributaries. However, we were focusing on the Thames Estuary itself, and we argued for some time about where the royal river ended and the Estuary began. I told the group I had been looking at eighteenth- and nineteenth-century Admiralty charts in the British Library map room: beautiful, hand-drawn documents covered in a mystifying array of complex lines. They were difficult to decipher, but at the top of a chart dated 1871 the Thames Estuary was described as being '18 nautical miles long from Gravesend to the Nore'. Some members of the crew thought it was much longer than this, starting as far upriver as Tower Bridge (the Victorian control centre of the Estuary), but most agreed that the historic gateway into the Thames was the shipping port of Gravesend, which sits at Lower Hope, the narrowest point in the river, a place of strong tidal currents, where the brackish, dirty water from London merges with the saltwater from the North Sea.

If Gravesend is the beginning of the Outer Estuary, the end reaches much further out into the North Sea: a hydrological survey dated 1882 shows the boundary line of the Outer Estuary going across from North Foreland, near Margate, to the Kentish Knock Lighthouse in Harwich, and our contemporary chart showed the outer limits of the Estuary extending even further, all the way up to Orford Ness on the Suffolk coast.

The boundary line for the end of the Inner Estuary is generally believed to be somewhere around the forbidden military zone of

Foulness Island, which sits opposite the site where the Nore lightship once stood. The starting point for the Inner Estuary was thought to be near the head of Sea Reach, south of Canvey Island, although I felt it could originate as far along the Essex coast as the Crow Stone, which sits just off the foreshore of Chalkwell Beach. This antique obelisk is one of two boundary stones situated on the opposite sides of the Essex and Kent foreshores to mark the end of the City of London's jurisdiction over the Thames. The first marker stone was placed on the Essex shore in 1197 and was referred to in official records as the City Stone of Leigh. The base of this medieval stone may still rest under the mud, but the original has long since disappeared. The monument that exists there today is made of granite and looks similar in shape to Cleopatra's Needle on the Embankment. It was erected in 1836, but an older version from 1755 sits amongst the rose beds in Priory Park in Southend. This stone replaced a much older stone, which was lost to the tides centuries ago.

You can walk out to the Crow Stone easily when the tide goes out. Inscribed on the north, east and west faces are the names of the lord mayors of London, who used to visit every seven years for the water pageants that once took place around this local landmark. In Southend library, I had read eighteenth-century descriptions of these ceremonies, which told of great processions from London by steamboat, with the lord mayor being accompanied by water bailiffs, sheriffs and aldermen of the City. The ceremonies were performed to large crowds of people and would begin with the City sword being placed against the stone, 'an act which signified the official maintenance of the claim of the City of London of the jurisdiction of the Thames at this limit mark'. At high tide, City officials would row around the Crow Stone three times before drinking to the toast 'God Preserve the City of London.' At low tide, entertainment was provided for the spectators, with the local sheriff being 'respectfully bumped' against the stone by watermen, after which he would obtain the Freedom of the Water.

THE CROWSTONE AT SUNSET, WESTCLIFF-ON-SEA.

The proceedings would continue with a large amount of drinking and merriment, followed by 'a scramble in the mud for coins'. The same ceremony would then be repeated on the other side of the river, at the London Stone, which sits directly opposite the Crow Stone at the entrance to Yantlet Creek on the Isle of Grain. The imaginary line between the two stones is called the Yantlet Line and denotes the final end of the seaward limit of the Thames. As a child, I was told that the Yantlet Line is the place where London ends and Essex begins.

The London Stone has recently become a pilgrimage site for a number of artists and writers, who have risked their lives to touch it at low tide. I first met Ben Eastop when he attended a talk I was hosting with the writer Iain Sinclair in the former drawing room of the old manor house of Chalkwell Hall, which overlooks the Thames Estuary in Essex. During this event, Iain spoke about his recent explorations around the marshland territory off the north Kent coast, during which he crossed to the London Stone on a swan pedalo with the artist Andrew Kötting:

In *Ghost Milk*, a book I wrote as a charm against monolithic Olympic enclosures in the Lower Lea Valley, I decided that I needed to actually touch the London Stone, as a physical marker for the start of the tidal Thames. I was going to walk the river, from mouth to source, as a way of taking the temperature of the softest part of Middle England. But you can't reach it! The Stone is on unmapped military land. I spent four days trying to get in and being turned back by razor wire and the wives of policemen. I finally managed it with the photographer Stephen Gill. We carried a kayak to the mouth of the Yantlet Creek. But we didn't need it, the tide was out. We walked across.

After Iain's event, Ben approached me and asked if I would be willing to be writer-in-residence for a multidisciplinary arts project he was organizing, the focus of which was responding to place. The idea was to take a five-day experiential cruise on *Ideeal* along the Thames Estuary with a mixed crew of visual artists, an archaeologist of the recent past, a musician, a filmmaker, a writer and an ornithologist. The journey would be deliberately slow-paced, a direct and immersive experience of the ancient waterway. We would amble downriver, drift on the tides, meditate on the unique seascape of that place.

The idea appealed to me immediately, as the Estuary and the mudflats of the Thames were the landscapes of my childhood. I grew up in Southend-on-Sea and spent my school holidays paddling, swimming and playing in the Estuary waters. When the tide went out I walked on the mud for miles, catching crabs and shrimp in the little pools of water left behind by the receding sea. I knew the dangers of the incoming tide and also something of the military history of the place, having visited the remnants of crumbling forts along the coastline. I had heard the stories of the ship filled with bombs sitting on the riverbed, but before my trip on *Ideeal* I had never spent any time on the water itself. Most Estuary dwellers haven't either. For the majority of people who live in the many towns and communities dotted along the Essex and Kent coastlines, the Estuary is little more than a much-loved scenic backdrop to their lives. It remains, for most, an unknown landscape, as it once had been for me.

After fifteen years living in East London, never more than a mile away from the river, I returned to live in my hometown of Leigh-on-Sea. Walking beside the Estuary became a form of daily meditation for me, a way of freeing my thoughts before returning to my desk to write. Even though I was writing about urban histories at the time, I became increasingly curious about the landscape I found myself living and walking through. I started to explore the stories of the place through a series of *Salon* events I hosted for arts organization Metal at Chalkwell Hall, to which I invited writers I knew to speak about their relationships to and investigations into this place. Iain came and spoke about the London Stone, Robert Macfarlane talked about his documentary *The Wild Places of Essex*, Ken Worpole read from his extraordinary book and walking project, *350 Miles: An Essex Journey*. These events were inspired by the informal evenings my Polish-Jewish grandparents once held in the front room of their house on the nearby Chalkwell Hall Estate with the Yiddish poets, writers and artists of the former Jewish East End. The discussions that ensued from the *Salons* started to inform how I was thinking about the place I was living in. When Ben approached me that evening, I accepted his offer without hesitation, intrigued to see what would happen to my perspective on and understanding of this landscape by physically being on the water.

It was late on that first night when we had finished with the nautical charts. I finally settled into my cabin in the stern, which I was sharing with the only other woman on the crew, the archaeologist Sefryn Penrose. I lay awake, feeling the weight of *Ideeal* in the dark water, listening attentively to the creak of old wood and the sound of water lapping against the hull whilst inhaling the strange odours inside: a mix of paraffin, rope, wood and dust. I had never slept on a boat before and, in truth, I was a little nervous about the journey ahead.

Eventually, I must have fallen asleep, as the vibration of the diesel engine above woke me at 6 a.m. Crawling out of my bed, I made my way into the former cargo hold next door. Abandoned sleeping bags and mattresses lay scattered on the floor; the rest of the crew were up already. I helped myself to the remains of the still-warm coffee in the pot and sat for a while in the belly of the boat, thinking about the merchandise that once filled that space: potash, tea, spices, bricks, hay – anything that needed moving from one place to another. Ben had told me that, when the vessel was used as a privately owned taxi service for shifting goods around the Dutch canals, the great, curved, solid-steel beams above me could be removed so that large loads could be thrown into the hold.

Tentatively, I climbed the almost-vertical wooden ladder up on to the deck. The sun was shining brightly and London looked magnificent. Ben was standing in the wheelhouse next to the musician John Eacott, the most experienced sailor on the crew. Everybody was in good spirits, and we were ready to begin our first day cruising along the Estuary: the start of what would become for me a deep exploration of that place.

PART I

Outbound

I

Ideeal

Forthwith a change came over the waters, and the serenity
became less brilliant but more profound. The old river in its broad
reach rested unruffled at the decline of day, after ages of good
service done to the race that peopled its banks, spread out in the
tranquil dignity of a waterway leading to the uttermost ends of
the earth . . . The tidal current runs to and fro in its unceasing
service, crowded with memories of men and ships it has borne to
the rest of home or to the battles of the sea.

        — *Heart of Darkness*, Joseph Conrad, 1899

After receiving permission from the Port of London Authority
(PLA) to depart, we left Hermitage Moorings and headed out towards
Queenborough. Ben skilfully steered the barge over to the starboard
side of the fast-flowing Thames, following the yellow steel navigation
buoys marking our passage downriver. The hull started to sway in
the water. The sense of movement was exhilarating – our journey
had begun.

As we turned away from the city, the river widened almost immediately. I sat on deck at the stern, next to Sefryn, and watched Tower
Bridge recede into the distance. We chugged slowly past hotels, modern flats and rows of nineteenth-century warehouses, since regenerated
into expensive riverside apartment blocks. Not a single building was
unoccupied, but they all looked empty.

As the river swept down towards the Royal Docks, we travelled through some of the oldest areas of the city, whose riverside had once been the core of the working Thames. Wharves and ports lined the river on both sides from the Tower to the docks until the 1960s, when the area became abandoned. Over forty thousand people had been employed at these docksides: bargemen and lightermen, porters, fishermen, boat-builders, sailors and stevedores. The place was once so congested with boats you could walk across them from one side of the river to the other.

The only other traffic we saw on that stretch of the river on our journey out of London were a few Thames clippers ferrying commuters up West. Most of the passengers were sitting inside reading newspapers; some stood at the back of the boats, folded jackets across their arms, enjoying the morning sun.

Ben called me over to the wheelhouse as we passed the Prospect of Whitby, one of many riverside pubs along the route, and asked me to keep a sharp eye out for drifting rubbish, which might clog up the propeller of the barge. I shifted focus and leant over the side of the boat, watching the swirling water beneath us, which was so dark it looked almost black. I thought about all the fragmentary traces flowing past, the particles of lost landscapes and other remnants from the city. Sefryn later wrote in depth about the obscured matter suspended beneath the boat, in an archaeological paper, 'The Charter'd Thames' (2013), where she describes how each entry in the Thames index has morphed into another form, visible or invisible, embedded or floating, material or remembered, then concluded that change was the only constant part of the continuous ebb and flow, past into present into past.

At Cuckold's Point, the river curved. Around the bend, I looked up to see the gleaming cityscape of the Docklands and Canary Wharf. Amongst the densely gathered skyscrapers and office blocks, it was impossible to identify any visible trace of the industry and crowded life of the docks that were formerly there. We sailed near to the

location on the foreshore where pirates were once hung on chains opposite Greenwich Hospital.

The river continued to twist and turn as we approached the loop of the Greenwich Peninsula, past empty loading sheds, luxury riverside apartments, hotels and leisure facilities. Large cranes stood on the water's edge at Deptford, pile-driving foundations directly into the water. There was evidence all along the route out of London of former industrial sites being demolished and replaced by new residential developments.

Just to the west of the prime meridian, the three tall masts of the *Cutty Sark* came into view. The famous nineteenth-century tea clipper, which has circumnavigated the globe four times, now sits suspended above a dry dock at Greenwich Pier. Beside her, on the former site of the fifteenth-century Palace of Placentia, sits the old Royal Naval College, Sir Christopher Wren's twin-domed masterpiece, and next to it the National Maritime Museum, with the Royal

Observatory beyond. This is one of the longest-occupied sites along the Thames, and the archives in the museum's library contain the most extensive repository of maritime history in the world, with charts, maps, manuscripts and books dating back to the fifteenth century.

We drifted over the centre point for world time – the dividing line between the eastern and western hemispheres of the Earth – then headed into Blackwall Reach, floating over road tunnels beneath. Ben with judgement turned the long, flat-bottomed barge around the tight bend near the O2. He explained that it was difficult to anticipate how the river is going to curve from the position of being on the water: 'Everything is flattened out on to the horizon. You are trying to see all the time where the course is going, and you need to make sure you have a good line.'

At Blackwall Point, he contacted London Vessel Traffic Services (VTS) on channel 14 on the VHF radio to let the coastguard know

we would soon be passing through the Thames Barrier. They responded by allocating an available span for navigation, indicated by green arrows and red crosses on the piers.

As we sailed past the O2 on the south bank and into Bugsby's Reach, the river widened again. We had moved beyond the city into an area now known as the Thames Gateway. The project became part of a government initiative of urban renewal and regeneration during the Blair ministry, and since then gigantic housing developments have been built on an immense stretch of marshland, as well as on former brownfield and industrial sites.

We moved through Silvertown; industrial chimneys, factories and cranes were still evident at Peruvian, Manhattan and Mohawk wharves. We passed the first of many power stations, a monstrous, grey, hulking structure next to a cement factory. A big ship from Cardiff moored alongside was spewing powdered cement into a large mound beside the dock. Large cranes lifted aggregate and sand into open-topped barges nearby. Another steel barge, piled high with rubbish, was being dragged upriver by two tugs. One of the tugs gave a long blast on her horn as she sped past. A lone Dutch sailing yacht on the other side of the river was the only other pleasure boat we encountered on our journey out to the estuary.

We stopped just north of Woolwich and waited for the radio signal that would allow us to navigate through the barrier. There was a pause whilst Ben awaited the correct instructions from London VTS, then we started to motor slowly through.

The view from the deck of *Ideeal* as we approached the Thames Barrier was spectacular. Sunlight bounced off the mirrored, sculptural sides of the shell-shaped piers, creating blinding, white reflections in the water. Dark shadows covered the deck of the barge as we moved through the span. On the river floor beneath lie ten gigantic hollow steel gates, which can be transformed when needed within an hour into one continuous steel wall stretching over 1,700 feet from one side of the river to the other. The complex mechanics of the barrier were mostly hidden inside the piers when we motored through, although the vast, yellow arms which lift the great steel gates from the depths below were just visible, curled up into the metal shells like the legs of giant hermit crabs.

As we passed through the barrier and out the other side there was a sense that the royal river had ended and we were moving into a different zone, into a wilder place of less predictable waters and stronger currents – into the cusp of the Thames Estuary. If a catastrophic tidal surge from the North Sea ever does take place, the low-lying coastlines from Clacton to Woolwich would be completely submerged. There are no man-made defences on the scale of the barrier to protect that land.

Moving up through Woolwich Reach, we passed a large freighter moored alongside the Tate and Lyle sugar refinery, which was probably either collecting or dropping off sugar products. Countless shipments of sugar and molasses have travelled upriver from colonies

in the Caribbean and beyond since the seventeenth century, when a multimillion-pound industry, built on the back of slavery, was established in Britain. Multiple syrup- and sugar-refining factories were built in Silvertown. The Tate and Lyle refinery is the only one left, and it still dominates the riverside there, although now greatly reduced in size from its former spread across a fifty-acre site.

We floated past the artificial peninsula of 'sugar mile' and a field of satellite dishes with high-rise flats beyond. The river narrowed again for a while as we neared the Woolwich ferry terminal. Ben slowed the boat down as we approached. The throbbing sound of the engine temporarily subsided as we waited for the double-ended ferry loaded with cars, trucks and lorries to depart. As the boat left the quayside, the sky became suddenly grey and overcast, and a light mist began to drift in from the sea. The water darkened again. I put on a waterproof coat, moved further into the wheelhouse and watched the diesel-powered boat move effortlessly across the strong tidal currents, reaching the north bank in less than five minutes.

As we cruised along Gallions Reach, on our port side we passed the Royal Docks, which were constructed in the nineteenth-century as a deep-water harbour for large vessels unable to travel further upriver to unload. The great, empty body of water shone like a black mirror as we drifted past. A large shadow flitted across the deck of the boat as a jet plane flew low overhead before landing on the airstrip of City Airport, which is situated on the quay between Royal Albert Dock and King George V Dock.

Further downriver, towards Barking, the buildings on the riverside became increasingly low-rise and residential. We saw the first bit of undeveloped land on our south side. We were moving out of London, into a different territory, towards the marsh country and a less-known landscape.

The water became choppier, more tidal. I left the wheelhouse and made my way gingerly towards the bow of the boat, shuffling along the side deck, holding on tightly to the grab rail around the edge of

the barge. I found crew member Simon Callery crouched down next to the anchor winch, grinning broadly, camera against one eye. Simon told me he feels transformed when he is near large bodies of water. His bright blue eyes flashed as he spoke. We sat together either side of the anchor, trying to avoid the spray coming over the foredeck.

We sailed past a former Roman burial ground towards the eastern limit of the Barrier Control Zone. During recent archaeological excavations there, the remains of oak and yew trees were found preserved in a bog, along with Roman coins, part of a canoe and the bones of a whale. As Simon pointed out the site of the graveyard, I realized that my own gaze had constantly wandered during our journey, from the water to the coastline. I kept referring back to the land, looking for recognizable landmarks. The river was almost devoid of them.

'The river doesn't have names for me,' said Simon. 'It only has changing weather.'

The landscape around Ware Point looked desolate, a mix of unpopulated marsh and abandoned industrial sites. Two steel cargo boats filled with scrap metal were tied up to a buoy. We passed a new riverside development at Beckton, on the edges of London, before coasting past the sewage works there. I thought about my trip underground with Thames Water a few years earlier, walking beneath the city through the perfectly intact subterranean Victorian landscape of Bazalgette's sewers, searching for the remains of the lost River Fleet. Thames Water's chief sewer flusher Rob Smith had told me then that most of London's sewage is still transported in a gigantic pipe to the Northern Outfall at Beckton, although now it is treated. When the system was first built, raw sewage from the city was pumped directly into the river at the Northern Outfall, which is thought to be the reason why so many died in 1878 when paddle steamer SS *Princess Alice* collided with a collier and sank near Woolwich Pier. Over six hundred and fifty people were killed in this disaster, the worst-ever loss of life recorded on the River Thames. Many passengers were trapped within the wreck, but the majority suffocated in the toxic and heavily polluted water after falling in the river there.

I stayed with Simon, sitting at the front of the boat, as the afternoon wore on. The sun was shining brightly as we passed London's lesser-known tidal barrier at Barking Creek, three miles downstream of the Thames Barrier. This massive concrete gateway acts as a weir, sealing off water levels travelling upstream. Fleets of fishing boats used to moor up in the creek there after depositing their catches in a Victorian icehouse, before they were transported upriver to Billingsgate Market. On the western edge of the creek sat cranes, pylons and a large gasworks. The tide was running strongly. We started to move faster downriver, increasing our rate of knots from five to seven by the time we reached Dagenham and the Ford Motor Works site.

Opposite the factory on the south bank sat the grazing marshes, criss-crossed by tidal ditches, of Erith – the last of the earliest pastures which once bordered the Thames on both sides throughout London, places where wild horses roamed and travellers gathered around campfires and caravans, the marsh resounding with their song.

As we moved into Erith Reach, we saw the beginnings of the Rainham Marshes along the north bank of the river. This former MOD land was transformed into a nature reserve after the Royal Society for the Protection of Birds (RSPB) acquired the site over a decade ago. I had first been alerted to the place whilst watching Robert Macfarlane's astonishing nature programme *The Wild Places of Essex*, during which he strolls across the marsh, marvelling at the ways in which wildness has returned to the dead landscape. Peregrines roost in abandoned cranes, and marsh frogs, reed warblers and endangered water voles live in the creeks, in groundwater once rancid with chemicals.

Historically, the south Essex coastline was London's rubbish tip for centuries. From Rainham Marshes to Two Tree Island near Leigh-on-Sea, there was a corridor of landfill sites, including Thameside, Wat Tyler and Pitsea, all of which in recent years have been transformed into verdant green parks and wildlife reserves, despite the polluted and often toxic ground beneath.

Turning into the straight section of the river at Long Reach, sewage works, power stations, cranes, logistic parks, container terminals and factories litter the riverside all the way from Purfleet to Dartford. I thought about the past lives of this place, which is now so heavily industrial yet was once wild, and the stories I had come across in various archives about these landscapes before taking this journey, such as the discovery by an amateur fossil collector in 1964 of some large bones in a clay pit in Aveley, near Purfleet. The Natural History Museum began excavations there soon afterwards and uncovered the perfectly preserved body of a mammoth in a seam of peat, on top of a straight-tusked elephant. Thirty years later, during road-building works for the A13, the same sediments were exposed and the bones of a jungle cat and a large lion were revealed, resting there from the time when enormous grassy plains once covered the Essex marshes and herds of wild animals grazed there, next to the fast-flowing river.

As we passed beneath the great span of the Queen Elizabeth II Bridge, the only fixed road over the river, there was a sense that another significant boundary had been crossed: the Thames had officially ended. The river widened significantly from this point onwards, and now, more than ever, I felt we were moving into the Estuary waters proper. Cars were fixed, as always, in a permanent traffic jam above. It was delightful to drift beneath, with all that space and freedom. We were the only vessel visible on the water. Soon after, the weather turned and it began to rain, gently at first, then more heavily. I spent the rest of the afternoon down in the hold with Simon, studying the nautical charts, examining the fantastical place names of the river – Black Deep, Gallions Reach, East Cant, Nore Swatch – trying to locate where we were on this huge expanse of water we were moving into.

A couple of hours later, Ben called down to ask Simon for assistance, as he was one of the most nimble and experienced members of the crew. We had reached Sheerness, on the Kent coast, where we would moor for the night beside a local-authority concrete pontoon anchored off the historic harbour town of Queenborough. It took a couple of attempts to get the barge through an avenue of yachts and safely tied up alongside the improbable floating structure, which was rough and pitted with utilitarian galvanized fencing. On the first attempt, a stiff breeze took the bow away from the mooring and we couldn't get close enough for Simon to jump off and tie up. Ben had to reverse out and do the whole manoeuvre again. Mud swirled up under the stern as the riveted steel boat displaced water around us. On the second attempt, Ben managed to steer the boat successfully alongside, much to the amusement of the harbour master, who had been watching us the whole time and who told Ben on the radio how much he had enjoyed the show. Although the Estuary might appear deserted, we were constantly monitored throughout our trip.

Dusk had fallen by the time *Ideeal* was safely moored up. The rain stopped for a while, and the whole crew sat briefly out on deck, drinking beer and listening to the waves gently lapping against the hull and the birdsong all around us. Ben's son Luke told us that the distinctive shrill, piping, repetitive call we could hear was the sound of oyster-catchers in the nearby marshes. The water in the harbour was clear and bright, slate green, different from the yellow upriver. Soon, night fell, and most of the crew went down below to start supper. I stayed for a while longer up on deck with James, talking about the collaborative film we were planning to make of our journey. The estuarine landscape gradually disappeared into the dark around us. Lights from the distant seafront of Southend opposite glittered dimly across the black river.

2

Mirror of the Sea

The sea-reach of the Thames is straight, and, once Sheerness is left behind, its banks seem very uninhabited, except for the cluster of houses which is Southend, or here and there a lonely wooden jetty where petroleum ships discharge their dangerous cargoes, and the oil-storage tanks, low and round with slightly-domed roofs, peep over the edge of the fore-shore, as it were a village of Central African huts imitated in iron. Bordered by the black and shining mud-flats, the level marsh extends for miles. Away in the far background the land rises, closing the view with a continuous wooded slope, forming in the distance an interminable rampart overgrown with bushes.

– *The Mirror of the Sea*, Joseph Conrad, 1906

We rose early the next morning to catch the tide and were underway before 8 a.m. The weather was changeable, spitting lightly in the early morning then stopping for a while; the sky was a blanket of grey clouds. I sat out on deck at the stern with Sefryn and James. Having left the mooring at Queenborough, we soon reached the mouth of the Medway and passed Garrison Point on our starboard side. A derelict semicircular Victorian fort with a radar tower on the roof sits above the busy commercial port of Sheerness Docks. Orange cranes lift multicoloured, rectangular containers off great tankers into the water. In front of them, a line of tugs was moored against the quayside.

On a spit guarding the river mouth sit the remnants of a Napoleonic battery tower. Behind us was the now defunct Isle of Grain power station, which once generated electricity from oil for much of Kent. From across the water in Southend, the giant smoke stack has dominated the horizon since the 1970s, with the grey-blue hills of Kent behind. Known locally as the 'upturned cigarette', probably because of the huge puff of smoke that was once a permanent feature above the chimney, the power station is for the most part a much-loved landmark. It changes colour constantly, depending on the light, from china blue to deep purple to black-grey, and features in thousands of local photographs and paintings. But most people have been unaware of the dangerous levels of toxic waste which have been emitting from the chimney and into the atmosphere for decades. Like much of the heavy industry along the Estuary coastline, the power station has recently been decommissioned, as the level of pollutants it releases is deemed unacceptable under EU law. It will soon be demolished.

Ben nervously manoeuvred his eighty-foot-long Dutch barge across shallow waters, away from Sea Reach buoy no. 1, which bobs around in the water, marking the site of a treacherous sandbank called the Nore: a place, Joseph Conrad wrote, that could 'conjure visions of historical events, of battles, of fleets, of mutinies'. The sandbank has been a major hazard for shipping for centuries – a wooden light-ship powered by sperm-whale oil was located there in the eighteenth century to warn vessels to steer clear of this dangerous area – but it was also an important anchorage and assembly point for ships coming into London. But of all its guises, the Nore is best known now as the resting place for the 'ship full of bombs'.

The SS *Montgomery*, one of the most hazardous wrecks in British waters, lies half buried in the shifting sands of the Nore. This American Liberty ship ran aground there on 20 August 1944, loaded with nearly seven thousand tons of bombs and explosives. The crew was rescued and, during the following few days, most of the volatile cargo on board was removed; but on the fifth day, the *Montgomery* broke her back on the sandbank and later that night sank in a storm, still loaded with unexploded bombs. Dubbed the 'Doomsday Ship' by locals, the *Montgomery* is a broken, waterlogged, ticking timebomb.

A number of warning buoys mark the edges of the 1,600-foot exclusion zone around the wreck, which is monitored day and night by the Port of London Authority. Shipping routes have been diverted around the submerged boat for seventy-odd years now, and pilots approaching Sheerness from the North Sea know to look out for the ominous sign of the ship's three masts above the waterline, as if warning of the dangerous presence below.

As Ben cautiously moved the barge away from the Nore into deeper channels, I looked through my binoculars, searching for the masts, before turning around to study the coastline of Grain. Apart from the petrochemical tanks and other industrial structures on the shoreline near the Medway, the only other buildings were some wooden chalets in the nearby All Hallows caravan park. I had never been this close to

the Hoo Peninsula before, even though I had looked across throughout my life at this rural landscape, which is situated just a few miles away as the crow flies from my hometown. Compared to the built-up shoreline of Southend, it looks like a different country – remote, wild and almost completely uninhabited.

Once we cleared the Nore and moved further out into the Estuary, we picked up speed. There was good visibility across the main shipping channel and not another vessel in sight. Big, ominous, dark-grey clouds arced above. The water, which looked like sheet metal from a distance, broke up into different planes of colour as we sailed towards Sea Reach; dirty jade-green, slate brown, pearlescent white, cadmium yellow.

We edged out across the wide-open sea on a north-west course towards Southend Pier, where we hoped to moor for the night. As we crossed the choppy waters, the bow hit the waves continually, dipping up and down throughout the hour-long journey. Ben stood in the wheelhouse the whole time, paying close attention to the Medway VHS radio channel, listening out for any big ships or tankers coming upriver. The radio buzzed with traffic coming in and out of the river, voices talking boat to boat, shore to shore. Our barge lacked speed and manoeuvrability, and the biggest container ships can travel at twenty-five knots; we moved across the main shipping channel of Middle Deep as quickly as possible. As we crossed, I scanned the waters again. Two container ships, loaded high, were coming in from the east, some distance behind us, making their way upriver.

Far out in the North Sea, faintly visible architectural structures punctuated the horizon: the elegant white masts and sails of an offshore wind farm and the tiny, mushroom-shaped silhouettes of the Red Sands Sea Forts, one of three sets of army forts erected at strategic points in the Estuary during the Second World War to guard against submarines, sea mines and possible invasion. The others were Shivering Sands Forts (still standing) and Nore Forts (destroyed). These defensive buildings on stilts were abandoned by the military in the 1950s and used as a base for pirate radio stations in the 1960s, but most have been empty since, although some have had periods of human habitation. The designer of these forts, Guy Maunsell, also designed a series of heavily armed naval forts in the Estuary to deter and report on German air raids. There were four naval forts: at Rough Sands, Sunk Head, Tongue Sands and Knock John.

As we moved towards Southend, I noticed the great black hulk known locally as Mulberry Harbour emerging out of the sea off the Maplin Sands. Built in the dockyards of Chatham, then towed upriver, destined for Normandy, this gigantic concrete caisson would have formed part of a vast floating deep-sea port for the D-Day landings, but it snapped away from the tug, crashing on to the mudflats below and breaking in two. It has remained there ever since, a seaweed-encrusted war relic.

The wreck is a well-known local landmark and a magnet for mud

walkers, who make a beeline for the dark shape on the horizon when the tide goes out. From a distance, it looks like an upturned boat. Southend coastguards constantly patrol the area, calling out to people through loudhailers, warning them to start walking ashore when the tide starts to turn.

As the boat moved nearer to the Essex coastline, the low-lying shore of Southend seafront came into view, underlined by a strip of deep-ochre sand running the length of the seven-mile-long promenade. Rising up behind the beaches, there is a mass of buildings – tower blocks, houses, pubs and amusement parks – broken up on occasion by patches of green on the gently sloping hills of Leigh and Westcliff.

From the water, I could clearly see Southend's most iconic landmark, the Victorian domed tower of the Kursaal, which is renowned for being the world's first-ever theme park and the place where female lion-tamers once performed. The Kursaal is also an important site in my own family history: my parents first met there in the mid-1960s, at a dance in the main ballroom. Today, the site has reduced dramatically in size and, despite attempts at renovating the complex, most of the building remains empty. Even the McDonald's next door has closed down for lack of business. A neon-lit bowling alley and some arcade games are the only remaining attractions in Southend's former palace of fun.

Moving up to the bow of the boat, I peered through my binoculars, trying to identify other familiar places from the water. I could just make out our family beach hut in Shoeburyness, the hotel next to my parents' house on the cliffs in Westcliff, the amusement park of Adventure Island and, of course, the pier, stretching more than a mile from the land out into the sea. This iron-and-wood Victorian structure is famous for being the longest pleasure pier in the world, but it was constructed as a working dock: a place for tea clippers, cargo ships and steamboats to offload, and to allow ferry passengers to disembark whether the tide was in or out.

To the far west of the pier, the tall chimneys of the decommissioned Shell Haven oil refinery rise up behind the gasworks on Canvey Island like the spires of a sunken, magical city. Clumps of green salt marsh sit out in the creeks around Leigh-on-Sea and Two Tree Island. Cockle-fishing boats bob in the water next to small sailing yachts and motorboats in the Ray. Behind fishermen's cottages dotted amongst the pubs on the beachfront, the white line of the c2c train flashed past on its way to London. I could see the ruins of Hadleigh Castle, a Norman keep built to defend this section of the Estuary from French attack, high on a ridge in the distance. My childhood memories of time spent at these places are filled with colour, noise and laughter but, seen from the water, this is a melancholy landscape of grey and purple; it looks unpeopled, abandoned, silent.

As we moved towards this familiar terrain, our navigator, the gentle musician John Eacott, joined me on deck. Sitting behind the anchor house, trying to avoid the spray coming up off the hull of the boat, he told me about his recent project, *Floodtide*, the sonification of water flow. Using a foot-long probe called an acoustic velocimeter, he mapped tidal movement in the sea, then transformed this data into a musical composition, which was performed live, on the water's edge, to the incoming tide.

We sat together, moving with the rhythm of the boat, staring at the great expanse of water and sky in front. Dark shadow clouds sped across the surface of the sea. The sun broke momentarily through and, for a few seconds, the water mirrored the soft blue tones above before quickly returning to the colour of grey clay. As the end of the pier came into focus, John made his way to the wheelhouse to assist Ben.

We anchored in shallow water some distance east of the pier head. Our skipper and John lowered the small, inflatable tender into the water then motored out towards the pier to check the mooring site. I watched them as they reached the pier head then disappeared out of sight. The barge drifted in the wind, turning on the anchor, swirling up blue-grey silt under the stern. I sat on deck with my notebook, documenting the scene around me.

After having spoken to the foreshore officer on the pier and arranged our mooring for the night, Ben and John returned by the dinghy to *Ideeal*. The water continued to ebb away beneath us. Eventually, we ran aground, temporarily, on the Oaze; time to pause and reflect between the tides. Ben and some of the others took the opportunity to have a nap. I stayed up on deck and watched the activity on the pier through my binoculars. A few people were braving the weather and taking the long walk across the boards to the end. The train rattled past every half-hour or so. I saw a group of men fishing with lines and rods. By late afternoon, waves started to creep back in over the mud. When the water was deep enough, we sailed cautiously towards the lifeboat station on the north side of the pier head. From a distance, the old steel structure seemed to weigh nothing; it was as if it were suspended on light. As we drew closer, the black ironwork of the pier legs became monstrous, the water dark with shadows.

The wind had picked up by then, and there was quite a swell. Ben manoeuvred the boat against the flow of water, with the bow pointing

towards the North Sea, then sailed alongside the spine of the pier, purposefully turning *Ideeal* eastwards, using the tide as a brake to slow down the boat, concerned all the time about crashing into the great iron legs.

With the help of a lone fisherman, we secured the barge with thick ropes to huge wooden pillars beside a platform known as the lower deck, which is situated underneath the lifeboat station at the end of the pier. Strong currents pulled the vessel around. It began to rain. Jumping off ship, we explored that extraordinary space: a dark, slippery, seaweed-covered area with rotting wooden planks encrusted with barnacles, and rusting machinery. No longer accessible to the public, the lower deck is lost under the tides repeatedly throughout the day and night. As we wandered around, picking up the shells and bones of sea creatures, examining the oysters, mussels and clams attached to the surfaces of this strange room, it felt like we were walking in a subterranean dream space.

We made our way carefully up some slimy, concrete stairs on to the upper deck and took the *Sir John Betjeman* diesel pier train to the pier head instead of taking the long, windswept walk back to the shore. 'Southend is the Pier, the Pier is Southend' runs a quote by the celebrated poet on the side of the carriage.

3

Soundings

The Thames should be like a great aquarium, in which a
certain balance of life has to be kept up. When aquaria first came
into favour such things as snails and weeds were excluded as
eyesores and injurious. But it was soon discovered that the
despised snails and weeds were absolutely necessary; an
aquarium could not be maintained in health without them, and
now the most perfect aquarium is the one in which the natural
state is most completely copied.

— *The Open Air*, Richard Jefferies, 1885

When we reached the end of the pier we took a walk along Southend
seafront, battling against strong winds, then marched up Chalkwell
Avenue and eventually arrived at the old manor house in the park
filthy and tired. I could barely stand up straight after just one night
and two days on the boat. The constant rocking movement of the
barge would stay with me for a further ten days after our trip had
ended.

The first guest to arrive was local fisherman Paul Gilson, who was
smartly dressed in suit and tie. I had contacted him after reading his
letters protesting against the dredging taking place at the time for the
new super port being built at Shell Haven in the local *Evening Echo*,
but this was the first time we had met. He shook my hand firmly, then
described himself as an author, an environmentalist, a 'killer of fish'

and a passionate advocate of the fisherman's way of life. He told me he is at least the sixth generation in his family to be a fisherman. 'This is my river,' he said, whilst eyeballing the ramshackle crew of *Ideeal* suspiciously. 'I make my living from this place and it needs more protection.'

All of us were fascinated to hear his stories about a lifetime spent working on the Estuary. He told us about navigating by the stars and the changes he had witnessed on the river. He spoke passionately about the seals, the birds and the fish, as well as the unique environment of the place itself, where he felt privileged to work.

As the rest of the guests arrived, he continued to hold court, amusing us with tales of things he had caught in his nets over the years – wheels and propellers, supermarket trolleys, pieces of railway track, cannonballs, a whole aeroplane and numerous body parts, including a human skull.

'Paul has donated many things that have been dredged up in the Thames,' said Ken Crowe, the curator of Southend Museum, who had quietly slipped into the room, along with local journalist Tom King, 'the most important being a series of seventeenth-century Spanish oil jars.'

'We once had a big Roman pot stuck in the top of the cod end,' said Paul. 'We couldn't see what it was, so we shook the net and this lovely pot whistled past, then fell to the deck and broke into a thousand pieces.' Ken visibly winced, then went on to tell us about the planned new museum of the Thames Estuary, which will be built into the cliffs overlooking the Estuary near Southend Pier. Exhibits inside will examine the story of the river from the time when the Thames was flowing further north, out towards Colchester, before

the great glaciation about half a million years ago, and include material recently dredged up by a team from Wessex Archaeology in the new deep-water channel which had been created for the London Gateway super port.

During the dredging operation, Ken told us, archaeologists recorded and examined a number of newly discovered shipwrecks, including a Tudor Thames brick barge, a nineteenth-century shrimping boat, a 1940s pleasure cruiser, a collier called the SS *Letchworth* and a prototype German bomber which was shot down in the war during an espionage mission. But the most significant find by far was that of the *London*, a seventeenth-century naval warship which accidentally exploded in the Estuary in 1665. The historic wreck HMS *London* was considered to be so important that the Port of London Authority redirected the route of the main shipping channel so as not to disturb it.

Paul turned the conversation around to one of the most contentious talking points in the area: the dredging operations. In 2005, heritage company Wessex Archaeology and the Port of London Authority began to survey the sea floor of the Thames Estuary using sophisticated scanning and 3D technologies, searching for vessels and artefacts of historical importance which might be disturbed by the dredgers used to create the deep-water channel.

The dredging was funded by DP World, the Dubai-based port operators who own the site of the new London Gateway, in part as a gesture towards conservation. But the organization had another agenda in funding this expensive procedure. There was potentially a danger that shipwrecks that have lain undisturbed for centuries could rip the deep hulls of the vessels which were to travel along the newly carved shipping channel on their way to the super port, so mapping the location and size of any wrecks on the sea floor was essential.

A heated discussion ensued on how the dredging was both partially recovering (through archaeological finds) and violently disturbing the deep history of the Thames Estuary. Paul has been a very vocal campaigner against the dredging, and told us he felt he was being criminalized by the authorities for raising questions about the environmental impact of the operation, which is one of the largest anywhere in the world.

'The fragile marine life of the river is under direct threat from this aggressive activity,' said Paul, 'which is literally landscaping the Estuary from the bottom up: 31 million cubic metres of material have already been removed from the seabed.'

From 2010 to 2013, trailer suction hopper dredgers operating in the main shipping channel of the Estuary hoovered up tons and tons of sand, sludge, gravel and other material resting on the sea floor with the long pipes that hung below them and dragged along the riverbed, sucking up everything in their path at great speed, under tremendous pressure, into funnel-shaped dispensers (hoppers) on board the dredgers. Most of this material was 'bottom-dumped' near the site of the decommissioned and partly demolished Shell Haven oil refinery on the Essex coast, where it was used to create new land for the London Gateway development. The leftover water was discharged overboard, back into the Estuary, in a spurting fountain of muddy-coloured liquid.

Environmentalists, including Paul Gilson, have been greatly concerned about the impact of this dredging on the ecology, water quality and marine life of the Thames Estuary. 'The volume of Dover sole we are catching at the moment is poor,' said Paul. 'The Estuary waters near Shell Haven are one of the most important spawning grounds in Europe for juvenile Dover sole. The Estuary is usually filled with juvenile skate as well, but they are disappearing. And the cockles on Marsh End, on the other side of the Ray, all died. There was a huge young cockle bed growing there. The herring were turning back and going out, sprats were doing the same; there were lots of things that you could not explain, and they just dismissed it. All around the coast, fishing stock levels are high, fishermen are steaming away for fear of catching too many, but in the Estuary it is going the other way. Maybe it's pollution coming out of London, but I believe it is the dredging. Effects started to happen about four years ago, we could see it – we are basically hunters. We know what's going on in the river. We alerted the authorities, but they totally ignored us. DP World claims the fish will return, but how are we to know if this will happen?'

Local fishermen were likewise concerned that age-old mussel and oyster beds would not recover from the substantial damage caused by the violent disturbance of the sea floor during the dredging. DP World compensated some of these fishermen for loss of earnings, and the dredging was monitored by 'a number of government agencies', including Europe's largest marine monitoring programme, according to the slickly produced London Gateway brochure on the environmental impact of DP World's project. It states that monitoring buoys were placed along the course of the dredge channel to feed back information in real time to marine experts who had direct links to the dredge masters. These experts could demand that work be stopped immediately if the water quality changed, though it was unclear to me from reading the brochure if this ever happened.

Others around the table that evening raised concerns that the dredging had caused land slippage along the Essex and Kent coastlines. We discussed DP World having commissioned various independent specialists to assess the 'predicted' effects of the dredging: they had conducted aerial and light-detection ranging surveys to map the surface contours of the Estuary before and after dredging, alongside bathymetric surveys by the Port of London Authority to monitor erosion and accretion in the river. From this evidence, they had concluded that the dredging would not have any significant effect on coastal erosion or accretion, yet Paul said that concerned residents in Southend had continued to notice excessive erosion of the foreshore and had raised complaints. The Environment Agency set up a working group to investigate their claims and also concluded that there was 'no observable difference in the pattern of beach evolution', but many locals, like Paul, are still largely unsatisfied. 'It's worse than we could possibly have imagined . . . Bait-diggers say there is no mud left around the Crow Stone. Toxins which have been trapped in the seabed since the Industrial Revolution have potentially been released back into the water.'

Simon Callery was sympathetic to the concerns of the locals, mentioning a similar deep-dredging project somewhere near the coast of Kent which had had to be abandoned a few years earlier when cracks that looked like those caused by earthquakes started to appear on the adjacent mainland. Yet Tom King remained unconvinced, gently attempting to undermine Paul's arguments and pointing out that no harm to fishing stocks could be proven. This line of reasoning didn't hold much water with Paul: 'The port authorities hired "academics" to do their research into the impact on fishing stocks, but the guy they are using to do their fisheries research couldn't catch a fish if he towed through Billingsgate Market before it opened!' We all laughed, but the conversation was heated. Tensions between corporate and local interests continued to wind their way through the evening until the subject changed.

We started to discuss the landscape of the Estuary as a place of interest for artists and writers. Tom King was an early pioneer in this

respect, having written a guidebook of sorts called *Thames Estuary Trail* over a decade ago, which describes his journey on foot around the Estuary coastline. During those walks he was talking to people, trying to capture the stories of the towns and villages along the coastline, but it was the extraordinary wilderness of the Hoo

Peninsula – 'England's largest nature reserve, just thirty miles from Piccadilly Circus' – which really surprised him.

Since Tom had completed his book, many of the rubbish dumps and brownfield sites that he passed through have been returned to nature, such as the brownfield site of the former Shell Haven oil refinery on the Essex coast, which has now become the Stanford Wharf Nature Reserve, created by DP World, in consultation with the Essex Wildlife Trust, to provide intertidal marshland suitable for wading birds.

After the refinery had closed in 1999, the toxic site quickly became a haven for wintering waterfowl, newts, lizards, avocets, adders, water voles and many other wild creatures. English Nature, Thurrock Friends of the Earth and the Shell Haven Project Environmental Action Committee all objected to the original proposals for the development of the new super port on this site, fearing its construction would have a significant and long-term effect on the wild creatures living there. But before DP World built on this land, they captured over three hundred thousand wild animals and relocated them to the site. Endangered newts were moved to nearby ponds, snakes and lizards caught in buckets and taken to homes in other nature reserves and on a new wetland site. This ambitious engineering project involved breaching parts of the sea wall near the coastline of Stanford-le-Hope and flooding forty-three hectares of marshland.

After the animals had been removed and before the area was flooded, heritage practice Oxford Archaeology (again funded by DP World) carried out extensive fieldwork on the site, uncovering a significant amount of Roman artefacts and important remains of middle Iron Age and Roman salt works. Simon told us about the three years he had spent working on the London Gateway site as an artist on a research project in collaboration with Oxford Archaeology before DP World began the process of construction there. He originally saw the project as an extraordinary opportunity to research the way in which contemporary art can respond to a landscape during a period of change. Oxford Archaeology offered Simon full access to all the sites during the archaeological works, presenting him with a unique perspective on that landscape, both on the surface and under excavation.

At the Mucking site, which has since become part of the new London Gateway Port development, archaeologists uncovered multiple artefacts relating to early Roman salt production, along with a number of 'red hills': mounds of ash made from burnt salt-marsh plants and sediment (the residue of very old fires used to heat brine for salt). These excavated remains were preserved before the archaeological site was flooded. Simon created a series of works called the *Pit Paintings*, a name which refers to the circular shapes of the excavated landscape – pits, holes where posts had once stood, trenches and ditches.

During the time he spent on site, Simon became acutely aware of the river and how little attention was being given to the Estuary itself. He wanted to switch focus from the landscape to the actual waterway and started to think about the character of the Estuary, its future and how we should respond to it. From there, he had the idea to find a group of people to undertake a journey from London along the Estuary out to the point where it meets the North Sea, and to use that time to talk and think about what the experience of being on the Estuary is all about. It was Simon who had originally thought up the idea for our cruise, something that came directly out of his residency at Mucking. He approached Ben and, together, they made a successful application to the Arts Council for funding, before inviting the rest of the crew to participate. Aside from myself, Simon Callery and Ben Eastop (who are both visual artists), there was also Ben's son Luke, an ornithologist (as well as being an excellent cook and an experimental cartographer), photographer and filmmaker James Price, musician and sailor John Eacott and archaeologist of the recent past Sefryn Penrose.

Soon it was time for the crew of *Ideeal* to return to the barge. We had left John Eacott at the end of the pier, looking after the boat. The wind had picked up again and I anticipated that we were in for a rough night on the water. Paul Gilson was unhappy about us returning to the barge that night. 'The tide's in at the moment,' he said sternly, 'but there is a strong wind. It will be rough, noisy, windy and not entirely safe. I strongly recommend you stay here for the night.' If only we had listened to him.

4

Sea Echo

The sun set; the dusk fell on the stream and lights began to appear along the shore . . . Lights of ships moved in the fairway – a great stir of lights going up and going down. And farther west on the upper reaches the place of the monstrous town was still marked ominously on the sky, a brooding gloom in sunshine, a lurid glare under the stars.

– *Heart of Darkness*, Joseph Conrad, 1899

After a short taxi ride we took the deserted diesel train back to the lifeboat station. By the time we reached the pier head it was nearly midnight. The rain was pouring down, lashed by the wind, which whipped around the open deck. It was hard to take a breath. We cautiously made our way down the crumbling concrete steps, to the eerie place below the lifeboat station, holding on to the wet iron railings for support. The lower deck looked even more ominous at night than it had when we left the barge earlier that evening. Shafts of pale moonlight cut across the floorboards in wide ribbons in between the columns of wooden pillars. Dark and light intertwined at the edges of the space, creating strange optical illusions in which shadowy figures seemed to flit between the pillars before dissolving into the gloom. In the half-light, the place looked reminiscent of the abandoned remains of an ancient Egyptian temple.

Wind and rain tore through the open sides of the subterranean space. The sound of the waves crashing against the pier echoed around us. The damp night air smelt of salt, rust, blood and mud. We walked tentatively across the slippery deck to the barge. Small fountains of water bubbled up through the gaps between the floorboards as the waves below rose and fell. The tide was coming in fast. We needed to get back on to the boat quickly before the deck became completely submerged beneath the sea. I pulled out my phone from my pocket and tapped the torch function, lighting a faint pathway in front of me. Suddenly, everything under that pier seemed to come alive. I saw huge clusters of oysters, mussels, sea anemones, crabs and all sorts of other sea creatures covered in wet, dripping, bright green seaweed, clinging on to the pillars. The torchlight bounced off glistening shells which appeared to be pulsating in time with the waves. I turned the beam of light on to the barge, which was rocking up and down violently in the swell of water beside the pier, straining against her mooring ropes. The black, choppy water surrounding the boat looked menacing and wild. John Eacott was standing on deck in his oilskin

coat, soaking wet, urging us to get on board quickly, grateful to see us return. One by one, we stepped on to the swaying boat and made our way out of the rain and down into the hold.

As I lay in my cabin that night, trying to sleep, I was aware that we were by ourselves out there. Paul Gilson's words of warning came back to me. I did not feel safe. At 2 a.m., a strong wind blew up and the sea poured through the dark underbelly of the pier, smashing against the side of the barge. I paid sharp attention to the sound of the water. It was under, over, against, beneath and all around us. Something kept banging incessantly against the hull, metal on metal. It felt like we were in a war zone. The barge was rocking so fiercely I could not stand up.

As that long night wore on, I began to hear other noises aside from the banging – the clamour of a great crowd of people crying out simultaneously in fear. I could distinguish a woman's scream, the dreadful noise of children sobbing – the sound of hundreds of men shouting. It went on for hours, unbearably loud at times, desperate, before drifting away for a time on the wind then returning with a vengeance.

At some point, Sefryn called out my name; she was wide awake, too, and could also hear the screaming. We tried to calm ourselves by coming up with rational responses to the sounds we could hear, wondering if it might be a flock of seagulls nearby, but we were sure the shouts were human. We also considered the possibility that the noise came from a violent argument on the seafront, but we felt we were too far from the shore for the sound to travel that distance. Eventually, we took our sleeping bags and crawled into the main hold, where the other crew members were sleeping. The voices were barely audible in there and, gradually, as dawn broke, the sounds stopped altogether.

I still could not sleep. As daylight slowly filtered into the hold through a porthole, I watched the mooring ropes stretch and strain to near breaking point as we dropped far down with the receding tide to another level beneath the pier, a second, hidden deck. I was afraid the barge would be left hanging from the pier head as the waters ebbed away beneath us. The tidal movement of the Estuary is one of the most extreme in the world. I hoped Ben had estimated the slack in the ropes correctly to compensate for this. I felt paralysed with fear, unable to take the short walk over to his cabin to tell him we might be in danger.

At 5.30 a.m., our skipper awoke and braved the storm in his dressing gown to loosen the ropes, where he discovered that the rudder had come loose, which had caused the banging noise we had heard all night. From the bottom deck of the pier, he watched the incoming storm at eye level, a cross section of the Estuary waters.

By six thirty, the weather had calmed, and I got up and went out on deck to take a breath of air. It was a beautiful, bright morning, and the sun shone on the water. Puffy, white cumulus clouds hung like mountains over the horizon. The view was so clear I could see Queenborough Harbour, over five miles away, where we had moored up the night before. As I looked east, towards the rapidly widening mouth

of the North Sea, I could just make out the distant silhouettes of wind farms and sea forts with my naked eye.

As Ben and John tried to assess the state of the engine, I sat and googled 'Southend Pier', trying to find an explanation for the sounds I had encountered during the night. My searches led me to 'Haunted Essex', a website which lists the end of the pier as a 'location for paranormal activity'. A workman claimed he had seen a ghost on the lower deck, and an investigator into the paranormal took photographs down there, which depicted lots of orbs. One dark autumn night, a policeman chased a tall, shadowy figure in a long, dark coat towards the end of the pier, then watched as he vanished into thin air. Someone else posted that they had seen a figure beneath the pier, 'a tall man in a long coat'. Another post read: 'I had the feeling of a man hanging from beneath the pier.' There have been many suicides at this location over the years, which, according to the website, is the reason for these 'haunting manifestations'.

Ghost stories are ingrained into the folklore of the estuarine landscape. Canvey Island is allegedly haunted by a lone Dutchman who roams across the marshes carrying a heavy sack on his back, and a Viking ghost who stands on the shoreline in traditional dress, looking out to sea. A phantom headless woman, a Roman soldier and a pirate ship offshore have supposedly appeared to many on the mysterious Foulness Island, and a ghostly hellhound is said to haunt Deadman's Island in Kent and to feast on the heads of nineteenth-century prisoners buried there after dying from malaria on hulks moored out in the Estuary. Many of these stories were known to me. I had grown up with them and had never before given them much attention or thought, but, after my extraordinary and, frankly, terrifying ordeal during that dreadful night moored up beside the pier, they were taking on new significance. However, as a historian and a researcher, I knew there had to be a logical explanation for the sounds I had heard that night and I was determined that, in time, I would find the answer.

We had planned to take the barge out to visit the sea forts that morning, but when Ben came back up on deck after inspecting the engine he told us the storm had further clogged the pipes with silt and debris. He made the decision to return to London. That trip would have to wait for another time. It was with great disappointment that we began our journey back upriver – although part of me was relieved not to be spending another night on the barge.

We motored cautiously westwards at a reduced speed towards my hometown of Leigh, past Bell Wharf, where a large, modern cockling boat, *Charlotte Joan*, was moored up, offloading her catch for the day. I could see about twelve other cockleboats tied up along the quay in the old town, beside trawlers and fishing boats. From the water, the place looked picturesque in the morning sun, with the wooden cockle sheds, pubs, sailing clubs and Victorian cottages near the foreshore and the boats bobbing up and down on their anchorages.

Ben manoeuvred the barge away from Leigh Harbour, heading further out into Hadleigh Ray Creek to avoid the rugged coastline of Two Tree Island. At the southern edge of the island, a fisherman was launching his skiff off the slipway into Hadleigh Ray Channel, probably on his way to his trawler, anchored out in the Estuary. A couple of birdwatchers waved to us from the towpath as we drifted past on our way into deeper waters.

We headed south-west towards the Yantlet Channel. Heavy, grey clouds hung over the Kent shoreline above a great strip of agricultural land, extending for miles along the coast of Grain, with a patchwork of yellow rapeseed fields and farmland occasionally broken up by industrial structures and the tall chimney of the power station, flanked by oil storage tanks and cranes, which, from the Essex coast, resembled the skeletons of giraffes. There were no visible towns beside the shoreline, only the white rectangles of the caravans in the far distance at All Hallows.

Looking east, back towards the North Sea, there was a great breadth of views over wide expanses of shimmering water. We were completely immersed in the estuarine landscape. I was sitting up near

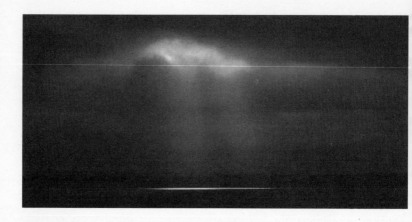

the bow with Sefryn, and she talked about how the pervasive presence of the water had, to her, started to feel overwhelming: there was just too much sea, too much wide-open sky. Every moment, the colour palette around us shifted as clouds rolled across the sky and light and dark interacted with the water.

I saw a big ship far in the distance in the deep-water channel as we headed upriver towards London. Looking at the Thames Estuary live shipping tracker website on my phone revealed that the ship was a general cargo vessel called *Brigga*, from Brunsbüttel in Germany, making her way to Tilbury Dock. Zooming out on the map, I found *Cymbeline*, a roll-on/roll-off cargo ship travelling from Zeebrugge, further downriver, and many yachts, tankers, container ships, fishing vessels, pleasure and high-speed craft clustered in the outer reaches, as well as a number of tugs and pilot boats. *Sea Echo* – a tug far out in the North Sea – was 'underway using engine', her destination unknown.

As we reached the outskirts of Canvey, waves splashed up over the bow. The low-lying land mass of the island appeared to float on the Estuary waters as we motored past. From the deck of *Ideeal*, I could see the oil storage tankers on the petrochemical site at the Occidental oil refinery and the chimneys in the distance at Coryton, along with the Labworth restaurant on the northern seafront, housed in a listed art deco building designed by Ove Arup, who was later involved in the early design of the Sydney Opera House. Norwegian crude-oil tanker *Navion Candia* was moored up at the end of the jetty near Hole Haven Creek.

Coryton oil refinery looked desolate as we drifted past, its multiple tall chimney stacks covered in steel rigging sitting amongst a tangled network of ground pipes and gigantic iron storage tanks. Perching on one of the chimneys was a lone bird of prey, which made me think of the Essex librarian J. A. Baker, who spent his life tracking the elusive peregrine falcon, in all weathers, across the Essex marshes, longing, as Robert Macfarlane said in his documentary *The Wild Places of Essex*, 'to leave humanity behind, to become a peregrine'.

As we headed towards the north bank near Stanford-le-Hope, I saw the vast area of new land in the process of being reclaimed for the new super port. Sloping banks of grey shingle edged a massive quayside, which was covered in high piles of sand and ballast. Acres

and acres of open land sat behind the quay, stretching as far as the eye could see, like a great, flat, sandy Martian desert. Enormous digger trucks shifting tons of material moved at speed around the site. Huge pipes flowed in and out of the deep-water channel, pumping dredged material from the bottom of the river directly back on to the reclaimed land. Steel cages enclosed parts of the quay; they had been filled with concrete to displace the slurry. Giant floodlights stood all around the construction site: work was going on twenty-four hours a day to ensure the new port was completed to deadline.

As we slowed down to take a look, a small tugboat came speeding out into the water towards us from the quayside. A man in a hard hat and a high-vis jacket came out from the wheelhouse and began asking Ben questions about what we were doing there. We were told not to linger; we had to move quickly on.

We reached Lower Hope, the first bend in the Estuary travelling upriver from the North Sea, an in-between place – not quite river, not quite sea. Local lexicographer Germander Speedwell describes the reaches and features, islands and inlets, settlements, creeks, sandbanks, towns and attractions of the Estuary from this particular bend in the river down to Foulness Island in her poem 'The Rise and Fall of the Lower Hope'. Many of the places named in her poem have long since disappeared: Tongue Wharf, Hook Spit, Skull Site, Gog's Berth.

We headed towards Tilbury, past the Lakeside Wall of Fame, an illegal gallery which has sprung up along the concrete wall beside this little-visited stretch of the river over the last few years. From the water, we had our own private view of some of the best urban street art in the UK, created by internationally famous graffiti artists from around the world. The brightly coloured tags and cartoons contrasted sharply with the monotone industrial landscape of the Procter & Gamble factory behind.

The river turned and twisted again, and soon we arrived at Gravesend Reach, the earliest recorded boundary of the Upper Thames Estuary, the narrowest point in the river, the gateway into London for millennia. An old Thames barge was moored up alongside Graves-end Pier, her red sails flapping in the wind. To the east of the pier head, beside a small wooden jetty, sat the *Princess Pocahontas*, the last pleasure cruiser left on the Estuary, named after the Native American princess buried at Gravesend. Looking across at Tilbury, I saw a cruise ship moored in the dock of the terminal. Large blue cranes lifted brightly coloured containers off the big ship *Hamburg Süd* in the dock at Northfleet Hope.

The river curved again as we continued our journey back towards the QEII Bridge. We drifted past more marshes, sewage works, power stations, burial grounds, new housing developments, oil refineries, riverside factories, wharves and wetlands. There has been a new phase of human intervention in this landscape: parts of the industrial Essex coastland have recently been demilitarized and reclaimed as public parkland; other areas are being turned into urban developments.

By late afternoon, we were back at Tower Bridge, where our journey ended. It was with some sadness that we said our goodbyes, back at Hermitage Wharf. There are particular kinds of friendships formed after spending time together in close quarters on a boat; we all promised to stay in touch. James and I had already started working on a film together about our journey; Ben and Simon talked about ways to expand collaboratively on the project; Sefryn would be writing a paper about the industrial landscapes we had passed through; Luke wanted to develop a digital map of our trip; and John had spoken about trying to organize a similar trip on a sailing boat out to the sea forts at some point in the future. I knew even then that the cruise on *Ideeal* had been the catalyst for a book project for me. Spending time on the river had made me deeply curious about the place. I wanted to know more about the people who had spent their working lives on the Estuary. I wanted to walk through those mysterious rural landscapes on the Hoo, to visit the sea forts and discover more about the mythology of the place, as well as hearing other stories of the river itself. And, despite the terrifying experience of the previous night, I was also determined to get back out on the water as soon as possible, to immerse myself in that landscape again.

PART II

Encounters

5

Black Water

As the deserted, grass-grown quaysides remember the busy tides
of other days which brought a bustling throng of sailormen to
moor along them, to lift their ringbolts and slip in the big
bowlines of head and stern ropes and then to lumber them with
dark coal or bright timber, straw in stacks or beer in barrels. The
mud in the channels sighs as the receding tide leaves it to bubble
and whisper. The ghosts of the old-timers haunt these places still.
          — *Last Stronghold of Sail*, Hervey Benham, 1948

It was an unseasonably cold October morning when I arrived at Hythe
Quay in Maldon, on the banks of the River Blackwater, a tributary
to the Thames Estuary on the Essex coast. Snow was falling as I stood
and watched a flock of white mute swans glide silently past the dark
hulls of about a dozen Thames barges double-berthed alongside the
wharf. The criss-cross of masts, wrapped and tied with red-ochre
sails, stood out against the indistinct landscape behind of wide-open,
heavy, grey skies and flat salt marsh fringed with clusters of
sea-lavender. Despite the weather, there were a number of people
sitting opposite the quayside outside the Jolly Sailor, enjoying the
picturesque scene. Hundreds of visitors come to the historic maritime
town every week to see the largest surviving fleet of Thames barges
in existence. Seafood stalls, oyster bars, cafés and ice-cream parlours
line the harbour now, replacing the docks and warehouses that once

filled this busy working port, in its time an important landing place for cargo vessels transporting goods up to London.

I joined a small queue of other people who had booked the boat trip; we stood near a row of black weatherboard cottages on the harbour before making our way cautiously along a wooden gangway on to a beautifully restored Thames barge belonging to local company Topsail Charters. The wooden deck was covered in a slippery film of sleet by the time we got on board. Snow had started to settle on piles of rope coiled up on the hatches. I went straight down into the oak-panelled hold, which smelt of tar, wood and paraffin. Long tables lined with chairs ran along each side of the large, open space; a roaring log-burning stove stood at the far end. After being given a welcome cup of hot chocolate, we were asked to sit down around the fire for a briefing before we set sail.

Our skipper, Paul Jeffries, told us that *Thistle* had originally been owned by a coal merchant from Battersea. The barge had had a regular passage transporting 'black diamonds' from the Humber down to the London docks. Sometimes she might have carried a mixed freight,

picking up extra cash delivering something specific to London – a piano, perhaps, or a single barrel of linseed oil. He described a tough working life on board, governed by the tides. Members of the crew were paid for by the freight, their income entirely at the mercy of the weather.

The first Thames barges were small lighters with sails and were used in the upper part of the river for moving goods to the London dockside from big ships moored further out. As the city expanded, barges started working down in the inner reaches and were built flat-bottomed so they could move easily around the tidal creeks and shallow waters of the Estuary. Gradually, the designs became more refined: the bows got smoother, the rigs grew larger, the lines became more seaworthy. The boats began trading across to the continent, down to Cornwall, up to the east coast, Newcastle and over to the Channel Islands. By the end of the nineteenth century, there were about two thousand barges working in the Thames Estuary and along the east and south coasts. They were highly economical, as they could sail without loading ballast with a crew of just a man (the skipper) and a boy (the mate). Most had a dog on board as well, for security, and some of the bigger coasting barges employed a third hand.

Every barge was slightly different, but they all had certain characteristics in common, such as leeboards on either side, a spritsail rig with a long diagonal spar holding up the mainsail, flat bottoms and red sails. Traditionally, these sails were dressed with a water-proofing and a rot-proofing material that contained a lot of grease, tallow and fish oil; red-ochre colouring was added to make them look more attractive. 'The old dressing never dried. It used to stink and, when you were stowing the sails, you'd be as red as the sail. Synthetic materials are used now, which are more user-friendly,' Paul explained. 'We do a lot of events on the barge. I'm sure you can imagine we wouldn't want people getting covered in red stains from dirty, smelly old sails sliding from side to side whilst they are in their wedding best!'

He led us back up on deck. *Thistle*'s mainsail had been set; the barge was rigged to depart. We were heading out on a two-hour nature cruise upriver, towards the remote Osea Island, which has become a haven for wintering birds, who migrate there every year in their hundreds of thousands to feed off the algae-rich saltings and tidal mudflats of the Blackwater.

By the time we slipped our mooring, it was snowing heavily. The majority of the group returned to the warm hold below, but I sat out on deck and watched as Paul effortlessly manoeuvred the heavy boat up the salty tideway. Soon, the tumble of old houses and pubs in the

harbour and the steep spire of the medieval church of St Mary's on the hill behind had been left astern.

The barge sailed almost silently along the narrow river, although the sound of the boat cutting through the water and the creak of old wood were ever present. There was barely any discernible movement up on deck, just a gentle rocking forward and aft. *Thistle*'s red sails billowed gently in the wind. The flat marshland landscape around us almost disappeared in the white mist. By the time we reached the spit at the far end of Promenade Park, I could make out through the fog only the outstretched arm of the bronze statue of the Anglo-Saxon leader Byrhtnoth, who fought against Viking invaders there during the Battle of Maldon in AD 991.

The course of the river twisted and turned. Soon, we reached Heybridge Basin, the entrance to the Chelmer and Blackwater Canal, where Dutch eel boats once sold live eels from boxes on the dockside and traders arrived in schooners filled with timber from Scandinavia. A few yachts and some old barges were moored in the basin as we passed by. I spotted one I recognized – an old coaster called *Raybell*, built over ninety years ago and long since fallen into disrepair. Her current owner, Rob Sargent, had been attempting to restore her single-handedly, making slow but steady progress during the past five years. Restorations like this are rare and ambitious projects. The passion and dedication of amateur enthusiasts like Rob are as vital to preserving the heritage of the Thames barges as initiatives such as those undertaken by Topsail Charters.

I sat up on deck, chatting with Paul Jeffries about the future of the Thames barges, as we sailed out towards the Estuary. I had told Paul about my book project before the journey, and he was keen to share his stories and considerable knowledge with me.

About a mile east from Maldon, on the banks of the Blackwater, we arrived at Northey Island; the site of the oldest-recorded battlefield in Britain, which was used by Viking raiders as a base during the Battle of Maldon. This uninhabited, wild place is cut off from the mainland at high tide. Access to the island is by private arrangement only. Birdwatchers are the most regular human visitors now, going there to see the great throngs of Brent geese who descend on the island every winter, along with redshank and plover. A low mist obscured the island from view as we passed, but we could hear seabirds calling in the distance.

Before the island became a nature reserve, it was one of many popular wildfowling spots along this coastline. Local fishermen and oyster-catchers once earned an extra living in the winter months by shooting marsh birds. Some made their own clinker-built punts, which they took out amongst the creeks; others walked out on the mud with eight-bore shotguns and a gun dog in tow to stalk the immense gatherings of Brent geese, widgeon, mallard and teal that used to arrive on the Estuary mudflats in hard weather. During particularly cold winters, the skies around these places would be darkened by thousands of wildfowl. Most fishermen-fowlers lived in the little villages dotted around the banks of the Blackwater, such as Maldon, Bradwell and Mersea, as well as in Wakering and Foulness, further down the Essex coast.

One such fisherman-fowler was Rob Smith, Thames Water chief sewer flusher. In his youth, Rob worked as an oyster dredgeman, picking oysters by hand at low tide from the Essex mudflats. His target was ten thousand oysters per tide. Occasionally, he wore gloves, but usually he would just plaster up his fingertips to protect them from the sharp edges of the shells. In the winter, he went wildfowling on the salt marshes. He comes from the small village of Wakering, from a long line of bargemen. 'One of them, for bets, used to swim underneath four barges tied alongside each other. There must be some of that madness left in the bloodline, as that is just the sort of thing that I would do,' he said. Once, in the middle of February, he shot two mallards, which fell into the middle of the creek. His dog was not with him, so he had to dive into the icy water and retrieve the ducks himself.

After sailing for about an hour, we reached Osea Island, which is surrounded by a long shingle beach covered in oyster beds with saltings beyond, home to Brent geese, shelducks, avocets and other waders. When wildfowling was at its height, there was an unofficial code of practice which meant the birds were never over-culled; in fact, the wildfowlers looked after these habitats: their livelihood depended on it.

Due to the thick fog and heavy snow, there was little to see, which was a bit disappointing, but the snow and mist made the landscape around us timeless and eerily beautiful. With help from his crew, Paul tacked round in the widest section of the river and, as we started to sail back towards Maldon, he told me more about his working life. Like Rob Smith, Paul had also grown up in Wakering. His family once owned a large fleet of barges there, which transported bricks from the local brickfields up to London. One of his earliest memories was of sitting in his grandfather's shed, watching him carve toy barges from pieces of wood, then cycling with him down to the creek nearby, where they would sail the toy boats out across the water amongst the working barges. His grandfather had been full of encouragement for Paul to continue in the trade, although his grandmother thought it was a dangerous and dirty job and did not want him to have anything to do with it. However, Paul was always drawn to the barges and started working on them as a teenager, volunteering with a preservation society based in Maldon which owned several restored boats. He helped out at weekends, at first doing general maintenance, and eventually became a skipper, learning from the older men who had worked on the barges all their lives.

Now Paul runs Topsail Charters with his wife. They own three other barges apart from *Thistle*, including a grain barge called *Kitty*, and *Hydrogen*, one of the last-surviving wooden coasters. Their fourth, *Reminder*, is a riveted steel-hulled barge which became the champion in the Thames and Medway Barge Match when she was launched in 1929.

Paul told me that Thames barges started to disappear from the river from the 1930s onwards, as more goods were being transported by road and rail. Then the introduction of motorized Dutch coasters, which were faster and could carry more cargo, took further business away from the traditional commercial sailing vessels. Over the following decades, the majority were taken out of service. Paul recalled seeing the *Cambria*, the last of the working sailing barges, making her way up to Stambridge Mills when he was a child in the 1960s. Today, there are only about two dozen seaworthy barges left, and most of these have either been made into houseboats or restored and are being used as charter vessels, like *Thistle*. Yet Paul seemed tentatively hopeful about the fate of the Thames barges. 'Enthusiasm and passion keeps the barges and the barge matches going today. Our biggest worry is finding people with the skills to sail them and pass those skills on. We're fortunate that we've got a number of youngsters who've adopted us . . . We encourage them a lot, so, hopefully, that's where the future is.'

6

Ship Full of Bombs

The sea and weather have removed the funnel, ventilators and most of the fittings from the midships island, but although she is barely recognizable as a Liberty ship, the three masts remain, and the slings and nets of the stevedores continue to dangle from the cargo booms as relics and reminders of brave men who raced against time to get the bombs out, before the sea overtook them.

– Published by Southend-on-Sea District Chamber
of Trade & Industry Ltd, 1972

A well-spoken octogenarian called John Cotgrove approached me after a lecture I gave at the Leigh-on-Sea community centre and politely but firmly corrected some of my information about the SS *Montgomery*. He told me the ship had run aground on the Sheerness Middle Sand at the height of the spring tide, on 20 August 1944, 'because she was told by the stupid people based at Southend Pier to anchor in the wrong place'. When the wind fell northerly at low water, she could not avoid touching the shoal.

The ex-navy man seemed extremely knowledgeable about the sunken ship but told me it was his late brother David who had been the real authority: he had been an explosives expert who spent years examining the story whilst working on Foulness for the Atomic Weapons Research Establishment. When David first became interested in the wreck, the public knew little about the disaster, and he was determined to investigate further. The inquiry into the loss of the *Montgomery* found that a number of lookout ships in the vicinity had seen her swinging towards the shoal in the pre-dawn light and blown their sirens in warning. And even before this, the deputy harbour master at Southend had noticed that the ship had been allotted a mooring too shallow for her draught; he tried to give the crew alternative instructions but was stopped by his superior officer, despite the cacophony of warnings from other ships. The captain was asleep when the *Montgomery* dropped anchor off Sheerness, and woke to find her stuck on the sandbank. He stubbornly refused assistance from tugs to pull her off the sandbank, and the stem of the ship soon began to crack.

David spoke to people who were on the *Montgomery* when she ran aground, and they told him that they had tried to take the bombs off her, hoping she would grow lighter and float on the next high tide. A tugboat from Chatham arrived with some lighters filled with dockers, and they used the tide to supply steam for cargo winches to haul the bombs up out of the hold in wire netting. They were wading in water that was up to their knees. As the tide ebbed, the strain on the *Montgomery*'s hull caused some of the welded plates to crack and buckle, creating an explosive snap as loud as a gunshot, which was heard by a fishing boat over a mile away. It was only then that the crew conducted an emergency evacuation of the ship via lifeboats and rafts. Of the 8,687 tons of bombs and detonators originally on board, half were successfully removed in 1944 – but an estimated 1,445 tons of TNT are still in the wreck, as well as loose bombs and toxic hazards such as white phosphorus smoke bombs.

Various people were suspended over the disaster, some vital evidence seemed to have gone missing and key witnesses were not questioned at the time. I later learnt that short cuts were taken during the construction of the American Liberty ships, which had been built by untrained workers in less than five days, using welded instead of riveted seams. This almost certainly contributed to the disaster, allowing the *Montgomery* to break in half so easily. The *Montgomery* finally broke her back on 8 September 1944, leaving her completely stranded.

There was a war on and many other things to do than recovering a wrecked ship, so she was left. After the war, all around the coast of Europe there were numerous warships, tanks and aircraft which needed to be removed. Various firms, most of them American, went around on massive salvage operations. But when they got to the *Montgomery* they were told not to touch it; it would be too dangerous. Years later, John's brother David became interested in the case and spent over a decade writing up his findings in a report.

The following week, I visited John in his bungalow near Belfairs Woods to see the report for myself. Inside the neatly kept home, nearly every available inch of wall space was lined with paintings: beautifully composed local scenes of working craft – sailing and fishing boats, barges and tugs, cockling and shrimping boats – the story of the Thames Estuary painted by John in oils. Sitting on top of the piano was a perfect miniature wooden model of the *Montgomery*. 'I made this for David when he was working on his report,' he said, pulling the model into two pieces, replicating the broken ship.

He led me over to a mahogany dining table at the far end of the front room that overlooked an immaculately laid-out garden. Covering the table were some neatly arranged folders and a large pile of printed material, which he opened out into a single document entitled 'The Cotgroves of Leigh'. The extensive family tree had been compiled by a relative and dated back to the birth of fisherman Benjamin Cotgrove in the early 1600s. Most of the family's male descendants spent their lives working at sea: as cocklers, seamen, dock agents, sailors, fishermen, bargemen, oyster dredgemen, sea captains, naval officers and mariners. 'One of my relatives joined the Napoleonic Navy in 1810,' said John. 'He was a foretopman, which meant he was quite a skilled seaman. He is described in here as having a crucifix tattooed on his arm, and a pockmarked face, and was once given six lashes for bad behaviour.' He flicked through some more pages. 'Look at this one,' he said, pointing to some notes and

laughing. 'PLA Lighterman Walter Cotgrove caught a whale in the Thames in November 1899, which ended up in the Natural History Museum.'

John's forefathers also feature in the annals of literary history. I told him that the American poet Justin Hopper had written about this incident in a poem for his series of works *Public Record Estuary*, which combined new writing with texts sampled from, and inspired by, nineteenth-century reports of minor sea disasters in the Thames. Hopper had become fascinated by the story of two young boys called Cotgrove and Noakes in the newspaper archives of Southend library when he came across a story of them rescuing a young girl in their rowing boat who had fallen into the Estuary. A decade or so later, he found a Cotgrove and a Noakes in the papers again; this time, they were going on an expedition to kill a whale that had been trapped near Tilbury. Towards the end of the century, a Cotgrove and a Noakes were killed when an iron-clad, steam-powered tug cleaved their little Leigh fishing smack, *Bertha*, in half. The resulting poems tell the story of the Estuary at a crucial period of change during the Industrial Revolution through the tales of these two families, Cotgrove and Noakes.

Florry Rand

Sources: 'Rescue by Boys at Leigh' from the *Newsman*, 5 July 1884

By the crimped, knotted wood of the old Billet Wharf,
'tween the gross summer's sun and the shifting Leigh sand,
Two young boys, full of Creek water's quaff,
Lifted the arms of the child Florry Rand.

A splash of the Thames on the Billet's old wood,
A splash of the ocean to deliver a band
Of slick green fluorescence that summer's eerie flood
Lay down at the feet of the child Florry Rand.

Young Cotgrove and Noakes saw her pirouette's arc
As they deviled the town with their boys' idle hands,
And plunged from the Wharf like smack or like barque,
And sparred with the mud for the child Florry Rand.

Young Cotgrove and Noakes, the boys of the day,
Who pulled from the water the sea's dark demand,
Knew not of their doings, knew not of their trade,
When they stole from the water the child Florry Rand.

— Justin Hopper

Gave Up the Ghost

Sources: Thomas Browne, 'Of the Spermaceti Whale', 1835; Herman Melville, *Moby-Dick*, 1851; 'Still They Come!' from *Chelmsford Chronicle*, 7 August 1891

The beast lurched against a Friday night tide,
Disporting itself in shallow water:
A whale, sparring with the mud.
Sixteen feet in length and girth,
Seven feet the breadth of tail from tip to tip,
Teeth only in the lower jaw,
Received into fleshy sockets in the upper.

A bituminous substance floating upon the sea:
What spermaceti *is, men might justly doubt,*
Since even the learned Hofmannus
Saith plainly, Nescio quid sit,
Not easily conceiving the seminal humour of animals
Should be inflammable.

Fishing off the Nore Lightship, they saw the beast beached:
Disporting itself in shallow water.
Johnson, Cotgrove, Noakes,
And a number more of Leigh fishermen,
Spied the great beast and lunged as it lurched.
And in order to effect its capture, a kedge anchor,
Attached to which were twenty fathoms of rope,
Was thrown overboard.
A running noose skillfully thrown over the giant's tail,
And the kedge taken to its extreme length.

John Johnson, armed with two knives,
Jumped into the water
And hacked a hole under the whale's left fin:
The men inserted a boathook three feet into the whale's head,
After which the leviathan gave up the ghost.

On Saturday morning
It was towed and tugged to Mr. Tomlin's wharf,
Where it has since been exhibited
With twelve-hundred paying, both child and man,
To see the great once-lurching beast;
Lifted in the air by the shifting Leigh sand.

> *Hand in hand, ship and breeze blew on;*
> *But the breeze came faster than the ship.*

Too Close to His Liking:
The *Violet* and the *Embleton*

Sources: Report of Court inquiry into *Violet* and *Embleton*, Westminster Town Hall, 25 May 1900; 'Wreck Inquiry: The Disaster to a Leigh Smack', from *Essex County Chronicle*, 11 May 1900; 'Leigh Fishermen Drowned', from *Morning Post*, 25 January 1899; other brief newspaper stories, 1899–1900; 'The Sinking of the *Embleton*', from *Liverpool Mercury*, 24 July 1900

1.

Each smack and barque
That slips from the Oaze
Into Ray Gut,
Touches with its shadow
The shifting, sallow
Outline of January's hollow

Chews its clewed-up fingers
Across sea dunes
And whale-roads
That rain, steam and speed

Gut in clunks and grunts.
They feint against January

With timorous gusts,
And counter with time-honed
Thrusts, but the sand's bones
They all become
In the shadow, becalmed
At stoic Crowstone.

Cold blows the wind tonight, and cold the drops of rain
Great grief has been occasioned upon the greening main.
The Violet, *the* Faith Roby, *the* Embleton *and* Goole,
A mourning tide becalms them all in January's pool.

2.
Cotgrove and Noakes,
The famous two,
Comprising captain and crew
Of the Violet,
Set course for Leigh
With eyes on the morning wash

Of dull January green
On the Hadleigh Castle hillside.
Cotgrove and Noakes trod
A good boat under them:
This smack, the Violet,
Steered the thick Estuary traffic,

Dense with trawlers,
With tugs and steams;
Groaning hemp

And pluming iron,
Terraced beside wood
And fretted sailcloth.

3.
Iron-shod and rope-towed
By the steam-tug the Goole,
With cargo weighed on its march
To Adelaide,
The bold swimmer Embleton
Eked her way

Through the heaving creek:
So close to each mooring,
So close to each cloud.
Elbowing through the pool
As through London Bridge's
Death-undone crowd.

'Too close to his liking'
Were the Embleton *and smack:*
So said the iron ship's mate
Of the fate befalling
His seaborne kin,
Who leapt from the Violet

As the greater ship's fluke
Felled the smack's mast,
A lumbered tree,
'No chance had they,'
Said the Faith Roby,
Neighbors on course for Leigh.

The fluke anchor dragged
Its prey to effect its capture,
A noose to the Violet's *throat,*
And Cotgrove and Noakes
Met the sea's dark demand,
Pulled lifeless from the shifting Leigh sand.

John was thrilled to hear about the poems but doubted that the Cotgrove and Noakes who rescued the girl as children were the same men who were killed by the tug. 'These two old fishing clans from Leigh were large families,' said John. 'That's why everyone had a nickname, so you could tell them apart.' We spent some time examining the annotated notes on the document, which included the fantastic-sounding nicknames of some of John's relatives: Lumpy and his son Bert Lump, Cockearlie, Seaman Tolley, Old Cockily, Snikey and Tottles, to name just a few.

Looking through the family tree, it was sobering to see how many Cotgroves had died at sea over the centuries. In 1874, William Cotgrove and his son were killed when their boat turned over in Woolwich Reach. In 1888, George Cotgrove's fishing boat capsized and he drowned. His mate, Alfred, survived by clinging to the mast throughout the night; he was rescued in the morning. Another fisherman, also named George Cotgrove, was killed by a torpedo off Canvey Island in 1941, and Harry 'Rat' Noakes (who married Ada Cotgrove in 1910) died on the Leigh-on-Sea cockling boat *Renown* during the evacuation of British troops from Dunkirk in 1940.

Moving on from tales of his ancestors, John began to reminisce about his own life on the water. Story after story poured out of the elderly gentleman, pictures were drawn on the back of napkins to illustrate his tales, paintings pulled down from the walls, books picked from crowded shelves. He told me tales of shrimping on bawleys, wide, heavy crafts particular to the Thames Estuary made to carry heavy loads and designed to trawl near the shore. He spoke about gun punting in the Swale, a form of hunting for waterfowl from a wooden boat, and he talked about wildfowling off the Broomway, and recounted many wartime memories of the river. Back then, the mudflats had been littered with barriers, iron scaffold poles, barbed wire, unexploded bombs and wrecks. John and his friends used to walk out on the mud from Thorpe Bay at low tide as young boys to the edge of the sea to collect free coal from a coal-burning tug which had been mined and driven ashore there. One time, they sailed their dinghies out to Mulberry Harbour. One of the boys had a pistol with him, a 9mm Luger which he had 'borrowed' from his father, and as a dare he fired right through the thick planks on board, just to try out the power of the weapon. 'We knelt down and felt underneath, and it had come right out the other side,' said John. 'It was thrilling.'

The adventurous gang also sailed out to visit the *Montgomery* in their EODs (Estuary One Design sailing dinghies) shortly after she ran aground. 'There were plenty of places to tie up a rope and climb on board back then,' said John. 'The danger of her being an unexploded bomb was in the future; to us, she was just another wreck to explore. We went looking for loot, for flags, bunting, copper and guns, but we didn't find anything. I remember lots of empty wooden ammunition boxes lying about, a lot of cargo nets and shrouds coming down. Because it was wartime, she was a bit grotty. We were disappointed that we didn't find anything good, but some enterprising Leigh or Medway men must have got out there first and taken the copper and the big bronze propeller at the back, which was worth a lot of money.' I asked him if he had taken any photographs of his trip, but of course they were just kids; they didn't have a camera. Instead, he showed me images of the *Montgomery* in another file from the pile on the table, black-and-white aerial shots of the sunken ship taken decades ago by an unnamed photographer. 'The shrouds, the stays and the derricks were all there back then. If you look now, there's nothing, except the odd cormorant sitting there, looking forlorn.'

Finally, he pulled out his brother's yellowing report, which is what

I had come to see – twenty pages of notes typed out in 1972. I had initially found John's story of getting on board the *Montgomery* hard to believe, but information within the report confirmed that his excursion to the wreck had not been unusual at the time; in fact, after the war, the *Montgomery* became a centre of attraction for hundreds, if not thousands, of visitors. The 'growth of public concern' about the ship full of bombs came decades later. It was not until 1952 that the matter was first raised in the Commons and then a further twelve years (autumn 1964) until the *Montgomery* featured in an article in *Wide World Magazine* as 'The Doomsday Ship'. The Ministry of Defence for the navy stated that the chances of explosion were remote if the wreck was left alone and that, as time increased, the 'risk of spontaneous explosion' would decrease.

However, David's report stated that, by 1965, the wreck was being monitored day and night, under constant radar watch and patrol. Anyone attempting to trespass on her was removed by force. Divers were sent down to examine the remains on the seabed and found that the two halves had sunk heavily into the mud, and, as expected, heavy silting had 'engulfed the remainder of the cargo'. The decision was made not to attempt salvage, yet the ship continued to create drama. In January 1969, students plotted to blow the *Montgomery* up as part of a rag-day 'jape', which resulted in the ringleaders' arrest. Questions were asked in Parliament, and divers checked the wreck for signs of interference.

David's report documented all the facts about the sinking of the *Montgomery* and her unlikely afterlife, but it also expressed serious concerns about the safety of the wreck. David visited the site himself in 1972 and concluded that, contrary to government investigations, the wreck was by no means definitely secure. He was particularly concerned about heavy bombs sitting on 'tween decks, which could collapse at any moment, dropping bombs on top of explosives on the lower deck and triggering a chain reaction. The report references eyewitness accounts of fishermen 'dumping' bombs from their nets near the *Montgomery*; it cites bombs 'visible at low water' and worries

about the unknown safe lifetime of the explosive material. And David warned darkly that, if the wreck were ever to explode, the blast could create a tidal wave engulfing the Isle of Sheppey, and possibly Southend, too.

I thanked John for allowing me to see his brother's report, which had given me a unique insight into the story of the sunken ship, and for sharing his own stories of the Estuary with me. Before I left, I mentioned my desire to hear the stories of other fishermen, cocklers and bawley men – and he had one last treasure to share. Shuffling out to fetch the item from the garage, he returned ten minutes later with a dusty file filled with photocopied pages of tiny, careful handwriting. This photocopied Victorian manuscript was the work of Dr Murie, a scientist who arrived in Leigh in 1888, straight from an expedition in Africa. Murie had been commissioned by the Kent and Essex Sea Fisheries Committee to write about the fishing industry of the Thames Estuary. His first volume focused on the molluscs, crabs and fish living in the river at the time, and in the second he planned to track the trades and industries on the water – but Murie died before it was finished. The doctor was a mysterious figure in the community. He lived in the old town in a small cottage overlooking the water, amongst the fishermen but never quite accepted by them. 'They rather held him in contempt because he was trying to write about things he didn't know about,' said John. After his death, Murie's handwritten manuscript languished in a garden shed for decades, hidden amongst piles of firewood and sacks of coal, until it was rediscovered in the 1940s. David somehow got hold of the original manuscript and copied it, planning to get it published one day. That manuscript has long since disappeared, but David's copy remains.

I scanned the photocopied manuscript and spent days trying to decipher Murie's papers. A lot of the pages were too water-damaged

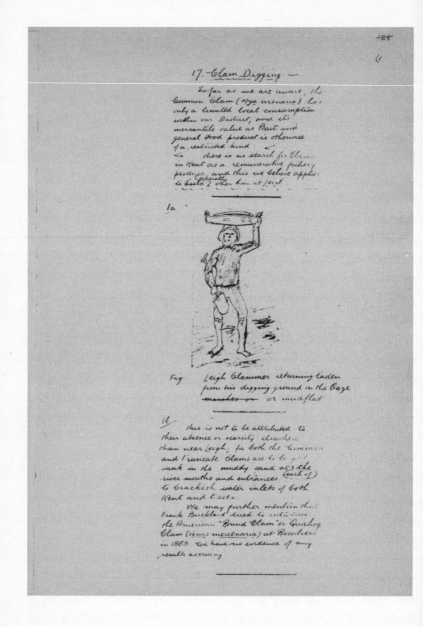

17. - Clam Digging. -

So far as we are aware, the Common Clam (Mya arenaria) has only a limited local consumption within our District, and its mercantile value as Bait and general food product is otherwise of a restricted kind.

there is no search for Clams in Kent as a remunerative fishery produce, and this we believe applies to Essex & other than at Leigh generally.

Fig. Leigh Clammer returning laden from his digging ground on the Ooze marshes or or mudflat

this is not to be attributed to their absence or scarcity elsewhere than near Leigh; for both the Common and Truncate Clams are to be sunk in the muddy sand at the river mouths and entrances (such of) to brackish water inlets of both Kent and Essex.

We may further mention that Frank Buckland tried to introduce the American "Round Clam" or Quahog Clam (Venus mercenaria) at Reculvers in 1869 We have no evidence of any results accruing.

to read, and there were many mistakes and crossings-out, but his notes were fascinating: little naive sketches and detailed accounts of starfish dredging, the age-old art of fishing with kiddle nets, eel

84

trawling and eel spearing, detailed notes on dialect, education, home life and even fishermen's nicknames. I realized that the doctor had attempted an even more ambitious exploration of the Thames Estuary than my own, well over a century ago, and with just as little prior knowledge of the place as I had. The connection was unexpected and deeply moving. Looking at those fading pages, I realized they might be the only surviving record of those long-forgotten ways of fishing on the estuary. Murie's papers gave me confidence to continue with my own project, as I recognized anew the value of this kind of research, however clumsy or unknowing it might appear at the time.

I stayed in touch with John Cotgrove over the coming months, and he alerted me to a talk at Southend Library which he thought would interest me. It was entitled 'The Wreck of the *Richard Montgomery*: Ruin and Regeneration in the Thames Estuary'. The event began with a presentation by contemporary digital artists Richard Whitby and Dave Charlesworth, who discussed their map-style publication, *31,838 Feet from the Wreck*, which includes an attempt to create a three-dimensional computer model of a life-size, copper-plated replica of the ship, which they imagined being placed in the centre of Southend as a permanent monument. They were exploring the idea that Southend might incorporate the threat of the *Montgomery*, known to locals as 'the Grand Old Lady of the Thames', as part of its future identity. 'In this imaginary location, the wreck becomes a heritage attraction and part of the town's iconography.' Their presentation also included multi-beam sonar images from a 2002 survey of the sunken ship.

The writer and academic Professor Patrick Wright spoke afterwards about his wider research into the Thames Estuary, which he described as a 'non-place' in the minds of popular culture, a liminal landscape of mud, waste, ruination, dereliction, danger, memory and collapse. 'There is nowhere where this culture of derision is more prevalent,' said Wright, 'than in Sheppey.' In the BBC4 film *The Joys of Essex*, the presenter Jonathan Meades sneers at Sheerness, describing it as a 'crap town' and a 'shithole extraordinaire'. Yet Wright went on to speak about the great German author Uwe Johnson, whom he has researched extensively. Johnson spent the last decade of his life living at 26 Marine Parade in Sheerness, the biggest town in Sheppey, refusing any public appearances and instead making friends in the local pub, who called him Charlie. From his seaside home, Uwe could see the *Montgomery*, which he called Sheppey's 'only spectacle'. In 1979, he published a lengthy essay entitled 'An Unfathomable Ship' in *Granta*, which remains to this day the most comprehensive article on the *Montgomery*.

Johnson, like David Cotgrove, was a sceptic about government claims that the *Montgomery* is, effectively, a safe site. In his *Granta* essay, he imagines the destruction if the ship were ever to explode: the north-west corner of Sheppey would be worst affected, with older buildings collapsing, gas and water mains rupturing and windows and roofs damaged in Sheerness and the nearby town of Sittingbourne. The exploding ship could produce a fireball at sea, hurling debris for more than a mile, which might even land on one of the super tankers, which carry 100,000 tons of oil. Further worries include the threat of a tidal wave caused by the explosion, which would bore up the Medway and the Thames, destroying the built-up areas along the banks. If the wind was blowing in the wrong direction, the effects could be felt as far away as Canvey Island, where there are tanks with a capacity of more than a million gallons of oil, as well as chemical and methane gas containers. When Johnson completed his essay, the local coastguard station had reported twenty-four near-collisions with passing ships. There is also the problem of pressure waves from low-lying jet aircraft triggering an explosion, or even deliberate targeting by terrorists. Weighing up this list of threats and outcomes, Johnson's essay offers a solution – to enclose the *Montgomery* in concrete.

The SS *Montgomery* remains a problem-child for the Port of London Authority: the wreck is now monitored day and night on radar.

The Maritime and Coastguard Agency collects data on the orientation and inclination of the wreck annually, and the most recent report concludes that, despite the unease of local residents, it is still stable, with negligible signs of deterioration. Despite the dangers, the *Montgomery* is, strangely, a much-loved local landmark, which has inspired creative projects and become embedded in the mythology and contemporary culture of the place: an alternative pirate radio station in Southend has recently been named the 'Ship Full of Bombs' and local writer Terry Smith has penned a fictional thriller, *Tide of Terror* (2006), about the *Montgomery* becoming the ultimate target for terrorists. Everyone living along both coastlines knows the story of the wreck. It lies there defiant, in awkward harmony somehow with both the landscape and other anarchic stories of this place, such as the origins of early punk on Canvey Island, the development of the world's smallest principality on a former naval fort in the outer reaches of the Estuary and the extreme beauty, mystery and danger of the Broomway on Foulness, Britain's most dangerous path.

7

Cambria

At the age of six, I accompanied my father to watch a yacht race at the end of Southend Pier. The race was cancelled because it was blowing a gale, but sailing up the river came a lone Thames barge. She was lying right over, the water was breaking over her deck, her sails were nearly touching the sea. I thought she was magnificent. My father said to me, 'Look at that, by the time you're my age there won't be any of them left.' I had that vision in my mind of that barge all my life.

> — Bargeman John Dickens in conversation with
> Rachel Lichtenstein, 2013

'A lot of the skippers were on the Thames barges because they were romantics, whether they admitted it or not,' said John Dickens, as he stepped off Gillingham Pier on to the deck of the *Cambria* for the first time in over half a century. The last time he had been on board was in 1964, when he finished a two-year stint as the third hand when she was still a working boat. Even then he had been aware that this way of life was coming to an end. 'It feels like I never left,' he said, smiling, as he walked around the deck of the newly restored vessel.

Cambria is a large coasting barge built of oak and pitch pine with a bowsprit, sprit mainsail and gaff-rigged mizzen. She began her working life in 1906 as a river and coastal cargo carrier, making regular trips across the Channel to the Netherlands and France, transporting pitch, coke, wheat, oil cake and any other cargo, from manure to sugar. Fully laden, she could carry 170 tons, which put her down to her load line, and her decks were frequently awash, making a hazardous working environment in the rough waters of the Channel and the North Sea.

By the early 1960s, the majority of these Channel crossings had stopped and most of her freights were delivered from London to Great Yarmouth. John described a difficult working life on board: 'Bloody miserable in the middle of winter, in the pouring rain, with hours before you got anywhere.' The river was still filled with shipping then: big freighters, little Dutch coasters, barges, tugs and strings of lighters, most of which were making their way back and forth to the London docks. 'We'd sail up the middle of the dock and the crews of the ships would come and watch us go by, especially the Scandi-navian ones, who were interested in sail. The Thames barges, or sailormen, were the last commercial sailing ships in Europe, and the *Cambria* was the last British-registered vessel to carry a cargo under sail, so she was a bit of an attraction.'

Bob Roberts was the skipper back then, an experienced seaman who worked as a deep-water sailor before becoming captain of the *Cambria* in 1954. He wanted to be remembered in history as skipper-ing the last sailorman. Life on board the working boat under Roberts had its own particular rhythm. It was crewed by just three men, and there was no fridge or electricity, no running water, or toilet except 'a bucket then chuck it'. The crew lived as if they were still in the nineteenth century. Each morning, Bob would be first up and would wake John and the mate by shouting down, 'Do you wanna piss?' They would get dressed and go to the cabin aft, where the skipper had already boiled the kettle, and John would make tea for everyone before going up on deck to help the others reduce the moorings, take some of the lines in, then release the lashings to set the sails.

'If the halyard got jammed on the way down, the mate or I would climb the rigging,' said John, looking up at the ratlines next to the main mast with longing. 'Go on if you want to,' said Basil, from the *Cambria* Trust, who had joined us on deck and was listening to John's stories with great interest. Within minutes, the septuagenarian had shunted up to the top of the rigging, smiling broadly all the way. He effortlessly made his way back down and moved to the bows, where he demonstrated how to pull the anchor chain across the barrel to shorten it. Basil passed him a winch to wind in the last of the chain and, as John cranked the winch, he told us a story about being laid up in Harwich on his second trip out on the *Cambria*. The skipper and the mate had both gone ashore for the night, and John was on board alone. He was sixteen. A force-ten north-westerly blew up, and the *Cambria* started dragging her anchor. The young lad coped all night alone, until the morning, when the skipper returned. He had to keep throwing chain until there were about forty fathoms in the water. The skipper came aboard in the morning and, when they hauled it all back in with the windlass, the rusty old steel chain had turned silver where it had gone through all the gravel.

We moved past the large canvas hatch cover in the centre of the deck and down the wide companionway into the hold below, where we found comfortable sofas, as well as tables and chairs. The barge had been restored after being given a generous grant from the National Lottery Trust and was now predominantly used for taking young carers out for respite weekends: 'Our consignments are human now.' John was deep in recollection, describing the ship's past life, when freight was lifted into the hold via big cranes on the dockside. Hessian sacks would come over in rope slings, guided into the hold by a gang of dockers. Theoretically, they pulled them out of the way of the crane with curved hooks and stowed them immediately before dealing with the next load – but this system didn't always go to plan. 'Some dockers didn't like stowing them under the mast case so, during their lunch break, we used to have to stow it properly, to make sure the cargo was all in. If we had a hundred tons of a light cargo like oil cake,

you usually had to have a bit of a stack, mostly on the aft end, to make it fit.'

On occasion, they would take a bulk cargo like wheat, which would come aboard through a tube from a silo. This was much easier: they could have the boat loaded in a couple of hours. John described the pungent odour of some of their cargo: 'Stray kernels of wheat would get stuck in the bilges, giving off a sulphury, rotten sort of smell. We did a cargo of horns and hoofs to Faversham twice, which were used for making glue, and the whole barge was full of these little insects that came off the sacks, and they didn't smell too savoury. Most of the time the hold smelt of linseed-oil cakes, which were used for feed, but we were out in the fresh air all the time anyway, so it wasn't impossible to live with.'

After the boat was fully loaded, John and the mate would cover the hold back up, wash the decks with buckets of water, coil all the ropes over the hatches, then make their way down the east coast, bound for Yarmouth. John talked about the joys of sailing at speed with a good wind behind them, and working the tide. 'If there wasn't much wind, the skipper would call it "piss-bollocky flat calm" or say, "Come on, Jesus, give us a little draught!"' If the wind was against them, they would drift with the tide, then anchor up and wait for it to turn again. John recalled the thick smogs that often descended on the river in the 1960s. He or the mate would stand on deck ringing a bell. 'We had no radar or ship-to-shore radio – you had to hope to be seen and heard.'

One of John's jobs as third hand was taking a tally, counting the sacks at the start of the trip and making sure the numbers matched when they got to their destination. 'If it was short, the cost would come off the freightage – the barge would have to pay.' Once they reached Yarmouth and offloaded, John and the mate would sweep the hold out with yard brooms. 'Every time we changed cargo, we had to clean it properly. We would have a cargo of coal one week, then wheat the next, so it had to be spotless. We got filthy dirty every day.'

John, Basil and I went into the former skipper's cabin aft, which used to have a separate little stateroom to the side with a bunk. John pointed to a small cabinet above the table. 'The aft locker was known as the Yarmouth Road. We kept emergency supplies in there in case we got stuck at anchor without any food,' he said. They did most of their cooking in there on the Victorian grate, but there was another big stove in the fo'c'sle, where they used to cook roast dinners and, occasionally, the skipper's plum duff, but breakfast was always in the skipper's cabin. 'We had a lot of fry-ups – bacon and eggs – if we did not have to get underway first thing,' said John. 'Afterwards, Bob would be sitting here with his feet up chatting whilst me and the mate, Vernie Parker, smoked our rollies.' Later, when the barge was underway, John would sit at the table in the cabin, polishing the brass binnacle and cabin lamps, cleaning the glasses of the four oil navigation lights with newspaper, topping them up with paraffin and trimming their wicks.

We sat around the table whilst John spoke with some sadness about how this whole way of life had disappeared within a few years of him leaving the trade: 'Containerization was the end of the docks. To unload a barge, you'd have to have a gang of six dockers – a container can be whipped out with a crane and stuck straight on the lorry.' After decades of faithful service, the barges just weren't commercially viable any more.

Cambria kept on trading until 1970, then became an exhibit at St Katharine's Dock, before being sold to the *Cambria* Trust in 1996 for £1; an exchange of money is required under early maritime law for ownership of a vessel to be passed from one person to another, so many derelict and unwanted boats are 'sold' for the nominal sum of £1 for the transaction to be legally recognized.

After a long, hard campaign by many dedicated individuals, the *Cambria* was eventually restored to her original condition, which has secured the future of this famous sailing barge. 'She is a unique vessel, one of the gems in our maritime history,' said Basil proudly, going on to tell us that the *Cambria* still competes in the traditional Estuary barge races.

The barge matches were started in the late nineteenth century by William Henry Dodd, who became known as the Golden Dustman after accumulating a fortune with his fleet of rubbish barges. Racing had always been part of every bargeman's working life: the barge that brought the freight to port first was paid first, so there was a lot of rivalry between skippers. The big companies took advantage of this and used the matches to show off the speed of their vessels; they even started making new barges, such as *Veronica*, just to win the races. She was a champion in the pre-war races but still functioned as a working boat. In the 1950s she was rigged purely for racing and could not have traded cargo with her huge rig, as she was grossly over-canvassed. The races usually started at Gravesend, Southend or Erith, then went down to the Outer Estuary. There were various classes according to the size of the barges, which made a difference to their design and increased public interest. The matches stopped during the Second World War, then restarted in the 1950s, and they are still popular today.

Basil has skippered many barges during the matches over the years. He described the excitement at the beginning, the barges jostling for position as the gun went off, and said the races could be quite hazardous with so many big vessels, which are fairly slow and difficult to manoeuvre, especially when they're all in the water together. He said that competitors do try hard not to hit each other but, sometimes, there are incidents. Last year, one barge T-boned another vessel and caused extensive damage. There could have been fatalities but, fortunately, they were able to beach the barge and pump her out.

John had never crewed in the races when he was working on *Cambria*, but he always used to watch them with great interest and often worked as a nightwatchman on the racing barge *Dreadnought*. Basil could see what it would mean to John to be a passenger on the boat during a barge match and kindly arranged spaces for us on board at their next race: the Southend Thames Barge Match.

A few weeks later, on an overcast day, in the early morning we took a small fishing boat from the end of Southend Pier out to the *Cambria*, which was moored up to the west of the pier head, along with six other historic vessels, including Topsail Charters' boat *Reminder*. The barges looked spectacular, lying low in the water together, waiting for the tide to rise, rigged to race. We stepped up on to the leeboards and met the rest of the racing crew. In the security briefing, we were given strict instructions that, as passengers, we were not to get in the way of the crew during the race.

We would race the triangular course twice, starting at the pier head then inside the Low Way, leaving West Leigh Middle to port, then across the Estuary, rounding West North Sand in Kent to port and back to the pier head as the outer mark, before doing the same circuit again in reverse. There were two classes of barge taking part: Staysail (the faster of the two) and Bowsprit; we were in the latter.

As we waited for the tide to rise, John got chatting to the skipper, Iain Ruffles, who asked John if he would like to crew during the race. He did not need to be asked twice.

When we were ready to start, the crew got into position and I went with the rest of the passengers to stand out of the way behind the line of the wheelhouse. On Iain's instruction, the main brail was let loose, which unfurled the sail, then the mate released the brake and John ran forward and hooked the block on to the traveller on the main horse, which runs across the barge just behind the main hatch, before pulling in the sheet to set the sail. The heavy topsail was set with help from John and others. It took three men to get the last couple of feet up and to wind the handle to make it secure. Iain stood at the helm. We were tacking to windward and the barge would not come about without assistance, so the foresail had to be held across the bow of the barge with the bow line. John held it fast before letting go as the barge's head moved across, away from the wind. The skipper shouted, 'Let go o' the bow line!' then the foresail whizzed across the horse

and set itself. 'One more on the halyard!' shouted Iain, and John was already in position for the topsail tack that followed.

We sailed up towards the start line. Crowds of spectators had gathered on the sun deck of the pier to watch the magnificent sight of so many Thames barges under sail. The first horn blasted out and we gybed around to get near to the start line, trying to avoid colliding into the other boats, all of which were doing the same thing. The air was filled with the exhilarating cries of skippers shouting similar instructions to their crews. *Adieu* was closest behind us, to stern. 'Ready about!' shouted Iain. Everyone hunkered down on deck as we gybed around. The final gun sounded, but we had misjudged our approach and had to restart, turning back, against the tide. *Marjorie* had the best start and sped ahead, followed by *Adieu*, and it was a few minutes later when we actually crossed the line. The crew collectively groaned.

By this time, I was standing beside the wheelhouse, so I could

speak to Iain and watch all the action on deck at the same time. We sailed on a broad reach past Leigh buoy at a speed of about six knots, but it was not fast enough to catch up with the other barges ahead. 'On a good blow, with a good sail up, she can reach about ten to twelve knots,' said Iain, 'but today is not our day.' We had lost too much ground to the others by then and were half an hour behind the lead boat. We altered our course slightly to avoid a container ship in the shipping channel as we headed over towards the Kent coast. *Princess Pocahontas* came by to port, filled with tourists taking photographs of the barges.

Cambria cut almost silently through the water, pitching mildly in the centre of the Estuary. It was such an extraordinary, timeless experience, racing under sail in such a historic boat. I was thoroughly enjoying myself, but John and the rest of the crew looked despondent. 'We are trailing too far behind now after that bad start, and the tide is running against us,' said John. 'We're not really in the race.'

We sailed close to the *Montgomery* as we turned back towards the pier on our first run of the course. We were heeling over quite a bit, close to the water. As we moved away from the Kent coast, we began to pick up speed. It was a high tide as we started the second leg. Distant music from the seafront could be heard on deck as we passed the pier head for the second time. The crowds waved and cheered us on, but the distance between the boats grew and, after the excitement of the beginning of the race, it felt like we were sailing solo.

Throughout the rest of the afternoon, we tried to catch the other barges: a couple of crew members were on the winches for the leeboards, raising one board and lowering the other as we tacked. Someone else was up on the foresail to hold the sail up as we came through the wind. But though the crew worked tirelessly, hoisting headsails, dropping sails if the wind increased, and taking instructions from the skipper, we were too far behind to make up the distance. We came in last, after a long afternoon on the water.

Despite our dismal ranking in the race, it had been a fantastic day for all involved, a really wonderful experience for me and the other passengers, but particularly for John, who was thrilled to have spent the afternoon sailing *Cambria* once more on the Estuary. 'I feel sixteen again,' he said, grinning as we disembarked on to the passenger ferry. The crew stayed on board for a little longer, preparing for the dinner and prize-giving ceremony later that evening, which would be held at the end of the pier, and was where all the barge crews would come together to share stories and their great passion for Thames barges.

Looking back on the day's exploits, one detail really stuck in my mind. Standing beside Iain at the helm was a young boy of fourteen who watched him like a hawk; the teenager was interested in training to be a skipper himself one day. 'He is the future for the barges,' John told me as we reflected on the afternoon's defeat. 'Without that interest from the next generation, these vessels just won't survive.'

8

Neither Land nor Sea

The Essex littoral: a shoreline which, though historically
embattled and often aesthetically derided, is today a place of
great ecological and cultural importance . . . the tidal shoreline
as a unique setting – an 'edge condition', if you like – where
the ecological, the ethical and matters of the spiritual and
the numinous, meet in a fruitful and prescient way.
   – 'Time and Tide: The Moral Theatre of the Essex Shoreline',
                        Professor Ken Worpole, Burrows Lecture,
                                       University of Essex, 2011

Between the railway track and the Benfleet Downs sits a sparsely
beautiful agrarian landscape of part-flooded salt marsh inhabited by
grazing cattle and wild horses, with the ruinous remains of Hadleigh
Castle on a hill behind. Beside it runs Benfleet Creek, a narrow inlet
of water that ebbs and flows with the tidal Estuary. In the mid-
nineteenth century, during the construction of the London to
Southend railway line, the charred remains of human skeletons and
ships' timbers were uncovered there: probable remnants of a battle
between the Saxons and the Vikings over a thousand years ago. Traces
of earlier marshes and submerged forests can sometimes be seen on
the foreshore at low tide, along with bones and shells from the prehistoric era.

One bright but crisp February morning I met the author and

cultural historian Ken Worpole outside Benfleet station, which over-looks the creek. As we began walking eastwards, Ken pointed towards the container ships drifting past in the deep-water channel beyond the flat terrain of mud, water and sky ahead. Canvey Island lay on our right. 'For me,' he said, 'Essex is special because it fails to conform to conventional ideas about what is beautiful in the English landscape.' Ken has written extensively about Essex as a place of significant cul-tural importance and as a laboratory of environmental, cultural and social change in the twentieth century. For *350 Miles: An Essex Jour-ney*, a collaboration with photographer Jason Orton, he walked the entire coastline of the county over the period of a year. Much of it was familiar to him already, as his family had moved to Canvey after the war, 'as part of that great exodus of people from the East End looking for a better life'. Ken spent his early years on Canvey living in a wooden bungalow on stilts near the sea wall, exploring ditches full of dragonflies and reed beds between the unmade roads. Every week he would read in the *Southend Standard* the list of ships and their cargoes that would be passing by. 'People were interested. Shipping was part of the landscape of our lives, along with the visual world of the refineries and the flat Thames.'

The family moved off the island the year before the Great Flood in 1953, then lived for a while in nearby Thundersley, opposite a chapel belonging to the Peculiar People – a group unique to Essex. 'It was a revivalist Christian sect started in the 1830s in Rochford by a drunken farmer who had an epiphany. They had quite a lot of affin-ities with the Plymouth Brethren, which meant they refused blood transfusions, which made them unpopular.'

We started walking towards Benfleet Marina, where a variety of boats were moored up on the muddy banks of the creek, next to a quirky pub on a former barge called the *Gladys*. 'Most of the boats here are very old,' said Ken, 'and some of them are still used for fish-ing, unlike the leisure craft at lots of very expensive marinas around the coast of Britain.' Benfleet Marina is also one of the only places

along the Estuary foreshore where people still live on the water, and quite a few houseboats can still be found there, from narrowboats to converted barges to beached hulls and ex-army landing craft. An earlier, much larger colony of houseboats once stretched from the creek right up towards the footpath of the castle in Leigh. These ramshackle floating homes were built from timbers rescued from bombed-out buildings and wrecked boats and housed a range of people, from travellers to those who had been made homeless by the Blitz.

'There is a culture in Essex of setting up DIY independent communities,' said Ken, 'from self-built homes in places like Jaywick and Canvey, to the plotlands in Laindon and Basildon. Land colonies were also a big feature of the late-nineteenth-century Essex landscape, partly because of its proximity to London and also because land was relatively cheap. This part of Essex has always been a place where social reformers in the East End established experimental communities.' Ken told me about some of these settlers: the suffragette on Canvey Island who set up a boarding house in which young seamstresses could recuperate from their work; and the Salvation Army colony established by William Booth at Hadleigh Farm, next to the castle, as a settlement for alcoholics and homeless men from London's East End. Booth's project is still going and is now the longest-surviving land colony in Britain. Today, they run a café there that employs young people with learning disabilities.

We moved on to a high, grassy embankment which runs through the marsh from Benfleet to Leigh. On one side, the tidal estuarine landscape stretched out before us, with the North Sea beyond. On the other side were the Benfleet Downs, dotted with sheep, cattle and other wildlife, and historic Hadleigh Castle up on the hill – the best place along this coastline to see fantastic panoramic views across the Estuary.

Hadleigh Castle is popular in the English imagination: it was painted by John Constable in 1828 soon after his wife died. The artist's earlier works are full of life and images of serenity – working landscapes with lush vegetation – but his painting of Hadleigh Castle depicts a ruin: all emptiness, with bleak skies beyond. At the time of Henry III's reign, when the castle was built, the sea would have reached the base of the hill and the marsh would have been completely flooded. The embankment we were walking on was a relatively recent construction built to protect the land from the incoming tide.

As we walked through the intertidal zone of salt marsh and mudflats, Ken spoke about the beauty of the landscape. 'Some people would call it desolate, but the fact that you have got the sea and the sky in a dynamic relationship to each other makes it pretty magical – at

least to me.' It was low tide, and the muddy banks of the creek were covered in the footprints of all kinds of wading birds, creating a beautiful kind of Cyrillic writing made by ducks, turnstones and curlews. We looked across the Estuary waters to the farmland in the far distance on the Isle of Grain, and the post-industrial wilderness of the power stations and silos, which we both agreed had a certain melancholy beauty of its own.

An article in *Country Life* once awarded Essex zero points out of ten for landscape quality. Irritation with this article, along with the 'continual drip-feed of nonsense about Essex being a wild, barbarian county and the knowing jokes about Essex girls or Essex man', inspired Ken to start writing a counter narrative of his own. In his superb essay 'East of Eden' (in the anthology *Towards Re-enchantment: Place and Its Meanings*, 2010), Ken focused on the particular qualities of East Mersea, one of several inhabited Essex islands, with its dusty roads and little cottages, where people still in the summer put out boxes of apples or plums on tables to sell or give away.

Towards Re-enchantment, a collection of specially commissioned

pieces by writers with a shared interest in the meanings and inter-
pretation of place, was published by Artevents. I had listened to Ken
read from the book during the launch at the *London Review of Books*
shop. Iain Sinclair spoke about Hackney and Springfield Park, and
Jay Griffiths brought wildness into the room with her sensuous and
passionate recitation of her brilliant essay 'The Grave of Dafydd'.
The lively discussion that ensued afterwards, chaired by co-editor
and maverick curator Gareth Evans, was a catalyst for me for a new
way of thinking about the Essex coast.

The book was part of the wider re-enchantment project which
focused around W. G. Sebald's *The Rings of Saturn*, which tracks a
long walk around the East Anglian coastline and explores some of
the lesser-known histories of Suffolk. Ken and I had both been asked
by Gareth to speak at the writers' symposium taking place in Snape
Maltings as part of an extraordinary weekend put together by
Artevents, which included the launch of *Patience (After Sebald)*, Grant
Gee's translation of Sebald's work into celluloid, which features the
book itself as artefact, as landscape. During the film, Iain Sinclair
gave a warning to would-be psychogeographers planning to walk the
route mapped out in the *Rings of Saturn*: it was a pointless exercise,
as Robert Macfarlane found on his attempt.

As Ken and I walked across the marsh that day and spoke about
the re-enchantment project and its impact on our work, I told Ken
how I had met Jo Catling after the screening of Gee's film at that
winter arts festival in Suffolk. Jo is an academic from the University
of East Anglia who worked closely with Sebald for decades. She compiled an anthology of essays, academic writings and newly translated
works by and about Sebald after his death. For the front cover, she
chose a photograph of Max standing outside a hotel in Aldeburgh,
holding a couple of books in his hand. She was curious to find out
what the titles of the books were, and when she looked closely
with a magnifying glass she discovered the small volume was one of
mine: a slim, limited-edition, alternative walking tour called

Rodinsky's Whitechapel. I was overwhelmed to hear this. I had felt
nervous about doing a presentation the following day at the symposium dedicated to Sebald, the person whose writing has had a deeper
impact on me than any other artist, and it felt as if he had given me a
blessing from beyond the grave that night. It was after that weekend
that I decided I would write a book focusing on Essex, and after my

trip on *Ideeal* that the idea for this book on the Estuary really came into being.

Ken enjoyed this story, with all its Sebaldian coincidences and recurring themes. As we walked through the sparse terrain of the Benfleet marsh, he gestured around us and said, 'Sebald helped revive interest in the agricultural interiors and bleak maritime landscapes of Essex and East Anglia.' Ken has continued to explore these places in his work. In his most recent book, with Jason Orton, *The New English Landscape* (2013), he discusses the need to reinterpret contemporary landscapes anew, particularly hitherto neglected areas such as the Thames Estuary. 'Landscape is still the largest visual component of our lives,' he said as we strode across the wetland, 'reflecting where we are today, emotionally and psychologically.'

We walked in silence for some time, then began to talk about Liverpool Street station, another recurring theme in Sebald's work. Ken remembered the place when steam trains were still operating. He recalled that coming into the station was like arriving at a vast, smoke-filled cavern – and, for a child, rather scary. In his guide to Essex, originally published in 1954, Nikolaus Pevsner suggested that people were put off visiting the county because Liverpool Street station had once been so unbearably grim. Sebald, too, felt discomfited by the associations of the station, and connected the history of East Anglia with the history of Europe, especially the Kindertransport: 'Liverpool Street was the main starting point for people going to Europe and coming from Europe at the outbreak of the war, as well as for Jewish refugee children arriving.' He notes that the station is physically populated by these ghosts: there is a sculpture of Jewish children with suitcases, and a marble memorial to the Great Eastern Railway employees who died during the First World War.

We talked for a while about Jewish settlement from East London to Essex. Ken's wife, Larraine, came from the Jewish East End, as had my family, and likewise settled in Westcliff. Then, as we continued our walk towards the edges of Two Tree Island, Ken spoke

about the volatile relationship between the coast and the sea, about that landscape being both a place under constant threat from climate change and flooding and a place of constant shape-shifting and evocation of past lives. 'The physical landscape is continually evolving here,' he said, 'and shaped daily by tides, resulting in a unique environment for particular plants, flowers, birds and insects, which thrive in these rich intertidal habitats.'

We reached the tip of Two Tree Island, one of many former landfill sites along this part of the Thames Estuary now turned into wildlife-conservation areas. When Ken was growing up here, Two Tree Island was still the main rubbish tip for Southend Corporation, and he remembers seeing endless convoys of dustcarts trundling past Leigh station, dumping rubbish. After it reached capacity, the tip was seeded, and successional overgrowth reclaimed the land. Subsequently, artificial lagoons – non-tidal and independent – have been constructed to the west of the island and have become one of the principal UK breeding grounds for avocets. The marsh sands around the island are covered in rough saltings and clumps of eelgrass, which from a distance make the mud look green when the tide goes out. Thousands of dark-bellied Arctic geese arrive at these salt marshes every winter to feed, before returning to the tundra to breed.

I often walk my dog on Two Tree and visit the bird hides scattered around the perimeter of the island. I had recently also visited the Lower Thames Rowing Club there, the headquarters of which (two shipping containers) overlooks the Canvey Yacht Club, on the other side of the creek. I spoke with Vanessa Bradford, a local woman from Leigh who has been rowing competitively on the women's racing team with this club for the last couple of years.

They race in Norwich, Brightlingsea and Richmond, amongst other places, but most of their training takes place on the Estuary, which she describes as an exhilarating environment. 'There are all

these hidden dangers in the Estuary you've got to be really aware of. Every time we go out it's different, and so much more challenging than being on a gentle river. You're dealing with waves and traffic and the whipping currents out in the channel.' She said the mud had changed since the dredging began, especially since the big container ships started coming downriver. Some sandbanks had shifted; others had appeared. 'It's a bit like sand dunes – it looks different every week, and when the tide's in you lose perspective of where the channels are – but learning in these conditions means that we win all the races.'

'It doesn't matter how many times I have done this walk,' Ken said as we reached the end of the embankment and started heading towards Leigh station, 'it's always different. The big skies and long vistas allow your mind to wander.' I waved goodbye and stood and watched three big ships out in the deep shipping channel queuing up, waiting for the tide to come in.

9

Estuary One Design

We study the sailor, the man of his hands, man of all work; all
eye, all finger, muscle, skill and endurance; a tailor, carpenter,
cooper, stevedore, and clerk and astronomer besides. He is a great
saver, and a great quiddle by the necessity of his situation.
— *Journal*, 'At Sea', Ralph Waldo Emerson, 2 January 1833

It was a cold March day and the water looked dark and uninviting. I
was standing on the deck of the Essex Yacht Club, which is housed
in a prototype glass-fibre minesweeper called HMS *Wilton*, which is
anchored up on the mud about a quarter of a mile from Old Leigh
Town. My friend Jonny Wells was with me, and we were waiting for
the photographer James Price, but he was stuck in traffic on the A13.
The tide was starting to run out and we only had a small window of
time before our planned sailing trip would have to be cancelled.

We were hoping to go out in Jonny's eighteen-foot sailing dinghy
Tango, an Estuary One Design based on the earlier Essex One Design,
one of the oldest classes of dinghies still racing, built in 1911 specifically for the shallow waters of the Thames Estuary. 'Back in the day,
they had them in Leigh, Whitstable, Margate and Ramsgate,' said
Jonny. 'They were originally heavy, clinker-built boats with five-inch
planks, built to order as pleasure boats and for racing near the shore.
By the 1960s, the wooden boats had become hard to maintain, so they
started moulding them in glass fibre, which made them a bit lighter

and less expensive. The new, lighter Estuary One Designs kept the same sail area as the old, making them over-canvassed and a handful in a blow. They have a relatively shallow draught and a lifting centreplate, which means you can sail over shallows.'

Jonny has been racing these boats for the past seven years with his father, Brian, and team mate Tim Browne. They are the holders of the coveted Velsheda Trophy, the award for the most important race in the EOD calendar. Any eighteen-foot dinghy can enter if she is kept on a mooring on the Essex foreshore. So far, they have won this competition four times.

We went below deck into the club room, a large, open space with a wooden floor, and a bar at one end with wide windows that wrapped around all sides of the decommissioned warship, giving panoramic views across the Estuary waters. Low tables and velvet-covered chairs sat in front of the bar. The walls were adorned with various sailing trophies, photographs and paintings, including pictures of the previous four ships – the *Gypsy*, *Carlotta*, the *Lady Seville* and the *Bembridge* – all of which had served as the headquarters of the club. Despite being inside a ship, the decoration of the interior was typical of many of the other sailing clubs along both coastlines of the Estuary I had visited whilst researching this book: a little eccentric and home-spun, but warm and inviting. 'For some people, being a member here is like being a member of a country club,' said Jonny. 'They meet up here to have a couple of drinks, attend balls and other functions but, for me and most others, it's very much about the sailing.'

Jonny has been sailing all his life. His father used to take him in the family cruiser; Jonny sailed up the east coast in a carry-cot when he was still a baby. The family spent most school holidays exploring the Dutch canals, living and sleeping on the boat, and Jonny was just nine when he got his first dinghy, an Optimist, which he described as 'a seven-foot-long box'. He kept it at the Thames Estuary Yacht Club and has fond memories of hot summers in the 1970s, sailing with his friends up to the pier and back. Some days, they would pack sandwiches, catch an early tide and spend the day beached on the southern mudbanks of the Ray Gut, playing football and swimming in the creek, before drifting back in on the tide around five. They occasionally got into minor scrapes, had the odd capsize and

sometimes struggled to get back to shore, but if they got into trouble they had to sort it out themselves.

Jonny started racing competitively at the age of fourteen, in an Express (a two-man glass-fibre boat with a spinnaker) before moving on to a Laser, a twelve-foot-long, Olympic-class glass-fibre boat. Around this time, Brian started ocean racing in a Contessa Space 38 called *Assassin*, competing in the Round Britain race, the two-man transatlantic and the Azores and Back race. 'My father is seventy-eight now,' said Jonny, 'and he's still winning competitions. Sailing is a sport that you can carry on well into your retirement years.'

Jonny stopped competitive sailing for a while when he left Essex to go to art school, returning to the sport in his early thirties, and sailing Wayfarers at the Essex Yacht Club before moving on to ISOs: fast, fourteen-foot two-man trapeze boats with asymmetric spinnakers. He competed in many local races, including the Nore Race, the biggest inter-club event on the Estuary, which has taken place annually since 1920. Over a hundred and fifty boats participate – every class of sailing dinghy and cruising yacht – leaving at 9 a.m. and taking a route all the way over to Kent, past the *Montgomery*, around the former site of the Nore lightship in Kent, and back. It's a long race, stretching to seven hours for some boats, and over thirty different trophies are presented at the end. Jonny recalled a particularly eventful year when the wind went from five knots gusting to over thirty knots. 'It was carnage, with capsized boats everywhere. We spent the whole day stuck on mud and watched the rest coming in with broken masts, sails down, getting towed along, then dumped on sand.'

One winter, he bumped into an old schoolfriend and they started sailing ISOs together. They won a few events, got a coach and a sponsor, and spent the next eight years competing at amateur level in sailing events around the country and in Europe. They were constantly on the road, staying in B&Bs in obscure little seaside towns, and racing intensively.

Even for experienced seamen, the races can be dangerous. At the Hoo Freezer in 2005, the wind was blowing thirty-five knots straight on to the sea wall behind the start line. Two hundred yards from the finish line, they were blown flat by a gust and couldn't get the boat upright. 'Every time we got the boat up it would go straight over again on top of us. We tried about fifteen times.' Jonny ended up wrecking his knee, tearing the cartilage and needing an operation.

As we sat talking in the clubhouse, Brian and Tim came in. James was ten minutes away, and Jonny and Tim went out in the rigid inflatable boat (RIB) to rig the EOD whilst I sat and chatted with Brian. When James finally arrived, Brian gave us both a safety briefing before fitting us with life jackets. Whilst we waited on the racks for Tim to come and pick us up in the RIB, we discussed the photo shoot. Brian suggested that James follow the EOD in the support boat, but James was keen to have a close-up action shot and, somehow, James and I managed to persuade Brian that James should come in the EOD, too. It was a decision we would all come to regret.

By the time we got on to *Tango* and started sailing east out towards the pier, there was a fairly fresh breeze of about sixteen knots. The sun had come out, but it was still cold and the sea looked quite choppy. The sailing boat sat low in the water and tipped over slightly to one side. Jonny and Brian were leaning out of the boat as we sailed along, with their feet under the toe straps. Brian explained that if they did not do this the forces of the wind on the sails would make the boat heel too much. Brian was steering the boat, working the mainsheet and the tiller, whilst Jonny was working the gybe. Brian let some of the mainsail out to spill the wind in the gusts. To me, it appeared as if we were travelling at great speed. The experience felt a little precarious, but it was also exhilarating to be sailing whilst looking back at Leigh-on-sea from the Estuary.

Whilst we moved, Jonny told me more about racing EODs. He explained that you might get ten boats out for a club race, closer to twenty if it was a championship. Crews read the course card in advance so they know where they are going. The race officers always try to set one of the legs to windward, which gives people the chance to play the wind shifts – get your tactics right on these legs, and you can come out on top. 'Success in dinghy racing is rooted in the physical – but the real race is often won tactically. A beautifully executed start, the correct race strategy, working the shifts upwind and down, knowledge of the rules – out-thinking your opponents is key!' said Jonny.

He said that every race is a challenge because the variables are so extreme. 'You can't all line up on the start line and go, you have to get yourself on the line at full speed, at the start gun, which is quite hard when you've got loads of other boats all fighting for the same piece of water and affecting the wind over your sails. Whoever can get the first shift and get free generally comes out well – but that's not always the case.'

The river could be busy, particularly at weekends. 'We keep out of the way of the cocklers because, if they are coming up the creek, they have restricted manoeuvrability. We don't really come into contact with kite surfers – they are normally out when it is too windy for us – but sometimes we have to shout at the odd windsurfer to get out of the way. If you're racing, you don't want to go around someone and lose half a boat-length. When we are short tacking up the shore towards the pier on a nice sea-breeze day, we see loads of swimmers and we have to whistle at them to stay where they are. Sometimes, we have to avoid the odd seal but they normally swim away from us, and we do have to watch out for the lines of anglers out there on boats – occasionally, we've accidentally got caught on someone's line and sailed off and got shouted at.'

Jonny used to sail the ISO in the evening series on a late tide as well but said that he had to stop because he kept hitting the mud. 'Even the EODs struggled to get round one of the racing marks just by the creek off Leigh beach, which is silting up.' He wondered if these changes had anything to do with the dredging for the super port.

Whilst we had been talking, Jonny and Brian had been constantly working the boat, releasing and trimming the sails relative to the wind direction, sitting in different positions dependent on the point of sail and making various other adjustments to keep us moving in an optimal way. They did all of this without discussion, anticipating the other's movements instinctively. This is not unusual: any good racing crew will execute their tactics and boat-handling with barely a word spoken; just a glance at the compass or the rig is enough for the other to understand the next move.

We changed direction and started sailing west down towards Two Tree with the wind behind us. By then I had finished my audio interview, and it was time for James to start setting up the camera. We had a maximum of twenty minutes on the same tack before we reached the island. James spent a long time fixing the camera in place behind the mast, and Brian warned him he now had less than ten minutes to take the picture. As we sailed along, James was always under the hood of the replica Victorian camera, desperately trying to focus and take the action shot of Jonny and Brian. The boat pitched up and down in a fairly steep chop as we travelled along at a speed of about six knots.

Time was starting to run out, and so was our sea room. Jonny kept asking if James was ready, and every time he said, 'Nearly there, nearly there.' I was getting anxious – the shoreline of Two Tree was looming up ahead. After another couple of minutes, Brian firmly told James to drop the camera immediately, but unfortunately the camera was attached to the boat by so many different tripods and clamps it took ages to dismantle, blocking the boom and preventing Jonny and Brian from tacking the boat in time – which caused us to crash hard into the marshes.

My memories of exactly what happened next are sketchy. I know James must have finally released the camera, because it somehow ended up in my lap. I remember clear, calm and very firm instructions from Jonny and Brian. We were told to keep our heads down and to keep our hands out of the way. Ropes flew around beneath me. Brian and Jonny worked hard, expertly pulling different ropes as they attempted to tack around to get us off the mud. They shouted instructions for us to shift our weight over to the other side, but we were not quick and we heeled over a great deal to leeward as we turned. I fell hard against the side of the boat as it angled down steeply towards the water, my recording equipment went overboard and the camera fell from my lap towards the sea.

It was a slow-motion moment. I remember tumbling towards the water and thinking quite calmly, 'Oh, we are going to capsize' as the boat started to rise up above me. James grabbed the back of my jeans and somehow yanked me back into the boat and back into normal time, then everything speeded up dramatically as *Tango* righted herself with a heavy splash and a thud. Somehow, in those few moments,

I had managed to flick the extremely heavy camera back into the boat with my left hand, but in the process I had injured myself badly. At the time, I was so overjoyed that we had not capsized I did not feel much pain. Jonny could see I was hurt and in shock and wanted to get me off the boat straight away. Tim was right beside us in the support boat, which he steered alongside and, somehow, I crawled on my belly from one moving boat to the other.

The next day, Jonny walked out on the mud in his boots and found my ruined voice recorder. He took the SD card out and put it in a bag of rice for twenty-four hours and, amazingly, it was readable. It took me a long time to be able to listen to that tape, which, thankfully, cuts off just before the crash.

Southend is the Pier

Imagine if you can, the silver specks and black, darting amongst
the clouds – the ships hobbling home with holes in their sides –
the Little Boats for Dunkirk streaming out and back – the blazing
tankers – the forts and the odd monstrosities slowly towing
out – the destroyers and the gunboats – the procession of
searchlights – the falling planes – the first Liberty Ship –
the doodlebugs – the German U-boat.

> – *The Battle of the Thames: The War Story of*
> *Southend Pier*, A. P. Herbert, 1945

During the night, deep-purple bruises emerged along one side of my
body, I could not sleep, my left hand was throbbing with pain. An
X-ray the following morning revealed shattered fragments of bone
floating around inside it. I had to have an operation. The surgeon
explained that he would drill through the remaining healthy bone to
fix a metal frame in place.

After the anaesthetic had worn off, it felt as if I had been stabbed
through the hand with a knife. They gave me liquid morphine – bottles
of it. I spent days in bed with the curtains drawn, staring unthinking
into space, and began unwittingly to abuse the drug, waking throughout the night, swigging straight from the bottle, then falling back into
a fitful sleep filled with disturbing, violent dreams. I was visited by a
nocturnal guest, a dark presence in my room, the sinister figure of the

surgeon performing DIY on my hand, standing with force, cutting through bone and gristle with an electric saw.

Other nightmarish visions drew me back to the eerie space beneath Southend Pier, that strange shadow realm filled with the wailing sound of restless ghosts, sirens of the sea luring me under. From the depths of my unconscious mind, I sensed there was real horror in the sounds of that night; black water flowed through my mind. I kept waking, paralysed with fear, thinking I could hear the creaking of rope stretching and rubbing beside me. I disappeared for a few weeks. The drug took hold of me for a while, then I came off it too quickly and spent days curled in a foetal ball on my bed, intermittently shaking and vomiting. I could not write, I could not eat and I could not get back on the water.

During those dark days, I thought about opium a lot, about the thousands of Chinese people who had become addicted to the drug in the nineteenth century, when the British had illegally imported it from India to China in vessels belonging to the East India Company. When the Chinese government began to confiscate crates of the drug stored in British warehouses in Canton, the Opium Wars began, with British troops attacking Chinese forces until they gained control of the trade, which they tried to legalize, keen to take advantage of its high profit margin.

I thought about the East End opium dens of Limehouse, which were established by Chinese seamen – the earliest ethnic East London migrants, who arrived in England via the Estuary and jumped ship at the docks. They were vilified for introducing opium to the UK. Some were undoubtedly involved in the trade; most were not, although the stories of the 'mean and miserable' ruinous dens have become legendary, mainly due to the literature of Conan Doyle and Dickens, who described unsavoury foreign characters wreathed in opium smoke luring in the innocent and the curious. I thought about opium a great deal for a long time. It possessed my mind, as did the mysterious lower deck of the pier.

When I had recovered enough to start working again, I spent days in the archives of the Maritime Museum looking for information on Southend Pier, which was erected in 1829. The pier quickly became a popular tourist attraction, and the lower deck was used extensively from the offset as a landing stage for getting on and off vessels arriving at and departing from Southend.

Throughout the Great War, the army and the navy commandeered the pier. Prisoners, soldiers and naval personnel replaced the day-trippers and tourists using the lower deck. German prisoners-of-war were regularly brought down to Southend by train, then marched along the high street under armed guard, along the pier down to the lower deck, to be transported out on to three former cruise liners moored just off the pier head, which had been leased by the British government and were used as temporary prisoner-of-war ships.

The *Royal Edward* and the *Saxonia* held civilians (many of whom were interned Germans who had been living in the UK; as well as other 'enemy aliens'), and the *Invernia* held military soldiers (who had been captured in France). Over five thousand prisoners were on these three vessels by March 1915. Those that could afford it paid for first-class cabins; the others slept in steerage. In the daytime, the prisoners could be seen relaxing on the decks of the boats; at night, they were locked below. A signal station was placed at the pier head and was manned by local Boy Scouts, who communicated with the prison ships using semaphore flags and bugles.

On 10 May 1915, the first major bombing raid in Britain took place over Southend. More than one hundred bombs were dropped by Zeppelin LZ 38, the first falling in the water close to the *Royal Edward* and only narrowly missing the ship. A direct hit would have meant certain death for those on board. I thought of the sheer terror of those German prisoners that night, who were nearly killed by one of their own, and imagined them screaming out in unison as the bombs fell in the water around them.

During the First World War, injured soldiers would have disembarked from war-damaged ships on to the lower deck before being

transferred on to the pier train, which operated day and night, carrying people, stores, ammunition and medicine back and forth from the boats to the land. Some carriages were adapted to accommodate stretchers for the wounded, who were taken directly to the Palace Hotel on Pier Hill, right opposite the shore end of the pier. It became a medical station known as Queen Mary's Royal Naval Hospital. Postcards from the period show injured servicemen leaning over the balcony, dangling tin cups on bits of string, which were filled with coins, cigarettes and sweets by members of the public gathered below.

After the First World War ended, the hotel and the pier reverted back to popular recreational sites, predominantly used by thousands of day-trippers from London's East End. My Polish-Jewish grandparents escaped the grimy backstreets of Whitechapel for a precious day beside the sea whenever they could. They hired deckchairs on the end of the pier, visited the sun-deck theatre to see popular variety shows, ate fish and chips and took trips on one of many steamships, such as the *Royal Daffodil*, which operated day cruises from the pier head to places including Margate, Clacton, Calais and Boulogne. They would have boarded these boats from the lower deck – another layer of memory on that space.

During the course of the Second World War, the pier became the navy control centre for the Thames Estuary and was renamed HMS *Leigh*. Projectile rockets and anti-aircraft guns were fitted on the pier head and manned by the Maritime Regiment. Some of the 135 Phoenix Units built to construct Mulberry Harbour were anchored off the pier head for a while before being sailed out along the Estuary.

No lights were allowed afloat or ashore during the first year of the war, apart from searchlights on the pier head, which scoured everything that came up or down the Estuary. The lower deck would have been shrouded in darkness, as black as ink, occasionally illuminated by the sweeping beam of light, which would catch fleeting glimpses of weary soldiers marching in line, getting quickly on and off the boats. Thousands of navy personnel and Trinity House pilots would have used the lower deck to board the convoys of military vessels gathered at the pier head.

On the night of 22 November 1939, Germans machine-gunned the pier head and dropped fourteen magnetic sea mines via parachute into the water. The navy retaliated – one German aircraft was brought down and fell into the Estuary in a blaze of flames. After this attack, doodlebugs roared constantly ahead, but that was the last concentrated assault on the pier. The mines were plotted and sought out by sweepers, then destroyed.

In July 1940, the Battle of Britain began, with focused attacks by the Luftwaffe on shipping convoys and ports. The Estuary became a primary target. Night after night, the bombers came. Parachute mines, magnetic mines, acoustic mines and other bombs fell into the dark river; distant dogfights speckled the sky. Little patrol boats fired weapons from the water and picked up pieces of burning planes. Rapid machine-gun fire from the pier head filled the night sky with streaks of orange light. Daylight revealed the wreckage: half-sunken tugs, holes in Tilbury landing stage, fires at Shell Haven. Many vessels were destroyed. In the outer reaches of the Estuary, wrecks littered the channel. Bomb-damaged ships came back into the river and moored up beside the lower deck to offload their dead and wounded. A large fleet of Sun tugs travelled back and forth to the pier head, salvaging damaged ships and planes. The battle over the Thames continued in darkness for six months. Minesweepers combed the channel daily. Southend was on the front line.

In May 1944, the Americans arrived in the Estuary, with powerful tugs, landing craft and Liberty ships, amongst them the SS *Montgomery*. Prostitutes worked the lower deck of the pier when American warships came alongside, 'and they were busy'. Over 27,000 ships were reported in the Estuary that year. There was no room for them all to berth; they were anchored in long lines down the middle of the lower reaches. From Sea Reach to Hole Haven sat 'an endless forest of ships – transports, hospital ships, landing ships, tankers and barges'.

The solarium at the end of the pier, built originally as a dance hall, was used during the war for naval conferences. The *Montgomery* was ordered to anchor off the Nore from there, and it was from the solarium that Commodore Champion told eighty-nine masters and twenty of their escort commanders where they would land at Normandy during the Battle of Dunkirk. As D-Day approached, the ships off the pier head 'began to be as thick as midges on the water'. Crews of an armada of 'Little Ships' willingly volunteered to rescue the thousands of soldiers stranded on the beaches. The very last vessel to leave

the Mole was a Ramsgate-class lifeboat from Southend pulling a cor-
vette whose propeller had failed.

Southend lifeboat station is situated at the pier head, above the lower
deck. The lifeboats were extremely active during the war: they were
launched on sixty-six occasions, rescued and landed over three hundred crews of various ships and helped save troops in Dunkirk. Paul
Gilson, like his father and his father before him, spent his entire working life manning Southend lifeboats. Over the many times I met with
Paul after our first meeting whilst we were on our cruise on *Ideeal*, he
told me many stories about the rescues he had undertaken during his
decades of service. One day, the Kent coastguard telephoned Southend
lifeboat station to tell them that Sheerness port control could see 'a guy
sitting in one of the machine-gun nests on top of the wheelhouse of
the *Montgomery*'. Paul and his team launched the motorized lifeboat
from their base at the end of Southend Pier and sped across the main
shipping channel towards the ship full of bombs, where they discovered
a lone canoeist, eating a cheese sandwich on top of the wheelhouse.
When the lifeboat called up to the man, he waved at them cheerily and

gave them the thumbs-up. After they told him exactly what he was sitting on, he very slowly and very prudently disembarked.

When he was in the lifeboat service, Paul used to tell young kids the lower deck was haunted to stop them from going down there. When I told him about the noises I had heard that dreadful night, he said, 'The pier is always moving. It feels like there is someone behind you there.' He told me the place has been a site of multiple suicides over the years; his brother once found a dead body drifting in the water near the lower deck.

The report of suicides was confirmed by Lynn Jones, Southend's first female foreshore officer, who works from an office beneath the eastern end of Southend Pier looking out on to the new RNLI lifeboat station. Over the years, she has been involved in multiple incidents on the pier, including many suicide attempts. She confirmed that bodies had been found hanging from underneath the lower deck.

Lynn originally crewed on the patrol boats, which was unusual for a woman: 'It caused a few raised eyebrows with the boatmen in the

town at first.' She now works alongside the lifeboat crews and the Marine Police, searching for casualties in the water, often responding to minor incidents ahead of the lifeboat team, such as rescuing swimmers and people on lilos who have got out of their depth. 'We have an all-terrain vehicle here, an Argo-Cat, so we can rescue people even at low water out on the mud.' During her twenty years in service, Lynn has been involved in many different incidents on the pier, including fires and boat collisions. She carries a VHF radio at all times, so she can contact the coastguard at any point to launch the lifeboat. Her job also involves monitoring the pier and the Southend coastline, allocating moorings to boat owners and acting as a source of information for visitors. It was Lynn with whom Ben Eastop had liaised when we spent the night at the end of the pier on *Ideeal*.

All kinds of events and activities take place on the pier, from music festivals to zombie walks and other community projects. Last year, a project organized by Southend Museum and the Nautical Archaeology Society took place at the pier head. Seventeen local volunteers were recruited and trained in basic principles of conservation first-aid for marine archaeology. A finds centre was set up on the end of the pier in the summer, then the archaeologists came directly from the wreck site of the *London* with artefacts for the volunteers, who sorted through them and practised preventative conservation in front of members of the public. The exact position of the *London* remains a closely guarded secret, but Lynn told me it is not far off the pier head: 'On a clear day, you can see the dive boat bobbing up and down from the end of the pier.'

11

The *London*

This morning is brought me to the office the sad newes of 'The London,' in which Sir J. Lawson's men were all bringing her from Chatham to the Hope, and thence he was to go to sea in her; but a little a'this side of the buoy of the Nower, she suddenly blew up. About 24 [men] and a woman that were in the round-house and coach saved; the rest, being above 300, drowned: the ship breaking all in pieces, with 80 pieces of brass ordnance. She lies sunk, with her round-house above water. Sir J. Lawson hath a great loss in this of so many good chosen men, and many relations among them. I went to the 'Change, where the news taken very much to heart.

        – *Diary*, Samuel Pepys, Wednesday, 8 March 1665

Remnants of many great ships still exist on the sea floor of the Thames Estuary, evidence of the long maritime and military history of this geographically important river. Multiple sea battles have taken place there over time, and hundreds of military vessels have met their fate in these waters. Some have been sunk by enemy fire; others have fallen victim to the shifting tides and notoriously treacherous sandbanks; and many others have been destroyed through some unlucky accident.

The seabed of the Thames Estuary is littered with more shipwrecks per square foot than anywhere else along the UK coastline. There are over six hundred known wrecks in the deep shipping channel alone, and the remains of many more are lodged in the sea floor. Recent finds include a Bronze Age paddle, a Roman cargo ship, a ninth-century Danish Viking longboat, an Elizabethan gunship and a Tudor Thames brick barge, but the most significant wreck in the Estuary is the *London*, a seventeenth-century warship located on the seabed not far from the head of Southend Pier. The *London* is in fact the most important post-medieval wreck anywhere in British waters.

Samuel Pepys and John Evelyn recorded the sinking of HMS *London* in the seventeenth century, and naval historians have always known the wreck was somewhere in the Estuary but, over time, the incident slipped out of living memory, and the remains of the ship were not formally located and identified until extensive diving investigations were carried out on the site by the PLA and Wessex Archaeology, working with DP World.

The *London* was just one of over thirty new sites on which wrecks had been found during the dredging operation for the London Gateway Port, along with the 'Gresham Ship', an armed Elizabethan merchant ship, believed to be a similar-sized vessel to the *Golden Hind*. Luisa Hagele, assistant curator for archaeology at Southend Museum, told me, 'From the museum's perspective, the dredging has been extremely positive: we now have a lot of new material to show the local community. Without the discovery through the dredging, the *London* would have remained unidentified on the seabed and, with time, erosion and biological decay, it wouldn't have lasted into the future.'

Evidence of the wreck was first found in the early 1960s, when the PLA's wreck-raising service investigated an echo-sounder contact on the north side of the Yantlet Channel between Sea Reaches 4 and 5. A diver was sent down and reported seeing 'a lot of timber ribs of an old wooden ship'. The next day, the site was wire-swept, which involves lowering a wire stretched between two ships until it catches on the top of the wreck. After the depth of the wreck had been recorded, divers went down and recovered a seventeenth-century bronze cannon, but the site was then abandoned. In 1979, divers salvaged the site again and recovered two cannons after spotting 'an unusual-looking feature' in a PLA hydrographic survey. The site lay undisturbed for another decade, until the Royal Navy, acting for the Chatham Historic Dockyard, deployed a minesweeper to survey the site. A number of 'cannon-like anomalies' were detected, but the data recorded has not survived.

The shipwreck was finally formally identified in 2007, after being cross-referenced with documentary material, as HMS *London*, a three-deck, second-rate, sixty-gun warship, launched in Chatham in 1656 for the Cromwellian navy. The *London* participated in the First Anglo-Dutch War and formed part of the squadron sent to collect Charles II from the Netherlands to return him to the throne during the Restoration in 1658, after the death of Cromwell.

More than three hundred people died on the *London* when she exploded in a ball of flames on 7 March 1665. She was sailing out of the Medway with seventy-six guns on board to collect her admiral from the Northfleet Hope near Tilbury at the start of the Second Anglo-Dutch War. Aside from the *Princess Alice* disaster, which

occurred further upriver, the accident remains the largest single recorded loss of life in the Thames Estuary. The explosion killed most people outright; others drowned after being trapped below deck, where they had been huddled together, trying to keep warm. It was such a cold day that, thirty miles north, a vicar in Essex reported that his water pump had frozen solid. Most survivors of the blast who ended up in the water quickly succumbed to hypothermia.

Naval historians have different theories about the accident. Some believe the blast was caused by a build-up of methane gas from rotting organic matter in the ship's bilges, others think a spark fell on a gunpowder keg in the hold, but the most popular theory is that the disaster was caused by the reuse of old artillery cartridges. The cotton in the reused cartridges often deteriorated into a fine dust, which then combined with tiny amounts of sulphuric and nitric acids in the gunpowder to form a highly explosive substance known as guncotton. If guncotton dust came into contact with fresh gunpowder, it could lead to massive explosions. After the incident, seventeenth-century salvagers managed to raise a few bronze cannons, but the bodies of the dead crew and passengers were never recovered.

When the wreck was first discovered, some cannons were stolen during an unauthorized salvage. To prevent further attempts, the site was brought under the Protection of Wrecks Act in October 2008, which means that only licensed divers can explore on it and that people cannot fish near the site or have any sort of anchorage there. A team of archaeologists has been excavating the site, but the number of dives they are able to conduct each year is limited, so they started working with three local divers to excavate the wreck. Steve Ellis is a local fishmonger, and he and his wife, Carol, are two of these licensed divers; they go out to the wreck most weekends. 'The *London* is well monitored. When we go out, we have to radio through to the Port of London to say we are on the dive site.' The dive team has been out there before to find Marine Police waiting for them; if anyone else had been on the site, they would have been arrested.

To reach the wreck site, the local team takes an inflatable RIB out from the pier head, then dives, pulling themselves down an anchor line. They have to remain attached at all times because the current is so strong; this causes the sediments below to blow up into something resembling a snow blizzard. They have only an hour to dive at slack water and have to be extremely aware at all times: 'If you came up on the surface when a container ship passes overhead, you'd be dead. The wreck is right in the dredge channel, right in the main shipping lane. The Port of London slow down the ships, which go directly above us; the noise is so loud below it's like being under a train, and with the vibrations it feels like you are being hit with a cricket bat. We have a procedure in place: if we lose a line, we have to fin as far north as we can until our air runs out and then surface away from the main shipping channel.'

The site is in two main sections on the sea floor, about 1,300 feet apart and splintered from the explosion. Most items are recovered from the forward part of the ship, which was carried in on the tide when she originally sank. The team excavates underwater with standard archaeological trowels and implements, but the divers also use their hands – they have to feel their way around. The best visibility is about six feet in high summer. Most of the time, it is near-zero visibility, even with commercial dive torches. Steve knows the site by touch: 'You have to keep your mask as close to the wreck as you can to distinguish anything. There is no ambient light below a few feet – everything is black.'

The first time Steve dived on the site, he saw what he thought were white pebbles. They turned out to be teeth, still attached to a human jawbone. The divers have brought up skulls, femurs, ribs and even a skull. Most of the smaller bones, like the fingers or phalanges, have been washed away. The concentration of human remains on the wreck site is highly unusual, and specialists are learning a lot about the lives of the deceased naval personnel from these rare seventeenth-century bones.

Over many dives, the team found a lot of ordnance, including

eleven early Stuart cannons (probably from the Tower of London), a musket and pistol shot, and a rare, nearly intact, wooden gun carriage. The gun carriage was discovered by Steve and Carol and eventually lifted out of the seabed using a twenty-ton crane barge whilst the dive team waited nervously in the water, hoping the fragile wooden structure would survive the exposure. But it is the personal items that seem particularly poignant, as they bear witness to the number of people who died during the accident: a perfectly preserved pocket sundial, buttons from an officer's uniform, a bronze tamper pipe ring (with a stalk on it for the sailors to press tobacco into clay pipes), as well as fragments of shoes, belts, pipes, candles and pewter spoons.

Luisa told me that the organic items from the wreck, such as leather shoes, have only survived because of the silty anaerobic environment of the Thames Estuary; creatures that would normally eat away at these objects cannot live in these waters. However, recently, warm-water organisms have migrated northwards, due to climate change, and they could potentially start to impact on the biological remains of the wreck.

The Thames Estuary is a mixed preservation environment: the lack of oxygen in the water conserves items but the strong currents wash them away. Some believe things were being swept away off the wreck site partly because of the dredging. Steve talked about having seen objects on one dive and finding them gone when he returned. He is now drawing out a plan of the wreck, an alternative mapping to the sonar and high-tech surveys being produced. For him, the *London* is the *Mary Rose* of the Thames Estuary.

The *London* has great significance for conservationists, historians and archaeologists, but it is also a site with a powerful imaginative pull. Luisa described the strange and eerie atmosphere out there: 'One minute you're on Southend Pier, with all the buzz and the noise, and then you're out in the middle of the Estuary, with the big ships gliding

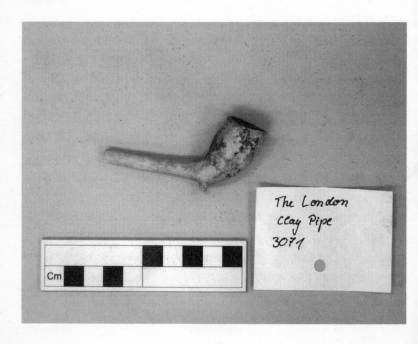

past, but apart from that it's silent and you know three hundred people are buried below in the mud.' She is haunted by a particular detail about one of just twenty-four survivors of the disaster – a woman who spent two hours on that freezing-cold day in March bobbing up and down on the water in the lifeboat, having just seen the great ship sink. 'It really made me think, when I was out there, how that might have felt.' I, too, felt haunted by the horror of it all: the explosion, the huge loss of life, the idea of all those people lying in their unmarked, watery graves, so near to the pier head and that strange lower deck.

Local artist Nastassja Simensky has also become obsessed with the story of the *London*. She has been out to the site with her perform-ance of *Colloquy*, which was played directly to the *London* wreck from the deck of cockle trawler *Indiana*, as it drifted across the breadth of the remains below, connecting the two sites. Nastassja had been working for some time with other local artists, such as Graham Har-wood, exploring themes around the recent changes taking place in the Estuary, particularly the impact of the dredging on the environ-ment and the cockle grounds. Graham mentioned the local dive team working on the *London* and introduced Nastassja to Steve Meddle, another licensee, who is also the skipper of *Indiana*.

On a visit to English Heritage's laboratory, she saw the strange and intriguing artefacts retrieved from the site: a mustard-brown Bartmann jug with a bearded face on it, leather shoes, bottles, pipes – alien objects kept in big tanks of distilled water to remove the salt content and prevent them cracking.

She started to form an idea about the relationship between these concrete objects being both scrutinized by archaeologists and histor-ians and looked at through a microscope on a molecular level. She envisaged combining this information with historical text from the period to create a piece of music – an audible map of the wreck.

The Port of London's UK hydrographic office provided her with numeric data, sonar scans and depth diagrams of the wreck and the surrounding seabed, which she passed on to composer William

Frampton, who produced a musical score using this information. The piece was written in five parts. The first and last movements use the raw data from the scans; the middle section takes the text from Samuel Pepys' diary for the libretto; and the second and fourth parts use information from English Heritage's laboratory about purifying the artefacts. The pitch, rhythm and range of notes throughout are dictated by data from the sonar scans and mechanical mapping.

The resulting composition was performed live on the deck of the cockleboat by a string quartet on 14 August 2014. The hand-crafted wooden instruments resonated for Nastassja with the idea of the ship below. She originally wanted to perform to the wreck with subaquatic amplifiers on the seabed, but it was too technically difficult. Instead, the boat drifted across the site and the musicians performed to just a small audience on board *Indiana* – the film crew and a couple of cocklers – and of course to the shipwreck on the seabed below, the hidden witness to so many estuarine stories.

12

Oil City

Much of the industrial shoreline of Essex has now been flattened.
There are no great cliffs or mountain ranges in this part of the
world, nor any man-made towering infernos – though there are
ruins. It is principally a world of horizontals, best seen from the
narrow aperture of a bird-hide, or looking out at a grey sea,
where the masts of distant coasters slowly crawl from one side
of the horizon to another.

– *350 Miles: An Essex Journey*, Ken Worpole, 2005

'Cut me in half, and it says "Canvey" all the way through,' said Chris
Fenwick, lifelong seafarer, Estuary enthusiast and manager of
legendary R&B band Dr Feelgood. It was a mild November morning,
and we were standing outside the Lobster Smack, a former haunt of
smugglers and bare-knuckle fighters on the southern edge of the
island, thought to be one of the locations used in the climactic episode
of *Great Expectations*. Chris was unsure if this was true, but he told
me that when Dickens published the novel he rented a steamship and
took journalists downriver to visit Canvey. But he did know that the
antiquated, white weatherboard building has always been a marine
pub. 'Licences included the rule that, if any sailor came in by boat at
any point of the day or night, they could demand a jug of ale, a leg of
ham and a loaf of bread.' He remembered seeing Norwegian sailors
in there when he was a teenager. 'People on the mainland think

Canvey is an insular place, but the opposite is true. We have always had international visitors to the island because we are so close to the water. There is a sense here of being directly connected out to the wider world.'

Climbing a steep, grassy slope, we made our way up to the imposing concrete sea wall, which runs for fourteen miles, right around the island, providing protection from both flooding and the backwash that occurs every time the Thames Barrier closes. The high wall dominates the coastline of the island, which lies below sea level and has always been vulnerable to flooding. Canvey originally consisted of five separate low-lying islands made of silt; the Dutch arrived in the 1600s and reclaimed acres of land from the sea by building a series of dykes and defences, creating one single land mass, which was called Candy Island. Most of the engineers were paid in land and subsequently settled on the island. 'Canvey was known as Holland-on-Sea,' said Chris, 'because the Dutch community was once so large.' Before the Dutch, there were other settlers – the Romans had a salt mine on Canvey and, before them, the Vikings had a camp nearby – but the Dutch were the first to inhabit the island in any great number. Many islanders still dress in Dutch costumes during the annual carnival; the street names reflect this history, and even the local secondary school is named after a Dutchman, the engineer Cornelius Vermuyden.

Chris's family first came to the island when his great-grandfather bought a plot on Canvey back in 1923. The practice had been started in the late nineteenth century by entrepreneur Frederick Hester, who purchased great swathes of land in Canvey and started chartering trains from London, promoting the rural, unmade plots as 'slice[s] of paradise beside the sea'. He constructed Winter Gardens, with miles of landscaped lakes and parks, built giant greenhouses filled with exotic botanical plants beside the shore and erected a model village.

Like many East Enders, the Fenwicks ended up settling on Canvey after holidaying there for decades. John Fenwick, Chris's grandfather,

an internationally known model-maker, built a perfect miniature replica of Canvey on the site of Hester's original model village, including the Lobster Smack, the Dutch cottages, St Katherine's Church and even the ruins of Hadleigh Castle, and with an electric train running through the marshes.

Canvey can be a volatile place to live. It has flooded many times, but the worst incident in living memory occurred during the night of the Great Flood of 31 January 1953, when a high spring tide coincided with a strong north wind, creating a tidal surge from the North Sea. The island was quickly submerged and fifty-eight people lost their lives. Most drowned in their sleep; others died from exposure after waiting in freezing temperatures to be rescued from the roofs of their homes. Chris is a 'flood baby', born in the year of the disaster, and much like everyone of his generation on the island he has grown up with an acute awareness of the vulnerability of the place. In the words of Wilko Johnson, the eccentric bass player from Dr Feelgood, there is a kind of 'submarine consciousness' that grows from living on Canvey.

Gesturing out towards a large container ship drifting by in the shipping channel on the other side of the sea wall at Hole Haven, Chris said, 'This is what my friends on the mainland just don't have. The waters here are always deep, which is why Canvey developed commercially, and big ships move closer to land here than anywhere else along the Estuary foreshore.' Twice a week, tankers offload refined crude oil, making Canvey a kind of gas station for the UK; they supply everything from the aviation fuel for London's airports to the pipelines that transport fuel all over the country.

When he was a teenager, Chris would come up to the sea wall at night to watch the tankers go by. 'It was just part of life on Canvey. We would have a smoke overlooking the jetty, the oil refinery was all lit up, it was fantastic – the authentic Thames Delta experience.' The cover photograph for Dr Feelgood's debut album, *Down by the Jetty*, was shot where we were standing. Wilko had described waiting for the wash of the tankers as being close to paradise in Julien Temple's extraordinary documentary film *Oil City Confidential* (2009).

Looking east, past the buoys, jetties and separation zones, we saw the gigantic cranes of the London Gateway Port – relatively new features in an already highly industrialized zone. Chris told me he watched the first super-sized cranes come up the river from China on a huge, flat vessel.

We started walking east along the sea wall, past the Calor Gas plant, where liquid gas, mainly from Algeria, is stored in vast circular tanks, then we took a short diversion directly under a large pipeline before rejoining the sea wall again. The industrial landscape around us was devoid of any human activity but, in between the gas pipes and storage tanks, nature was thriving on Canvey. Chris told me that, on the other side of the island, there is a brownfield site on a former oil refinery which has recently been dubbed Britain's rainforest – Canvey Wick supports more biodiversity per square foot than any other place in the UK.

'Most people think of Canvey as a bleak, rough place,' said Chris, 'but parts of the island are beautiful and wild.' He talked about an enchanted childhood playing out on the marsh on the north side of the island with childhood friend and neighbour Lee Brilleaux: they built secret camps on stilts which flooded when the tide came in, made hand-drawn maps to buried treasures and launched their boats directly from their back gardens into the creeks and inlets beyond. 'The landscape was a fantastically exciting adventure playground for us as children. We were the last of the kid pirates, really, playing at Swallows and Amazons every day.'

As we walked, he talked about his long friendship with Lee Brilleaux, which developed from mucking about on boats to starting a skiffle group with another friend, John Sparkes, when they were just fourteen years old: 'I played the washboard or the jug, Sparkes was on the banjo, Lee was always the frontman. We'd start the evening busking outside Admiral Jellicoe, then we'd go to another working man's club called the Corner Club for a twenty-minute set before moving across the road to the Canvey Club and finishing with a

late-night set at the Oysterfleet. Sometimes we made up to eleven quid each. It was great money – that's why we went into show business!'

By the time they were sixteen, they were playing gritty rhythm and blues and hitting the punk scene in London. Wilko joined and began writing their songs and, soon afterwards, their unique, hard-hitting sound, high-energy performances and anti-fashion look made them into internationally renowned rock legends. Chris has been the manager of Dr Feelgood for the past forty years, although none of the original members is in the current line-up. Tragically, Lee died of cancer back in 1994, at the age of just forty-one. 'It broke my heart,' said Chris, who can still barely talk about the loss of his friend without breaking down.

We passed Thorney Bay static caravan park and paused to look out across the water. It was a beautiful day, the tide was going out, an expanse of mudflats lay directly in front of us; further out, the water was grey-blue.

We stopped at Thorney Bay Beach, known locally as Dead Man's Bay, where bodies of sailors whose ship had been wrecked at sea used to drift in on the tide. 'When the tide is in this is a severe piece of water,' said Chris. 'There is a ferocious tidal flow here on the flood and on the ebb.' Chris grew up swimming in the creeks against the tides and worked as a lifeguard at Thorney Bay in the summer holidays, patrolling the coast. Back then, Canvey was packed with day-trippers. The roads on the island became impassable in the summer holidays with all the extra traffic, and the beaches were always rammed. As we followed the circular path around the island, we noticed some graffiti on the sea wall: CANVEY IS THE NEW LOURDES.

Just east of Thorney Bay Beach, there is a small, white, windowless building, which was originally built as a Cold War Admiralty secret facility. It has recently been declassified and now functions as the Bay Museum and Research Centre. It is occasionally open to the public, although some of the technology used inside remains top secret. The building once monitored the Canvey Loop: two thick circles of cable which sat on the riverbed out in the shipping lane and measured the magnetic signature of naval and merchant ships passing overhead. Wrens (Women's Royal Naval Service) inside the building recorded this data and sent the results by radio or semaphore back to the ship, warning the skipper to degauss the vessel (decrease the ship's magnetic field to ensure that metal mines cannot attach to the hull). Magnetic mines destroyed so many ships in the Estuary during the Second World War that the river was closed to shipping at certain points and minesweepers constantly patrolled the waters throughout the war.

We carried on walking east, heading towards Canvey Point. The sea was calmer there, there was nobody else around and, as we walked past some old wooden stumps down by the seashore, the Isle of Grain in Kent seemed close by. 'On a twelve-hour sail from here you can reach continental Europe,' said Chris, pointing out towards the North Sea. He has been sailing his entire life, starting as a cabin boy for his Uncle Jack, who was a pro-delivery skipper. 'He'd skipper any boat anywhere – he might pick up a boat from Calais and bring it to Henley, or take a boat from Hamburg to Newfoundland.' Jack originally wanted to be a Port of London pilot, but he is colour-blind so he became an ocean master instead and spent his whole working life at sea. 'He delivered tugs, catamarans, fishing boats and million-pound yachts – it was all the same to him,' said Chris. 'He is the most experienced and skilled seaman I know.'

Chris described going to sea with Jack as his antidote to rock and roll. 'Under the command of my uncle, there was no messing around. He could get twenty-five hours out of a day.' Over the years, they took multiple transatlantic trips together. One time, they hit a storm in the channel when they were bringing a twenty-five-foot sailing boat back from Oslo. 'We were smashed about all over the place. I was so scared, but I just shut up and did exactly what I was told. That was the only way to survive.'

Jack retired some years ago, and Chris no longer works delivering boats, but he is still sailing, and has just finished his third season crewing on *Marjorie*, a hundred-year-old Thames barge which competed in the same Southend Thames Match as *Cambria*. He was surprised to hear that I had been on board as a passenger and spoke for some time about the thrill of crewing these historic vessels and how hair-raising the events can sometimes be. Like many bargemen, Chris had his own stories to share: in the 2007 Swale barge match, *Marjorie* was involved in a collision with another barge which opened up a four-foot hole in her side.

We continued walking around the perimeter of the island, which was littered with crumbling military installations and gun batteries — remnants of the central role Canvey played in protecting the Estuary from attack during the Second World War. Chris told me that his mother trained as a radar operator and, by coincidence, she was stationed in Canvey. She spent her tour of duty sitting in a caravan about a mile away from the coast, giving coordinates of German aircraft to gunners in the gun batteries, who would then try to shoot down Luftwaffe planes flying along the Estuary from London.

By the time we reached Canvey Point, the easternmost place on the island, it was nearly midday. We were directly in line with the end of Southend Pier, as far out in the Estuary as you can physically be on land. Chris remembered going on trips on the *Royal Daffodil* steamboat to Calais from the end of Southend Pier when he was a child: 'My dad had a haulage company, and he would take his workers for their beano on this boat. I remember the saloon, which was filled with a mix of Londoners and locals who were always heavily drinking and surrounded by a great cloud of cigarette smoke. The *Daffodil* was like a giant mobile pub.'

The sun was shining brightly on the great vista of water in front of us, giving no indication of the dangers lurking beneath, in the form of the Chapman Sands — a notoriously dangerous and broad sandbank that is part of a wider band of sand that fringes Essex. Roman beacons, lightships and an iron lighthouse have all occupied this sandbank over time, warning sailors to avoid the area. Joseph Conrad, who lived for a while in the nearby town of Stanford-le-Hope further up the Essex coast, mentions the Chapman lighthouse briefly in *Heart of Darkness* as a 'three-legged thing erect on a mud-flat' whose light 'shone strongly'. I wondered if the Chapman lighthouse had been the setting for Paul Gallico's melancholic novella *The Snow Goose*, which tells the story of Rhayader, a lonely artist hunchback who lived in an abandoned lighthouse on the Essex marshlands and kept injured wild birds in enclosures. Gallico's marshlands are a place where 'time shifted land and water'; they become a metaphor for loss, loneliness and death. Rhayader is killed towards the end of the story, after attempting to rescue soldiers trapped on the beaches in Dunkirk. The ghostly presence of the hunchback and the long-forgotten Chapman lighthouse seemed to haunt that sandbank still as we continued our circular walk past the Point and through a landscape of muddy creeks and desolate salt marsh directly opposite Two Tree Island.

In between the tidal Estuary and the mud sat a silver streak of water, the Ray Gut, which was filled with windsurfers. Jan Tickell had told me that people from all over the world come to kite-surf and windsurf in the Ray because of the unique environment: the high mudbanks on either side of the creek protect the water left when the tide goes out from the onshore prevailing wind, creating the perfect conditions for exhilarating, fast sailing, with flat water and lots of breeze. Jan also grew up on Canvey; he is from an old Dutch family called Vandersteen. His mother, Jean, ran a well-known canoeing club on the island in the 1950s; she used to swim right around the island. 'A love of water and watersports is not uncommon here,' said Chris, smiling, as I told him Jan's story.

Commercial haulage and timber yards, boat builders and sail makers line the quayside of Smallgains Creek at the eastern end of the island. We stopped outside Prout Brothers, a world-famous boat-building company, where Jack Fenwick worked for many years.

The Prout brothers, Francis and Roland, represented Britain in the 1952 Olympics in two-man canoe sprint kayaks and went on to develop a prototype catamaran called a Shearwater; orders for these craft soon came in from ports all over the world. Over the years, the Prouts built and designed various pleasure boats, including forty-five-foot-long powerboats, racing boats and cruising boats as well as many different designs and styles of catamaran, and Jack delivered many of them. 'Jack took the biggest – eighty foot – catamaran ever built from Canvey to Nice,' said Chris. 'I was seven years old at the time. I tried stowing away, but he found me.'

Jack lives in a small bungalow about a hundred yards away from the home where he was born, near Smallgains Creek. Like Chris, he grew up mucking around with his friends on boats, rowing, sailing and shooting. He told me about heading out on the marshes with an old Canvey wildfowler called Charlie Stamp to shoot ducks and geese in the 1930s. 'You could make a living from it . . . Those days are long gone.'

He started working as a pro-skipper in 1956, when he was asked to deliver a boat back from the Mediterranean one Christmas. Over the following forty years, he delivered numerous vessels across the Atlantic, to Florida, all over Europe and the Caribbean. Most of his working life was spent travelling from the Prout boatyard in Canvey out into the Estuary then all over the world. In later years, he started delivering tugs and small commercial boats from Orkney and Shetland out to the North Sea oil rigs, then, when the fishing industry collapsed in England, he got involved in taking old fishing boats to Africa, where they were being sold cheaply. 'They were in a terrible state of repair – if a fishing boat fails its MOT, it means it is really clapped out. They were such decrepit wrecks, but if we managed to get them safely to their destination, it felt good. Every trip was a bit of an adventure.'

However, despite having travelled to so many exotic places, Jack describes himself as a 'Thames Estuary fanatic' and thinks that

Smallgains Creek is the most beautiful spot in the world. 'It's all been interesting, but I'm never sorry to get back to Canvey,' he said, before inviting me to come and see his current boat, *Kittiwake*, a twenty-five-foot sailing yacht with an auxiliary motor which he keeps at the local yacht club.

With great effort, the nonagenarian walked to his car, almost bent double. It took him some time to get inside. After we had buckled up, he drove us a short distance to the end of his road, then got slowly out of the car to open the gates of the Canvey Island Sailing Club, of which he is a lifelong member. Parking up, he led me along the creek, which was filled with small sailing yachts and dinghies. 'Mind how you go,' he said, as I held on tightly to the rails and made my way down some rickety wooden stairs on to a narrow jetty where *Kittiwake* was moored up. As soon as Jack got on board, he seemed to move differently, like an agile crab, side-stepping around the boat with confidence and at speed. He took my hand as I stepped gingerly on board, it was the first time I had been on a sailing boat since my accident, and I felt nervous, even though we were in the harbour and the tide was out. He told me he had sailed around Britain in this boat on honeymoon with his wife. After being single for most of his life, Jack met Shirley at a bus stop – he was already retired, well into his sixties, when she agreed to marry him. He showed me how the table inside the cabin dropped down to make a comfortable double bed. 'You could sleep six in the cabin,' he said. 'We have everything we need.' He told me he only takes the boat out for small trips now, mainly along the Estuary; often up to Shell Haven and back. I asked him about the new London Gateway Port and he was sceptical: 'It's just big container ships or nothing now. Traffic on the Estuary has been dead for almost half a century.' He offered to take me to visit the port on his boat, going up on a morning tide and back on the mooring before the tide went out. I was genuinely keen to do the trip but never mustered up the courage to call him back.

13

The Fishwives Choir

In the *Fishing News* every week there is a list of names of fishermen who have died. Commercial fishing during peacetime is the most dangerous job in the world – not just loss of life but loss of limbs, arms caught in winches: it's really deadly. If you try to get life insurance, one of the things you are asked is, 'Are you in the military, or do you work aboard an airline or a trawler.'

– Jane Dolby

Most, but not all, of the fishermen I met who worked on the Thames Estuary loved their job despite the dangers, the financial hardships and the long hours. They used expressions like, 'It is in my blood,' 'I've got saltwater in my veins' or 'My whole life is being on the sea,' and said they could not imagine doing anything else. They talked about the joy of seeing the sunrise on the water in the early mornings and of the particular experience of night fishing, 'and how that blackness and emptiness goes into your mind'. Paul Gilson told me about one memorable occasion when he was fishing off the Gunfleet Sands and witnessed the aurora borealis on the northern horizon.

The fishermen spoke of the knowledge passed down from generation to generation, such as how to navigate by the stars and the secret locations of the best fishing grounds, as well as the dangerous sandbanks and wrecks, which were often drawn out on hand-made maps that were passed on from father to son: 'When they got a bit wet, you copied

it out and made another one.' They talked about the weather, of course, and their different methods of predicting the forecast, from 'feeling seaweed' to watching the clouds and the wind in the trees. They all spoke about their great respect for and fear of the sea, which they never lost, however experienced they were, and many stressed that they would never put themselves at risk, because fishing was their living and they needed to go back out there the next day. They all said the skipper's word was law, they talked about the laughs, the camaraderie, of being part of a crew and told tales of the things they had caught in their nets aside from fish: a dead body, an upright piano, a VW Beetle, a live bomb . . . One fisherman trawled up a cow, and another caught a live dog and kept it for years; it used to go fishing with him. Many were superstitious and had stories of strange happenings out by the sea forts, of phantom ships appearing in the fog, and tales of violent storms and near-misses. Paul Gilson dedicates an entire chapter of his memoir *Sole Searching* to 'spooky happenings' on board his boat *Janeen*. Over the years on this boat, tools mysteriously disappeared, doors opened and closed by themselves, and strange tapping noises were heard during the night. One time, he was out hauling alone when he heard a voice shout, 'Jump!' and he reacted to the order without thinking, just as a wire flew across the deck. If he had not jumped, he would have been severely injured.

The fishermen I spoke to were also extremely knowledgeable about and respectful of the natural world of the Estuary and described multiple encounters with birds, seals, whales, sharks and dolphins. One dolphin turns up in the stories of lots of the local fishermen, feeding off the bass which themselves feed off the mussels that cling to a buoy near Canvey Point.

They spoke about fishing as a drug, as an obsession, as an extremely precarious and dangerous occupation, and also as a threatened way of life. Nearly all of them come from a long line of Estuary fishermen who have been working on the river for centuries, but most of their sons were not going into the trade and their daughters never had. During the five years I spent writing and researching this book, I didn't come across a single woman who worked directly on the fishing boats. When I asked why, the fishermen all said it was bad luck to have a woman on a boat, 'because they make the sea angry', but they also said that it was not a 'fit environment for a woman', being too smelly, dirty and dangerous. However, most fishing boats on the Estuary are named after female family members – mothers, wives, grandmothers and daughters – all of whom have played and continue to play a crucial role in the industry by supporting the men out at sea, 'keeping the home fires burning' and working in the associated trades on the shore.

Going in search of the voices of the Estuary women, I came across the rich audio archive of Sorcha Daly, who interviewed a number of Essex fishermen's wives for her project *The Seagull That Lived in the Shower*. Amongst them was Lara Hurley, whose mother worked in the cockle sheds in Leigh; when she was pregnant, Lara ate bowls and bowls of cockles every day – she had a craving for them. Now, she works in the sheds in the family business, as generations of women

in her family have, selling cockles directly to the public. Her great-grandfather Arthur Dench originally owned the shed, but he never fully recovered from his traumatic experiences during the Second World War, so her great-grandmother took over the business. She was known as 'the Cockle Queen of Leigh-on-Sea' and used to tell the men to 'get out of the pub and get on with the job'. She worked down there for years, sitting in the back of the rickety old shed until she was very old, keeping the whole thing going but never working directly on the boats.

Paul Gilson's wife, Heather, worked in the family business in later years, when their children were older, keeping the books, staying on top of the accounts and even 'hauling around boxes of fish off the boats as they came into shore'. In the early years of their marriage, she stayed at home, looking after their children. She described herself as a traditional wife and always tried to ensure she was there when her husband returned, to make him a hot meal, to look after him.

Before the days of mobile phones and ship-to-shore radio, there was no way for her to get in touch with Paul. 'We were like ships in the night. Depending on the tide, he would come in as I went out, and when he got home I had to try and keep the children asleep.'

'Fishing is a tough life for a man but even tougher for a woman,' said Linda Spurgeon, who described being the wife of an Estuary fisherman as a 'very lonely life; if fishing was good he would not come home'. Sometimes, she would wake up in the night and he would be gone; other times she would wake up and he would have returned. Financially, it was a precarious existence; the wage was unreliable. She 'would not recommend it for a young wife'; she often felt like she was bringing up the children alone and she constantly worried that something would happen to her husband out at sea and she would have no way of knowing that 'he never went out on an argument.'

Nola Baker had similar stories to Linda. She talked about how hard it was to plan any family activities, such as holidays or birthday parties, as her husband's job was so dependent on tides and the weather. She also worried all the time about her husband having an accident: 'He always worked solo. Any time, bringing the nets in, he could get his foot caught and go over.' In the end, her husband sold the boat, because 'there were too many government restrictions; he could not make a living. Fishing is a dying trade in this area: there are no youngsters going into it; many old families are leaving the industry.'

Rosemarie Godbold described a life onshore of 'worrying and waiting. If the weather was bad, I would really be afraid. It is such a dangerous job. If anything happened to him, I always used to think what would I do and what would the children do.' But, despite the danger, she knew that her husband, Daryl, loved his working life. 'He was out in the fresh air all the time. He could have been in a factory.' Every day, she would stand and wait at the kitchen sink and look out of the window for his van to arrive and, when it did, she would say, 'Thank God for that.'

'If you're somebody that needs your husband to do things with you all the time, then don't marry a fisherman, because you'll spend most of your life on your own,' said Jane Dolby, laughing, as she bravely spoke about her short-lived but passionate marriage to Colin. I met Jane initially through Facebook, after she posted a very moving account of being a fisherman's wife. I was so touched by her story and so impressed by the quality of her writing, I asked her if she had ever considered writing a book. We started communicating, and I discovered she lives in my hometown of Leigh-on-Sea and that we have many mutual friends. We met for coffee, and a friendship ensued. Jane is an extraordinary woman, a charismatic and inspirational person, who has faced many hardships in her life but remains to this day one of the most positive people I have ever met. She described herself as very independent, so the loneliness of Colin being away at sea much of the time did not affect her too much; she knew he was always there for her. She told me, 'I liked being Colin's wife. I liked saying, "My husband's a fisherman." I thought it was romantic.'

She met Colin after her youngest son befriended the shy fisherman next door by chatting with him over the garden fence. Encouraged by the child, Colin eventually asked the vivacious single mum out for a day-trip on his boat. 'It was not like going out on a yacht or a pleasure boat. It was dirty and smelly, but it was also real and exciting,' said Jane. 'I loved it immediately. I really miss it.'

Before that day, she had thought Colin to be a rather awkward, quiet man but, in his own environment, she witnessed a completely different person: he was confident, in control, at home. Colin had been the last of the Dolby fishermen – his family had been working on the Thames Estuary continuously for over three hundred years. He had learnt the trade from his father, Ken. When she first knew Colin, father and son used to fish together, but after Ken retired Colin had to skipper and crew solo; he did not earn enough to pay a second crew member. Ken used to catch shrimp, but Colin predominantly caught cod and Dover sole. After a lean winter, he would be desperate to get back out to work as soon as the blossoms were out on the tree, in March – the sign that the Dover sole were back in the sea.

'Fishing is a hand-to-mouth existence. People don't realize how hard it is,' said Jane. 'Colin used to work twelve-to-fourteen-hour days and sometimes not even come back with enough to cover the cost of the diesel, but he would not have wanted to do anything else. I knew the job was dangerous, he knew it was dangerous, but it's just one of those things, like getting in a car: you don't think it's going to happen to you.'

Colin's boat was a ten-foot-long steel-hold trawler called *Louisa* with two derricks on either side from which the nets would hang. When he was fishing, the derricks would automatically come down and the nets would drag along the seabed behind the boat. They would often get tangled in debris, which would cause the trawler to tip suddenly to one side, and Colin would have to run out of the wheelhouse to right the boat.

Quite often, Colin's nets came up filled with rubbish: plastic bags, condoms and food wrappers. Other times, they came up with holes in them, which he would have to patch up quickly, with a large plastic needle. On a really good day, he might catch twenty-five stone of fish, which he had to gut on board. 'He was an Olympian fish-gutter,' said Jane. 'He would throw the guts in the air, and hundreds of gulls would follow the boat and catch them before they hit the sea.'

His boat used to be on a mooring by the pier, so to get to work he would row a tiny wooden boat from Two Tree Island out to his skiff, before fixing a huge engine on to the back of it and motoring out to his trawler, in all weathers. On the way back, it was even harder, as the boat might be loaded down with a heavy haul of fish. Colin was often away overnight, taking one tide out and returning on the second tide coming in. 'I'd be trying to keep the kids quiet, 'cos he was knackered when he got in,' said Jane. 'If the weather was good in the summer, I just didn't see him. His whole life would be working and sleeping.'

On the morning of 10 November 2008, the sea was flat calm. There was no indication that the weather would turn. Colin had gone to the bottom of the garden, as usual, to 'feel the seaweed' and look at the trees to try to work out what the weather was going to do. The forecasts for the day were normal and everything looked fine. He had gone out to work about midday but, as the afternoon wore on, the weather became increasingly stormy. 'It was the sort of rain that stung your face,' said Jane. 'It was absolutely lashing down.' She recalled that the kids were going to a birthday party that day straight after school and Colin was supposed to be back by three o'clock to take them. 'He was late, so I left a message on the phone and took a taxi to the party. Whilst we were there, I noticed that I'd had about twenty missed calls from his sister. When I eventually spoke to her, she was semi-hysterical, saying, "Colin's not back, Colin's not back."' She told Jane that there was no sign of Colin's boat and the coast-guards had been called out. Jane knew then that she would never see Colin again.

The coastguards went out that night – all the fishermen went out, the cocklers; there were helicopters searching above the Estuary; lifeboats in the water; friends walking up and down the seafront with binoculars. They called off the search at about one o'clock in the morning and resumed it again at first light. They searched for two or three days and eventually found the wreck of the boat on the bottom of the Estuary, but when they pulled it up there was no body inside. 'That was the point when I had to tell the children,' said Jane. The police had advised her not to say anything before then, just in case Colin had sought shelter somewhere, or might be wandering around in Whitstable, not remembering who he was, but when they found his wrecked boat she knew for sure that he was dead. 'We couldn't have a funeral because we did not have a body, so I arranged this big memorial service.

'We had no money, I couldn't prove Colin was dead, I couldn't pay any bills and I was getting awful calls from mobile-phone people, banks, credit cards. There were journalists phoning my kids' school and my church, saying, "Is he really dead?" My really desperate, bleak, blackest times were about two years after he died. The daily grind of dragging myself through every day, bringing the kids up,

dealing with their arguments, not having any money . . . I just wanted Colin back. It's never really been OK in the way that it was when he was here.'

Jane spoke at length about the fishing community, the neighbours and the church, who pulled together and rallied around her. 'They were everything that you could want a community to be. I had people that I didn't know putting Sainsbury's vouchers through my door.' One friend, Michael Bates, organized a collection and Jane used the money to learn to drive and buy a car.

She said she would not have coped without the Fishermen's

Mission, a charity that arrange emergency living grants and food parcels for people like Jane. Tim Jenkins from the Fishermen's Mission was somebody she could ring when she felt like she absolutely could not go on; they even arranged a holiday for her and the children. 'They were my heroes. I always promised Tim that if I got back on my feet I would do some fundraising for them.'

Jane's background was in music, so she had the idea to do a karaoke-style recording in memory of Colin and raise funds for the mission. She put a notice on Facebook, looking for women to sign up to the Fishwives Choir, which would be made up of the wives and widows of fishermen. Within forty-eight hours, she had messages from a hundred women from all over the UK: 'I lost my husband'; 'I lost my father'; 'My uncle's a fisherman'; 'I can't sing, but I'm married to a fisherman, can I join?' One of the women called her from Scotland and told her the story of how her father had gone to sea when she was five and she had never seen him again. She also had ladies from Northern Ireland, Wales and most of the other fishing-fleet regions in England. They all met for the first time in Hastings a few weeks later and recorded a single together, 'When the Boat Comes in' / 'Eternal Father'. It was a huge success and even came close to the Christmas number-one slot. A book deal soon followed and, since then, the Fishwives Choir has performed at the Maritime Museum and many other places, as well as making multiple media appearances on *BBC Breakfast* and other shows. I was fortunate enough to witness their first live performance, at Shorelines Literary Festival of the Sea in Leigh, where, on stage, I introduced a nervous Jane to a roomful of people from the local fishing community. When she sang 'My Love was Ocean-bound', there was not a dry eye in the house.

14

Prince Michael

I can see the dark shape of our target, growing larger by the second. We are screaming in at 120 mph and the deafening roar of jet turbines and the clattering of whirring rotor blades produce a cacophony of noise and vibration that hammers my senses. Levelling off, the pilot tips the machine nose down for maximum speed and we are racing into our final objective towards little more than a metre above the foaming wave crests.

Fumbling in the wind-filled aircraft, I snap open my safety harness, reach under my camouflage jacket and feel the reassuringly heavy weight of a sawn-off shotgun, hung around my neck on a parachute-cord lanyard.

– *Principality of Sealand: Holding the Fort*, Michael of Sealand, 2015

A beautiful young woman with long, dark hair who looked like a cast member from *The Only Way is Essex* opened the door of the immaculately kept bungalow, holding a wriggling miniature schnauzer under one arm. She led me down a narrow hallway into a large, open-plan, bright, white kitchen, then invited me to sit on a high stool beside the breakfast bar whilst she went to find her dad. 'He'll only be a minute,' she said cheerily, as her high heels clacked along the tiled floor.

I sat apprehensively and waited, unsure whether to take my recording equipment out or not. The interview had taken months to arrange and would not have happened without a personal introduction from

Jane Dolby, who told me that Michael had been extremely kind to her after Colin had died. I had no idea what to expect: the stories circulating about him are wild, of armed sieges at sea with sawn-off shotguns and helicopter raids.

Shortly afterwards, a tall, broad-shouldered man with a closely shaven head, large, black, bushy eyebrows and a killer smile appeared in the doorway, wearing a black, open-neck shirt and jeans. 'I see you've already met my lovely daughter, Princess Charlotte,' he said, shaking my hand firmly. We moved into the front room and sat opposite each other on large, white sofas. Michael said he was happy for me to record our conversation; he was very used to being interviewed – over the years, there has been a great deal of media interest in Sealand, a former naval sea fort in the outer reaches of the Thames Estuary which has been occupied by the Bates family since the 1960s. Michael had just returned from a business meeting with an Austrian TV company who want to produce a feature-length movie about the place, and the following week he would be flying out there to film a promo with a prominent music artist. 'I've been invited all over the world to talk about it,' he said. 'People are fascinated by Sealand.' I thought Michael lived out there permanently, but he said that had not been the case for decades. He was too busy now, running his cockling business in Leigh, so his time on the fort is restricted to frequent visits. 'There are all sorts of interested parties wanting to set up businesses there,' he said, grinning. 'The place is just outside British territorial waters, which means we are free from the hands of the law.'

Michael first visited the naval sea forts at the age of eleven whilst on a fishing trip with his father, on the day Winston Churchill was buried. The legendary adventurer Paddy Roy Bates had formerly been a major in the Royal Fusiliers, and he wanted to go and have a look at Knock John Fort – previously, a Maunsell naval fort – in the mouth of the Estuary. 'We climbed up this rickety metal ladder off the boat and had a walk around,' said Michael. 'It was derelict inside and very dark. There were loads of cormorants about the place. We explored the officers' mess and the captain's cabin, then went down to the machine room, where we found two old wartime generators and some live ammunition on a workbench. There wasn't much else left; others had been before and looted all the gunmetal and brass fittings from the place. They loaded so much copper wire on to the old boat that it sank on their way home!'

This was the mid-1960s, the time when Screaming Lord Sutch and others were operating pirate radio stations on other sea forts and boats out in the Estuary. Roy soon joined them and started broadcasting from Knock John. The system was makeshift and imperfect, using converted radio-beacon transmitters from the American Air Force and ex-National Health blankets nailed into the corners of the walls for soundproofing. It was a twenty-four-hour radio station – the original Radio Essex. Whereas all the other stations tried to go national, Roy decided that local radio was the way forward. Michael told me about the coded messages the DJs used if they were running low on fuel or water: 'They'd play certain records or make particular comments, and the old man would know he needed to get things sorted.' Roy stayed on the fort for extended periods of time; the rest of the family used to join him for Christmas. 'We even took Fruitcake the cat,' said Michael. 'We got to know all the disc jockeys and the engineers; there were about a dozen people, all young lads, a lot of them only sixteen or seventeen. I'd go out on the supply boat sometimes without my father, to deliver the stores – I was only about twelve – and they'd all come and tell me all their problems. You can imagine, being a bunch of young lads stuck out on a fort in the middle of the Thames Estuary . . . but it was interesting.'

In 1966, the government brought in the Marine Offences Act, which made it illegal to supply offshore radio stations with food, fuel, staff, wages or advertising. One by one, the 'pirates' were taken to court and the stations shut down. Roy looked for a better option and visited the Sunk Head forts first, which were even further out in the North Sea, but decided on Roughs Tower instead, which is situated

seven and a half nautical miles off the coast of Harwich, just outside British territorial waters. 'Instead of putting a station on there, which was his initial plan, he decided to declare independence,' said Michael.

'It was on my mother's birthday, 2 September 1967, and he named her the princess of the smallest principality in the world.'

The family lived there for different periods of time over the years. Michael fondly recalled the many Christmases he spent out at Sealand, but he also admitted that they could never fully relax. 'There's a picture of me at about twenty years old – it's like something out of *Goodfellas*. I've got a can of beer in my hand and I'm sitting round with the family under the Christmas tree with a shoulder holster on.'

Over the decades, the Bates family have had constant problems with warships turning up from various nations, including some from the Royal Navy. Michael and his father both ended up in court in 1968 for firing on an English merchant vessel, but the judge ruled that the court had no jurisdiction as they were outside territorial waters. More seriously, another incident involved Germans and Austrians coming out in a KLM helicopter and holding Michael prisoner.

This particular incident took place in August 1978, when Michael was twenty-five years old and guarding Sealand alone. His father had gone to Austria to meet some business associates who wanted to turn Sealand into a casino, but the meeting was just a ruse to get him away from the place.

A helicopter arrived unexpectedly with some of the Austrians and a German film crew. It hovered above the helipad for a while, asking Michael for permission to land. He refused, already suspecting something was not right, but the passengers came down, one at a time, on a winch wire anyway. They tried to convince him that a deal had been sealed and that his father had handed Sealand over to them, then the situation quickly escalated; Michael was kept prisoner in a steel-lined room on the fort for the next three days.

At one point, they let him out, but his hands and elbows were bound together. A scuffle ensued. 'They jumped all over me and tied my ankles together, then picked me up and carried me to the side. They said in German, "Let's chuck this bastard over the side. He's too much trouble."'

The following morning, a Dutch trawler turned up with reinforce-ments. Michael was given the option to stay on Sealand or go to Holland. Initially, he wanted to stay, but the thought of his father coming out and getting himself killed trying to rescue him made him change his mind, so he went to Holland on the trawler, then made his way back to England soon after landing. When his father returned, they quickly came up with a plan of action.

'We had a small, rigid, inflatable RIB. Our first plan was to go out in that and scale Sealand in the dark but, as it was a fortress which we had made quite impregnable ourselves over the years, that wasn't going to be the easiest thing to do.' They had a phone call from a German who was involved with the Sealand invaders, warning them that, in two days' time, ten Belgian ex-paratroopers with Uzi sub-machine guns would be helicoptered out to Sealand, 'and if they got there, we would never get near the place again'. Desperate, they phoned a friend who hired out helicopters at Southend Airport and, straight away, he agreed to help.

Planning a dawn raid, they bought some lengths of rope and rehearsed sliding down them off a twelve-foot-high bracket attached to the front of the family factory in Wickford Road. 'It wasn't the way you would normally practise a helicopter assault, but it was the best we could do.' Michael and his father took two close family friends, Gordon 'Willy' Wilkinson and Barry Harcus, dressed in an assortment of camouflage fatigues and equipped with various weapons, but no life jackets. 'One other lad, Robbie Dawson, wanted to come, but we had to leave him, in floods of tears, at the airport because there wasn't enough room in the helicopter.' They took the doors off the helicopter and tied the ropes on to the back of the airframes of the seats, then flew up past Felixstowe, straight into the wind, to keep the noise down. As luck would have it, the German on watch, sitting in a chair in a yellow oilskin coat, was drunk. The pilot put the helicopter in between the two sixty-foot masts on the helipad and they rappelled down the ropes on to the fort.

The first man down was meant to collapse the masts so the helicopter could land but, as there were armed Germans running out of the building on the lower deck, Michael dashed straight to the edge of the helipad, shouting in German and waving his sawn-off shotgun. His father had got down his rope by now, and Willy was climbing along the outside of the helicopter after him. The situation reached crisis point when Roy climbed down the ladder to the lower level and Michael, not wanting to take his eyes off the enemy whilst he used the ladder, jumped off the roof, about twelve feet up, after his father. 'My shotgun hit the ground with a crash and went off. I nearly committed patricide and, instantly, everyone stuck their hands in the air.'

The next morning, with the Germans safely locked up, the press started to arrive. Reporters from the *Daily Mirror* and the *Sun* turned up on boats, and the victors brought out their captives for a photo op. 'They must have fallen over, because they had fat lips and black eyes. My father wasn't particularly happy about the way they'd treated me when I was held prisoner out there.'

The prisoners were released soon afterwards, apart from a lawyer who had a Sealand passport, which Roy had given him the year before. They tried him for treason and kept him prisoner for a month, during which time they made him clean the fort, make coffee and give them free legal advice. An official from the West German embassy flew out to the fort to demand his release, but Prince Roy refused and relented only after the prisoner threatened suicide. 'He drove us bloody mad,' said Michael.

'Sealand is third generation now,' said Michael, and told me his two sons are heavily involved with the place today. 'People travel all over the world on Sealand passports, and we have our own stamps, coins and visas – basically, all the trappings of state.' Prince Michael still has dynastic dominion over the principality of Sealand, which is the smallest micro-nation in the world. He occasionally takes people out, but the family is understandably nervous after past events, and keeps visits to an absolute minimum. I asked if there was a possibility I could go with him one time, and he said, 'Maybe – we'll see.'

15

Shivering Sands

Senses sometimes feel over-heightened in this unusual environment where I 'hear' myself with a different degree of sensitivity. Light and shade are palpable presences, solids are dense vapours and thoughts are a fine mist. Sounds can make me happy or irritated. The south mark bell is a slow, water-borne torture. It rings randomly all night and day in the slightest swell, and echoes of it go to most parts of the fort.

— *Seafort Project*, Stephen Turner, Friday, 19 August 2005

Kent-based artist Stephen Turner has been deeply engaged with the seascape of the Thames Estuary for decades. He regularly explores the foreshore of the Medway, the Swale, Sheerness and the Isle of Grain in his eight-foot dinghy, making drawings, notes and observations on the way. When the waters recede, he walks across the mud to the little islands that reveal themselves amongst the marshlands: Dead Man's Island, Bedlams Bottom, Barksore Marsh, Horrid Hill and Slaughterhouse Point – places that reverberate with military occupation, prison ships and quarantine vessels.

Turner's artwork resonates with these journeys. For *Time and Tide*, he made three thousand boats out of London clay, which were 'sailed' on the water before gradually dissolving back into the Estuary mud. For *Grotta*, he built a cairn of oyster shells on Whitstable beach, which eventually washed back into the sea, close to the oyster beds, in recognition of an old local custom.

His profound connection to the estuarine environment has led him to spend long periods of time in complete isolation in abandoned buildings and military installations in the area. In 1996, he spent 240 nights living alone on Fort Hoo, a derelict nineteenth-century garrison situated on an island in the middle of the River Medway that he first read about in Dickens's essay on Chatham dockyard, in which the author describes seeing a young boy there who says he is the spirit of the fort.

Stephen spent a long time in residence on Fort Hoo and installed a series of 'river maps' on the neighbouring (and identical) Fort Darnet, which he made by taking a sightline from the centre of the circular fort out through each of the eleven gun bays to the shore. At each point, he fastened canvases on to the riverbed and, as the tide washed over them, they captured patterns of erosion as well as the tiny bacteria that live in the mud. Stephen hung these eleven works inside the fort for a period of one lunar month. Visitors could reach the exhibition only by boat and the opening hours changed daily depending on the tides. The 'time-based happening' became both a study of the life of a tidal river and a piece of performance art. 'Visiting the fort was like an induction into a natural cycle and, when people came, I was the spirit of the fort somehow, and I'd escort them around,' said Stephen.

Stephen's most extreme Estuary project to date took place during August and September of 2005, when he spent six weeks living alone in the deserted searchlight tower of the Shivering Sands Sea Forts, which are situated eight nautical miles off the Kent coast. The idea for his residency had started years before his first visit, when he noticed the strange pinpricks on the horizon of the sea whilst sitting outside his beach hut in Whitstable. Curiosity led him to his local library, where he discovered what these intriguing structures were: one of four sets of observation platforms and anti-aircraft defences which were installed in 1943 in strategic positions in the outer reaches of the Estuary.

They were built at Gravesend, completed in the tidal basin of Tilbury, then towed upriver and sunk, so that seven of these platforms, connected by light, steel gangways, became a fortified island. They were heavily armed platforms, equipped like a ship and each accommodating 265 men for a tour of six weeks at a time. During the war, twenty-two planes and thirty flying bombs were shot down from these platforms, and they were instrumental in the loss of one U-boat. After the Second World War ended, the forts continued to be occupied by the military for some years and were then maintained by a skeleton crew of about six people until 1956. They were used briefly in the 1960s as the location of an episode of *Doctor Who*, but the longest post-war occupation of Shivering Sands was by pirates operating 'Britain's First Teenage Radio Station', which was originally set up by Screaming Lord Sutch in 1964 and became known as Radio City when new manager Reginald Calvert took over. Controversy ensued when Calvert was shot dead during a dispute over the station, in the

aftermath of which other illegal pirate stations on nearby forts were forced to shut down. Radio City came off the air in 1967.

Since then, the Shivering Sands Sea Forts have been empty. The walkways have been removed and the derelict buildings are now slowly rusting into the sea. One of the forts has already collapsed into the water, after being hit by a boat lost in the fog. Aware that they might not survive for much longer, Stephen became determined to spend some time on them.

His first attempt took place in the year 2000 and was in the form of a telephone call to HM Coastguard. He politely asked if they would take him to Shivering Sands in their helicopter. The initial response was promising, as the coastguards were interested in seeing the forts for themselves, but the next day he received a call back from a senior officer, who refused him categorically: 'They are dangerous derelict structures. We exist to rescue people in peril, not to imperil them!'

The idea fell away like a wave, disappearing for a time, until it resurfaced five years later when Stephen received some research funding from Creative Partnerships in Kent, which led him to find curator Sue Jones (now the director of the Whitstable Biennale), and, together, they collaborated on a successful bid to the Arts Council.

As part of his research, Stephen managed to track down John Proctor, who had worked as the medical orderly on the Shivering Sands Sea Forts in 1944. He was in his eighties when Stephen interviewed him. On the forts, some of the men could not read or write, and one of Proctor's jobs was to write their letters and read the replies to them. He acted as a kind of counsellor, listening to the soldiers who came to see him. Some found their tour of duty at the forts stressful: they weren't front-line troops, they were Royal Artillery Reserve; they did not like being out at sea, they felt incredibly cut off and isolated. Grown men came to him in tears.

Many of them suffered from a syndrome called 'fort madness'. To combat this affliction, everyone serving on the fort had to have a creative hobby, and so art exhibitions were organized in the men's

mess room at Shivering Sands. No one was dismissed on leave until they had presented their artwork: a piece of wood whittling, for example, some embroidery, egg decoration or painting. The winner of the art competition would receive a box of cigarettes. Stephen loved the idea of creating new artwork in the same space decades later. He began planning his residency and the work he would make on board.

Behind the scenes, Sue Jones started asking around locally for a way of getting on to the forts. A number of people pointed her towards Tony Pine, who knew the Shivering Sands Forts intimately, having been part of the Radio City crew in the 1960s.

With Pine's help, the day finally came for Stephen to leave shore for 'his experiment in twenty-first-century isolation'. He took a letter from Prince Michael of Sealand, wishing him good luck on his adventure, in his pocket. A fishing boat was chartered from Whitstable and a motley crew consisting of Stephen Turner, Tony Pine, Sue Jones, an internet technician, a photographer and a BBC journalist left the harbour early one morning after spending hours loading up the boat. 'Stephen was staying for six weeks,' said Sue, 'but we needed supplies for eight to twelve weeks, in case he got stranded. We had to take enough water to sustain him for this amount of time, along with lots of non-perishable foodstuffs in tins. When we finished loading, we motored out to the forts, which looked enormous from the water, with these massive legs and rusty old ladders coming down. The swell of the sea was violent, the boat was rocking up and down, it was impossible to anchor up, and there was nothing to attach the boat to, so we just had to pull up alongside and get on. It was incredibly precarious, but exciting, climbing thirty-odd feet up these rusty old ladders above a moving boat. The ladders were so fragile, if you stood in the middle, the rungs would break.'

Tony went up first with an angle grinder, to try to gain access, which resulted in a piece of rusting steel falling down from the underside of the fort, hitting Stephen on the head and injuring him slightly. After a while, Tony crawled along the underside of the fort to get in

through an open door at the side, then the rest of the crew climbed up the ladders and into one of the forts.

'When we reached the top of the ladders, we went directly into the tower,' said Sue, 'which is a building of two floors. Inside, it was full of rust and dust and all sorts of rubbish. Nothing really gets taken away from the forts because it is so hard to unload back on to boats, so they are filled with strange bits and pieces: posters, tin mugs, papers, saucepans – a trail of stuff from those who have occupied the place at different points in time.' The forts contain debris from and evidence of their having been manned in the 1940s but also from their second life as pirate radio stations in the 1960s. The forts haven't officially been occupied since Radio City stopped broadcasting from there, but they have become a draw, like mountains; people want to explore these extraordinary spaces in the sea – getting on to them becomes a quest for adventurers. So, over the years, people have visited, even though the authorities try to discourage this, which is why they are locked up against any but the most organized incursion.

Stephen was winched up into the tower from the boat by a rope-and-pulley system on a bosun's chair constructed by Tony. Once the artist was safely installed, the crew had to winch up all the supplies, including a generator, a wind turbine, a tent, lights and cooking equipment. 'It was really hard work,' said Sue, who did the lion's share of the hoisting, as the others were busy installing equipment. 'When everything was on board, it was a race against the tide to make sure everything was working before we left Stephen. We had to check communications back to shore were functioning and set up the wind turbine. We were there for hours, and all the time the tide was turning, which meant the boat was dropping further away from the end of the ladder. The most difficult bit physically was jumping about eight feet back on to the moving boat. It could have gone very badly wrong: we easily could have broken our legs, or missed the boat, or worse. But there was no time for fear or to settle Stephen in. We just had to leave.'

Terrified the rest of the crew would be stranded at the forts and therefore prevent him from spending his first night alone, Stephen was relieved to see them go. By that time, it was dark. He managed to light a paraffin lamp and clear a small space on the floor of the room with a broom, sweeping up dead seagulls and rubble into a pile. Then he pitched his small tent and went to bed. Most of the windows were blown out. The wind whistled through the space. The tower swayed in the wind; rust fell on the tent like rain. He was driven mad by the sound of the south mark bell chiming throughout the night, and when he awoke in the early morning, fog had seeped through the open windows and made everything wet. He patched up some of the windows with plastic sheeting and gaffer tape in an attempt to keep out the elements.

In the dawn light, he began slowly exploring his strange new environment. For the first four days, he limited himself just to one room, which turned out to have been the men's sleeping quarters. He noticed that the asphalt floor was indented with the impression of bed legs. On the wall beneath a rusting metal bedframe hung the fragile remains of a group of post-war pin-ups, curling at the edges – a soldier's private collection. He told me about other personal belongings he found inside the decaying building: a photo album in a drawer, fragments of newspaper clippings, cigarette cards . . .

When he felt he had adequately investigated this space, he let himself into the next room. He would ration himself in this way throughout his residency, to maintain a sense of excitement and anticipation. 'I felt like an explorer in my own little world,' he said, 'as I found new ways of examining every square inch of this lost world.'

Beside his tent, he created a dust mountain, a great pile of dirt and rubbish, out of which he pulled pottery fragments and other bits of ephemera left behind by the soldiers, then bagged and catalogued them. He spent days forensically inspecting these artefacts, slowly building up a picture of the fort's past occupants. Amongst the rubbish one day he found a ball of cotton covered in a thick layer of dust. When he split the ball open hundreds of tangled, brightly coloured cotton threads were revealed, a remnant of the embroidery classes once taken by the men during their tour of duty on the forts. Another day, he pulled 'the leg rings from weary homing pigeons that never made it back' from a mound of feathers on the floor.

He had taken binoculars to the forts, intending to sit on the roof looking at the sea, the passing ships, the constellations overhead, the moon rising and falling, but instead he became engrossed in a landscape of interior desolation. His residency turned into a deep psychogeographic project, picking up on the resonating spirit of those who had left.

In the washroom, he found toenail clippings and an old Silvikrin packet with fragments of hair attached to it. The bath was filled with mud and rubble. He cleared it, hauled up buckets of seawater from forty feet below and bathed just as the men in the 1940s would have done. All the time, he was mapping the landscape as he explored it in sketchbooks, which he transferred on to more formal architectural drawings on his return – a record in red marker pen of particular finds of interest during his stay.

Sometimes, at night, 'the ghosts of other people' felt real. He experienced difficult days, when the rain lashed relentlessly against the fort, but most of the time he was deeply content in his self-imposed isolation at sea. However, like many hermits before him, Stephen was attracting unwanted attention. His residency had received a huge amount of press coverage, and he had over sixty thousand hits on his daily blog. 'People are fascinated by hermits,' said Sue Jones. 'They want to go and look at them, so lots of boats came to the forts. The fishermen we went out with started chartering their boat to curious tourists and, once, the Thames river cruiser *Pocahontas* came with about eighty people, all taking photos of Stephen when he came to the window.'

The fort became both prison and sanctuary for Stephen, insulating and isolating. I interviewed him the day he returned to land after six weeks at sea, following a dramatic journey back, with gales and aborted helicopter rides. He had a strong sense that time had slowed whilst he had been there, of having been able to connect to both the past and the present. After weeks of total isolation, he began to hear voices on the wind at night. He wondered if they came from the foundations below, which had been built from tons of dumped material, the gathered remains of buildings destroyed in the London Blitz.

He told me that, in retrospect, the only negative thing about the experience was leaving the fort; he said he would happily retire to Shivering Sands and spend the last ten years of his life 'as a strange hermit looking out of the griddled window, waving to the passing ships'.

16

MT *Kent*

At tide-time you would see one of the loaded ships with battened-down hatches drop out of the ranks and float in the clear space of the dock . . . at the opening of the gates, a tug or two would hurry in noisily, hovering round her with an air of fuss and solicitude, and take her out into the river, tending, shepherding her through open bridges . . .

— *The Mirror of the Sea*, Joseph Conrad, 1906

I found the MT (Motor Tug) *Kent* moored up opposite the Ship and Trades pub near historic Chatham dockyard. The sturdy-looking boat had been immaculately restored: her bright red hull glistened in the brackish waters of the basin, her large black funnel looked freshly painted. On deck were a number of elderly men in jeans and sweat-shirts, polishing and cleaning various parts of the boat. I stood on the quayside and asked for Keith Toms, who appeared a few moments later and welcomed me on board. 'Most of the people here are former tugmen like me,' he said. 'We are all passionate enthusiasts and mem-bers of the South Eastern Tug Society. Once, we had nearly ninety members but, because of the age profile, we've obviously lost a lot of people. Collectively, we have spent over 200,000 man-hours working on this vessel over the past eighteen years.'

When she was launched in 1948, the MT *Kent* was the most power-ful diesel-propulsion single-crew harbour tug in Great Britain. She

egan her working life on the Medway, berthing ships in Sheerness
nd the Port of Rochester, and when the BP refinery opened on the
sle of Grain, she assisted the first British tanker into the dock. She
was taken out of service when the industry contracted in the 1980s
nd moored up in Chatham dockyard, where she remained in a poor
tate of repair, slowly deteriorating, until 1995, when the South East-
rn Tug Society purchased her for the sum of one pound from
wners J. P. Knight under the condition that they would preserve and
estore her.

'She is now the oldest working tug on the river,' said Keith, 'and
he's been involved in many special maritime events, including the
Queen's Diamond Jubilee Pageant, the annual Dunkirk celebrations
nd, more recently, Richard Wilson's *Ships' Opera*, which began with
he lone blast of the MT *Kent* out in the Thames Estuary and ended in
he Pool of London, with hundreds of historic ships taking part. The
nusician Jem Finer was on board with us, playing horns from the deck.'

Tugs were traditionally built as powerful small units for assisting
arge ships into docks or on to berths by pushing, guiding or towing
hem. Keith said that most modern ships still take a tug with them in
ase of mechanical failure and to help them manoeuvre in restricted
reas, but that now towing by tug is a dying industry. When Keith
tarted on the river, there were over thirty ship-towing tugs; now,
here are only six operating in the Thames Estuary.

Keith comes from a long line of tugmen from Gravesend. His father
went afloat in 1926, the year of the General Strike, and worked on
he tugs all his life, as had his father before him and all his father's
brothers. Back then, all the river trades were family orientated; most
boys from Gravesend followed in their father's footsteps as watermen,
lockmen, river pilots, tugmen, lightermen and bargemen. I asked
Keith if he had ever encountered any women working in the trade,
nd he said never, not during his working lifetime, although he had
heard there was one female tug operator working at the PLA today,
on a modern boat, but he had never met her.

Keith started on the tugs as a boy, after leaving school in 1961 at the age of fifteen, and soon acquired the nickname Tommo, which has stuck with him ever since. 'In a flash of a second, you could get a nickname that would stay with you for ever. Harry the Pud got so named because he was a bit rotund. We had another chap called Pony Moore who got his nickname after a milkman asked him to hold his horse and cart one day. Everyone working on the river had a nickname, probably because there were so many men from the same families.'

Keith's duties as the boy on the boat were cleaning, shaking mats, making tea, scrubbing decks, cooking and looking after all the needs of the nine-man crew. 'If they wanted a beer, you had to go ashore and get them one. In the East End of London, I would end up in some rather unsavoury pubs that would frighten the life out of you now, because they were tough places then. The dock area was a rough

environment.' He saw many youngsters leave after a few months because the work was so hard, but he kept going and gradually worked his way up to skipper. 'That was the beauty of traditional river trades – you could go in with no academic qualifications and progress through learning from those above you. This was the way of the industry; it was part of the slow structure, and it stood the test of time.'

Back then, the Port of London was a massive industry, with 20,000 dockers, about 6,000 lightermen and at least 4,000 others working on the tugs, on customs launches and as pilots. In total, over 70,000 people were involved in the port industry in the 1960s, including those who worked in the cafés, pubs, shops and transport systems around the docks. The port was an exciting place to work: 'on the bubble all the time, always something happening and a bit of friendly banter between different tugs, the dockers and other boats'.

Apart from assisting ships in the docks, the tugs could be asked to go further afield to help ships in trouble anywhere within the working area of the Thames Estuary, from the Pool of London up to Margate and Yarmouth. Crews could earn good money from salvage jobs if they performed their duties well and saved a ship. 'If a ship was aground, we would tow it off; if she was damaged and taking water, we would put our salvage pumps in and pump her out. Sometimes there might be a fire – all tugs had fire-fighting capacity. There was a great deal of excitement with salvage jobs – the adrenaline was running.' But salvage work could be extremely dangerous, too: often, the tugs arrived before the fire and rescue crews.

Keith recalled one particular incident on a cold, foggy October night in 1964 when East German freighter *Magdeburg* was in a collision with Japanese ship *Yamashiro Maru* near Tilbury. *Magdeburg* was carrying a cargo of ex-London transport buses bound for Havana. She had sailed from Dagenham and reached a place called Broadness Point when the bow of the Japanese ship hit her starboard side, near the wheelhouse. A hole opened up in her side, she heeled right over and started to sink. Keith was only nineteen at the time and working on the tug on duty. He remembers hearing people crying and calling out for help. The salvage operation continued throughout that long night and the ship was successfully evacuated.

The collision was the most significant to have taken place on the Estuary since the Second World War. After being beached, the wreck lay on a sandbank for over a year before being eventually righted, towed away and scrapped. There were all sorts of rumours about the CIA being involved in the crash, because Leyland were selling buses to Cuba during the Cold War, when there was a US embargo against exporting goods to the country, but Keith discounted the idea. 'There were lots of collisions on the Thames back then. It was a very busy river, with up to three thousand shipping movements a week. We used to say that the only way not to do any damage was never to leave the wall.' He said he had been involved in many other salvage jobs during his forty-six years in service on the river, some of which had involved loss of life, but he said solemnly that he did not want to discuss these occasions.

We went into the wheelhouse, and he showed me where the skipper would stand and how he would steer, using the wheel and the compass, whilst also working the ship's telegraph: a heavy brass instrument beside the wheel that communicates orders about direction and speed from the bridge to the engine room via a system of levers and bells. On the face of the telegraph were a number of instructions: STOP, FULL ASTERN, FULL AHEAD, SLOW AHEAD and SLOW ASTERN. When Keith rang the telegraph, a deep metallic sound echoed around the bridge. 'Every time I pull that handle I still get a buzz,' he said, grinning.

We went down into the engine room, a claustrophobic, low-ceilinged room which sits below the waterline. Inside, a British Polar slow-revving, long-stroke diesel engine took up most of the space. 'Major breakdowns in these types of vessels are rare,' said Keith. 'Tugs like the *Kent* are extremely well constructed – over-engineered even. This vessel is over sixty-five years old and still in reasonably good condition.'

At least two people worked as below-hands in the engine room whenever the boat was underway. Crew member Guss recalled, 'When she's running, it's hot, noisy, smelly and dangerous down here, particularly in rough seas, but you get used to it. We were often living and working together for weeks at a time. We had to rely on each other for our lives. The crew all work together. It's a bit like the fishing industry in that respect: everyone has their separate roles but we work as one unit. If I did not react when the telegraph is rung, for example, I could sink the boat. I have had a few close scrapes over the years.'

Another role of the tugs working on the Thames Estuary has always been to pick up river and dock pilots from outward- and inward-bound foreign, manned, big ships. This is a highly skilled operation and involves great teamwork from the entire tug crew. First of all, the tug needs to position herself directly alongside the huge,

moving ship. The pilot then steps off the tug, up on to a pilot ladder running down the side of the ship. If conditions are rough, a second tug will come out and assist in case of any problems. The tug stays in position until the transfer is complete.

The two retired tugmen talked about various near-misses they had been involved in over the years and went on to tell war stories that had been passed down from family members, from salvaging bomb-damaged warships wrecked in the outer reaches to being active members of the fleet of Little Ships that rescued so many during the operations in Dunkirk. Over 1,300 Little Ships took part in Operation Dynamo, the official name for the Dunkirk evacuation, including yachts from the upper reaches of the Thames, sailing barges, pleasure cruisers, fishing boats, lifeboats and over fifty tugs.

Most of the Sun tugs (owned by the firm Keith and his father worked for) went to Dunkirk, along with many other Gravesend tugs. 'If they had been hit, whole families would have been wiped out,' said Keith.

Not everyone who answered the call of the Little Ships fleet came home safely that year. Six Leigh cockleboats were among those in the fleet. All successfully made their way thirty miles across the North Sea to Normandy but, on the way home, *Renown* hit a German mine and the entire crew was lost in the resulting explosion. Frank Osborne, Leslie Osborne, Harry Noakes and Harold Graham Porter are remembered on the war memorial at Leigh church by Arthur Dench, a fellow cockleman from that fateful day: 'Any of them boys who went to Dunkirk – who answered the call – they weren't in the army or navy, they just answered the call – all of 'em were heroes.'

'Gravesend suffered some casualties later on in the war, but during the Dunkirk escapade all our tugs safely returned,' said Keith. 'The popular belief is that people knew what they were going to be expected to do, but that's not true,' he went on. 'My dad said they were given orders in stages. Some left the Thames with orders to go to Ramsgate;

when they got there, they were only told to proceed to Dover. Then, in Dover, they might be told to stay and assist the shipping in the Channel, or go out and assist damaged vessels back to England, or they might have had orders to leave for Dunkirk.

'My dad's tug, *Sun XV*, was one of the last ones to come back. They were given orders to go to Belgium, making their way to the coast with no navigation lights, and out of the darkness, coming the other way, roared a British Destroyer going full speed. Dad said the naval officer on board said that "If it's good enough for him to turn and run, it's good enough for us," so they immediately turned around, which was probably lucky.'

In the stories of the ordinary men at Dunkirk, it is sometimes hard to distinguish between bravery and foolishness. 'My Uncle Buster was only a youngster of seventeen. The tug he was on had a rifle mounted on a stand. Buster said, "I'm gonna have a go," and he jumped up on the gun and started to fire at aircraft. He was dragged off by the other crew members immediately, as the Germans were picking out the armed vessels . . . I know it was grim for the troops, but people like my dad and Buster were just ordinary people. I think they were extremely brave.'

Tilbury Riverside

On the misty morning of June 22nd 1948, a former German cruise boat, the *Empire Windrush*, steamed up the Thames to Tilbury Dock, where she disembarked some 500 hopeful settlers from Kingston, Jamaica . . . many of them were ex-servicemen, who had served in England during the war. The new arrivals were the first wave in Britain's post-war drive to recruit labour from the Commonwealth.

    – *History Today*, article by Richard Cavendish, 6 June 1998

As we stood on Tilbury Town railway bridge, looking out towards the docks, the cruise terminal and the Estuary beyond, the writer Iain Sinclair told me he had been repeatedly drawn back to this place, with its 'different energies in conflict', since first visiting in the early 1990s whilst researching his novel *Downriver*. He came initially to engage with the site of the *Princess Alice* disaster, which had happened nearby. Later, he found a junk shop in Tilbury and, within it, an old colonial photo album filled with strange photographs of people who had contracted various diseases in Africa. He also found a family connection to the place: his Scottish great-grandfather, Arthur Sinclair, had boarded a ship from Tilbury in 1856 to start a new life in what was then Ceylon (now Sri Lanka). 'I have a map that he drew of this journey, which took months by sea,' said Iain.

We started walking along the main road – a sort of no-man's land stretching out in the distance, filled with boarded-up pubs, a fried-chicken shop and a dubious-looking yard piled with second-hand white goods. Iain commented on the unexpected mirror image of what had happened during the classic period of colonialism, as we watched dead-end London trash being shipped off to Africa. We passed a Japanese-car salvage yard, a tattoo studio, a mini-cab office, a few cafés and an Irish Social Club that appeared to be shuttered up. 'The place is schizophrenic,' said Iain, as he strode along, 'with the grand projects still thriving in the distance, then you go into the shadows of it and it looks reminiscent of Romania or Albania.' We stopped briefly outside a shop selling air rifles, catapults and other weaponry, situated next to a guest house in Dock Road called Rorke's Drift, after one of the battles in the war against the Zulus, the high days of imperialism manifesting themselves in Tilbury. Across the

street, a new gym and a primary school looked, comparatively, busy with life.

Iain had walked this route numerous times, right along the length of the A13, through to Southend, to the sea, shadowing the road and following the river, marching through scrapyards, landfill dumps, big container parks, bits of motorway up on stilts and wildlife habitats. He tells me about the Dracula mythology in Purfleet: 'where Bram Stoker sets his abbey and distributes coffins of Transylvanian earth from there to specific addresses, including one in Chicksand Street – and now Purfleet is this distribution centre for oil and petrol. These metaphors run very deep in our culture.' We continued on, and he pointed down towards the river, where we were headed. 'Out here, where there's not much to distract you, then you begin to see the shape of how the energies of a city work.'

We walked at pace down towards the water's edge through a classically liminal landscape, past sheds and logistics centres, next to mountain-high piles of brightly coloured containers from Hamburg and China. Great lorries thundered past along the road beside us. To our left sat the monumental art deco brown brick building of the Tilbury cruise terminal; to our right was the dock itself, enclosed by a high protective fence, with hundreds of cars lined up, ready to be exported, and huge wind turbines spinning slowly in the distance.

'The working dock must be a completely self-contained universe,' said Iain, who told me he had walked repeatedly around the perimeter but had never been inside. I had recently gained access into the port, interviewing a third-generation river pilot on a large Grimaldi ro-ro vessel – a big, 700-foot-long ship.

There were tight security procedures at the entrance barrier. After showing my passport and receiving verbal confirmation from the harbour master, I was given a visitor's pass, as well as a high-vis jacket and a hard hat, before being driven round to the quayside, where the massive ship was temporarily moored. With my recording equipment

firmly strapped to my body, I climbed about forty feet up a precarious-looking rope ladder that was dangling off the side of the ship, then stepped on to the vessel through a small, open door about three floors up, into a cavernous, empty space, big enough to hold hundreds of parked cars, before being led along a series of narrow, steel-lined corridors and up various stairwells to the spaceship-sized bridge. I was quickly ushered through the control centre and out on to the upper deck. The view of the working port from that height was almost aerial, with matchbox stacks of containers stretching into the far distance, flanked by blue quay cranes.

The ro-ro had taken on local dock pilot Andrew Francis, who was on board to advise the Italian captain how best to bring the big ship safely into berth. Andrew told me that ships of this size often needed two pilots – as one person can't necessarily see everything fore and aft at the same time. Tugs assist in manoeuvring the ship around the docks. During his forty-six years in service, Andrew had not encountered any major incidents but told me about a time when tug lines towing a big ship into berth without an engine had broken, 'which was a little unnerving when you've got so much tonnage behind you'. Like many of the older men I had spoken with, Andrew had trained as a Thames waterman first, then progressed to pilotage, one of the most highly skilled jobs on the Thames Estuary. He came from a long line of river pilots from Gravesend and said that many of the jobs in the port had been handed down from generation to generation.

Tilbury Docks and the London Tilbury cruise terminal have both been major employers in the local area for over a century. Stanford-le-Hope resident Pauline Judd has worked in the cruise terminal for over twenty-five years, checking visitors and passengers on to the cruise ships. She told me there were thirteen security officers and about fifty porters, managers and other staff working there, nearly all from nearby Essex and Kent towns and villages but hailing originally from East London. Operations had reduced considerably over the years, as many of the bigger cruise ships now left from

Southampton and Dover, but there are still weekly cruises from Tilbury to places like the Norwegian fjords, Spain, Portugal, Amsterdam and Belgium.

Over the years, Pauline has witnessed multiple drug busts at the port and, more recently, asylum seekers and refugees arriving on containers. 'Last week, there were seventeen found by port police; last year, we had fifty – children as well. No one was dead that time, but it was terrible. The people had been in there about ten days when they opened the container. We looked after them, fed and watered them, got them in the cruise terminal. We rang the Salvation Army,

who brought clothes and blankets. We made beds here for them until the next day. Everyone pulled together.'

Pauline led me through the customs hall and down to the old watch-keeper's room on the dockside of the cruise terminal, where I met eighty-six-year-old Malcolm Hall, the buggy man, who drives passengers' luggage up from the quayside to the luggage hall and back. Malcolm spoke with visible pleasure of the camaraderie of the place: he loved his job. He remembered a time after the Second World War, when the cruise trade was booming. 'Cruising was a gentle art, and ocean-going liners were the way to travel. They used to have a lot of high-class ships here then.' When the Cold War ended, Russian cruise ships would come into Tilbury from the Black Sea Shipping Company; the engineers would disembark and go around local scrap-yards, buying up old washing machines and cars. They put them all on the boats, repaired them and took them back to Russia.

I was curious to hear Malcolm's thoughts about the next generation and the London Gateway Port. We talked about it for a while; Malcolm did not see the port as a threat to Tilbury Docks. 'We are adaptable enough to survive well into the future,' he said.

Malcolm drove me in his buggy into the former railway terminal of Tilbury Riverside station, a vast, empty brick building which once housed four train platforms but is now used only as an occasional car park. The station was operational until 1969, and it's now a listed landmark. I said goodbye to Malcolm and went to find Alan Mills, the cruise operations officer who looks after the old station building. His father used to work on the railways, fixing all the mechanical equipment, including the clock on the roof. 'He would climb up the ladder, then raise it so no one else could get up, and sit up there, eating his sandwiches, watching the ships go by.'

White metal arches curved across the dirty glass roof above our heads and pigeons flew around inside the huge space; it reminded me of that other great hallway for new arrivals at Ellis Island. This building would have been the first place that five hundred Jamaican

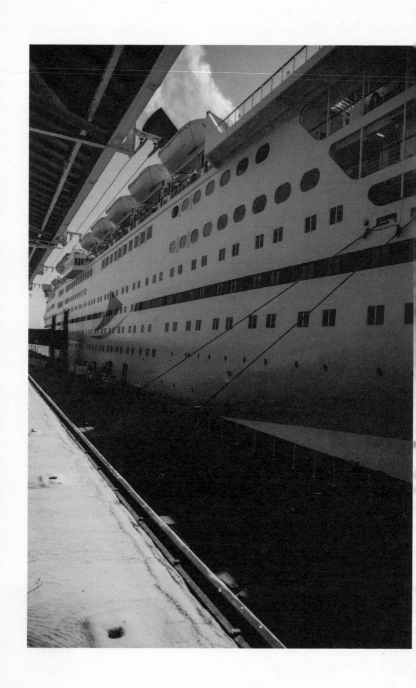

passengers saw after landing at Tilbury in the *Empire Windrush* in 1948. It was also the last place the Ten-pound Poms would have seen before embarking on their long journey from here to Australia, having been encouraged to emigrate after the Second World War. The place also has a special resonance for me: my maternal grandmother worked at the cruise terminal in the 1960s, collecting data on the countries of origins of those arriving at the quayside from all over the world.

Back on the perimeter of the dock's closed world, I described all that I'd seen to Iain as we walked past the cruise terminal. He remembered visiting the 'ghostly cathedral of immigration' decades ago, when the place looked completely abandoned, its former railway tracks still visible but overgrown with weeds, and porters still hanging about.

We carried on walking towards the ferry terminal and the river, then stood down by the glittering water, where Iain spoke about the magnificence and potency of the Estuary, the light on the waves, the lift you get in your soul because the water is connecting with the sky. 'Turner pushed on round to Margate, and Constable spent time at Hadleigh Castle to connect with the best skies in Europe.'

We stood on the quayside, imagining what it must have been like to step on a boat from there and make one of those overseas departures to Australia, New Zealand, Sri Lanka. And how must the place have appeared to those coming into London? Conrad describes it in such sparkling terms: travelling upriver and witnessing the immense energies of these docks; seeing London on the horizon, the world capital of industry and investment.

The weight of so many stories and lives rests in this place. Across the water, we could see the church where Pocahontas was buried; she hadn't wanted to leave London but was forced to take the journey, and she died at the point where the river becomes the Estuary. Iain spoke about General Gordon, who was killed in Khartoum but lived in Gravesend, and about Queen Elizabeth giving her famous Armada speech at Tilbury Marshes.

Iain pointed across the water. 'These two places twin beautifully. Gravesend was where you waited on the tide to go downriver and off into the world's oceans, but you had to pause here first. You get a real sense right here of taking the decision to go out or to come in. If you've arrived, then you're expectant that London is somewhere upriver, but you've also got the opening out. It's all out there, somewhere beyond. Your mind is at its best just at this place, moving in two directions at once, flowing in and flowing out.'

18

Graves Enders

At Gravesend all foreign-going vessels are compelled to stop and embark pilots, while homeward-bound ships take aboard a customs house officer. The Thames narrows to half a mile width, day and night the channel is full of every class and description of shipping – from the stately and majestic ironclad to the fussy little steam tug; from the clean-cut China clipper to the Dutch galliot, schooner yacht, deep-laden hay and coal barge.

> – *The Thames: 'Waterway of the World': A Literary, Commercial and Social Review, Past and Present*, 1893

A few months after my visit to Tilbury with Iain, I returned to that same quayside to take the ferry across the water to Gravesend. The Tilbury–Gravesend crossing has connected the Essex and Kent coasts for centuries. In the medieval period, sheep fattened on the marshes were moved in rowing boats from one bank to another; now, a motorized boat transports workers travelling to and from Tilbury Docks. It is the last public river crossing before the Estuary becomes open sea.

The *Duchess* was just leaving Tilbury as I approached. It took less than five minutes for the ferry to motor across the swirling, brown waters of Tilbury Reach to Gravesend Pier, where she docked briefly to let passengers disembark. From Tilbury, the historic maritime town of Gravesend looked charming, with its old hotels, stone church, riverside pubs, iron piers and Regency-style buildings – remnants of a time when Gravesend was a popular holiday destination for Londoners, with pleasure gardens, water baths and elegant promenades – but the place has a darker history, as its name suggests. Those who died at sea were once unloaded from incoming ships at this border point and buried in the town to stop the spread of disease into London.

Because of its geographical location, Gravesend has been the first and the last port of call for inward- and outward-bound vessels for centuries. All ships headed for the New World in the seventeenth century, including the square-rigged merchant ship *Mayflower*, filled with the first English settlers to establish a colony in New England, stopped at Gravesend to load goods and passengers 'and be examined by the Minister of Gravesend'. The passengers took oaths of allegiance

to the monarch and swore to follow the state religion before proceeding on their long sea journeys. Foreign sea captains from around the globe have anchored at Gravesend before travelling upriver; waiting between tides, offloading goods, changing crews, taking on board supplies, customs officers and passengers. River pilots board in-bound ships here to help steer them safely into the docks, and Trinity House pilots board outward-bound vessels at the same point, navigating ocean-going ships safely across the treacherous Estuary waters. Today, these pilots are trained from a bridge simulator in a specially designed building on the waterfront – the headquarters of the Port of London Authority. The PLA also monitors ninety-five miles of the Thames from Teddington out to the North Sea, tracking both commercial and leisure vessels with radar radio equipment and keeping the river open to vessels in all weathers. It also conducts underwater surveying programmes to map the ever-changing riverbed and provides divers to remove obstructions from the sea floor. PLA vessels travel up and down the river daily, both policing and supporting traffic on the Thames Estuary.

I watched the *Duchess* motor back over to Tilbury and stepped on board. It was too late in the morning for commuters and there was just a handful of other people making the crossing: two cyclists, an elderly couple and me. Inside the sparse interior of the ferry, large wooden blocks served as makeshift seats. I bought my return ticket, then made my way up to the wheelhouse to meet Gravesend resident Dave Simmons, a freeman of the river, who can navigate any vessel wherever the tide flows within the PLA limits. He currently pilots the Gravesend ferry and occasionally runs the *Pocahontas* pleasure cruiser as well, but over the years he has skippered every craft you could think of, including tugs, barges, salvage and rescue boats. 'Any freeman of the river of my age will give you roughly the same story,' he said, as he steered the ferry effortlessly across the water. 'The only thing I've done different was becoming a diver in my mid-twenties. I was navy-trained; it was exciting – I lived on adrenaline.'

Over the years, Dave has dived in most reaches of the Estuary, all the way around to Margate, halfway across the Channel, under Southend Pier and in the docks. He learnt to dive in the early 1960s, with a forty-pound brass helmet and fifty-six-pound weights on his back, his chest, on each of his feet. It was hard to walk on land but, as soon as he got into the water, the suit filled up with air and he became like an astronaut on the riverbed. 'I could literally run along, it was almost balletic. If I wanted to go up, I'd pump more air into the suit. If I wanted to come down, I hit the knot valve. If I had a stay line from the surface, I could go up and down in about a hundred feet of water like a lift.' Most dives lasted no more than an hour and then the tide would pick up. He showed me a video on his phone of him wearing the diving suit, which looked just like something out of a Jules Verne novel. It seemed incredible to me that, when I was a child, people

were still diving in outfits like this. The suit looked as if it should have come from the Victorian era.

Most of Dave's work involved recovering sunken craft, although wrecks were often left on the seabed after being identified and charted if they were not a danger to shipping. Sometimes, the diving team went down with archaeologists. In his time, he has recovered cannons, stone wine bottles, boxes of copper plate with fancy little signatures on them: 'all sorts of oldy stuff'.

Throughout the early 1970s, he dived on the *Montgomery* numerous times, checking the progress of the wreck. She was opening up and her ribs were working outwards, so there was concern that the moving decks would slowly squeeze the explosive percussion caps and set them off. Dave crawled around the crumbling decks and the holds, filled with waterlogged munitions, for six years before his diving team got twitchy and stopped accepting the work. 'We just weren't earning the money to make it worth the risk,' he said.

Dave was a PLA diving supervisor for twenty years and was in charge of two teams. They often dived on the wrecks out at Shivering Sands and Red Sands forts. The PLA hydrographic survey boat would go out first with side-scan sonar and draw a 3D picture of the riverbed. Sometimes, a wreck would appear on a dive which had not shown up on the survey, particularly at Shivering Sands, 'so-called because every now and again they move, the sand tumbles, it rotates and occasionally gives up a wreck. They reckon there's probably about sixteen wrecks down there, on top of each other, right down to Spanish galleons.'

He spoke with sadness about the disappearance of a way of life on the river which his family had been involved in for generations; he feels that the Estuary has changed irreversibly in recent years. Dave has worked for the PLA for over forty years and still remembers when they employed thousands of workers. 'We had about four canteens to feed people in Tilbury Docks, and gangs of blokes marched on board the boats, picking up stacks of bananas, or individual frozen sheep . . .'

I travelled back and forth numerous times that morning, listening to Dave's endless, fascinating tales of the river. I finally disembarked and wandered around the town for a while before heading to the Three Daws Inn, a fifteenth-century pub near the pier, where I had arranged to meet activist, artist, sailor and local resident Jane Trowell.

Together with her partner, James, Jane runs Platform, an arts/environmental/human rights group based in London. The couple met whilst working on a project about London's buried and polluted rivers: *Still Waters* was a month-long series of performances along four different buried rivers, uncovering and exploring the history of each. They recently celebrated their twenty-first anniversary with an epic journey from the source of the Thames to its mouth. They walked the first section, then hired a Thames skiff and rowed downriver for two weeks before picking up their sailing dinghy at Limehouse and finishing with a day-trip on the *Pocahontas* from Gravesend to Southend. The Thames is still ever present in their lives; they live in Kent, overlooking the river, and sail every weekend on the Estuary.

Over the last few years, they have sailed along every inch of the Kent coast – all the way to Grain and back – and have got to know the creeks, tides, histories, conflicts and natural world of the Estuary, building up a complex picture of the place from both water and land. Slowly, they have overcome their fear of the big ships out in the shipping channel which loom over their fourteen-foot yachting dinghy. Jane told me she and James were extremely cautious sailors who were interested only in gentle weekend sails along the backwaters. She offered to take me out and, whilst I loved the idea, I knew I wasn't ready to get back on a sailing boat, even though it had been well over a year since my accident.

Jane and James live on the Hoo, in Lower Higham, by St Mary's Church. Jane told me that, every year, the local church organizes a marsh day to get people out on the wetlands. The annual ritual has echoes of a much earlier tradition, when fifteenth-century nuns from nearby Higham Priory used to run a ferry across the Thames. 'There are loads of women in the story of the river,' Jane said. 'In terms of employment, the Estuary has always been a male domain, but there are other stories to uncover. All those men were sons, lovers, husbands, fathers. There's that whole story of what happened onshore, and that was the women's role.' Even more so than when she related the female history of the Estuary, Jane spoke passionately about its present and future as a creative space. 'There are more and more women making artwork around rivers and estuaries. I want to charge women to take on more industrial landscapes.'

There's no shortage of women answering Jane's challenge. She introduced me to *Thames Portraits*, a fantastic book by E. Arnot Robertson, a woman in disguise. It is filled with river journeys and conversations with people who worked on the water in the 1930s: a similar project to mine in some respects, except Eileen was an extremely competent sailor herself. Jane's neighbour Sarah rebuilt a Thames barge (a joint project with her husband, a captain of coastal freighters) and lived on it on the Medway for years. And another neighbour, Fiona Spirals, is an artist fascinated by the mud, creeks and low water of the Estuary who makes work on the rotting stumps of piers and the landscape of the North Kent Marshes. Female artist Fran Crowe collected 46,000 pieces of plastic rubbish from the beaches north of Aldeburgh – roughly the amount of plastic to be found floating in one square mile of ocean across the planet at any point in time. And Jane is a committed member of the Friends of the North Kent Marshes, a protest group made up of female activists campaigning against the planned Estuary airport. I was fascinated to hear about so many different female responses to this landscape, which has been, traditionally, male territory.

We started walking along the promenade to meet Helen Skellorn, a sailor in her nineties. As we walked, we discussed some of the other great creative responses to the Estuary by women taking place now, including the work of Leigh-on-Sea author Syd Moore, who has conducted extensive research into the Essex witch trials and uncovered disturbing information on Matthew Hopkins, the Witchfinder General, who was responsible for the deaths of hundreds of women in Essex and East Anglia during the English Civil War. We also discussed the new body of work focusing on riverside rituals by photographer Chloe Dewe Mathews. During the last four years, Chloe has been walking along the Thames in sections, interacting with people along the way and photographing events. She has documented African Pentecostal baptisms on Southend beach, attended by hundreds of worshippers dressed in white robes; the scattering of ashes by Hindu communities near Eel Pie Island at Twickenhan; the activities of a lone Druid, Chris Parks, who made a coracle by stretching animal hide around a wooden frame and paddled down the

Thames with an ostrich egg in his boat. The egg received blessings and prayers from Druids, Christians, Jews, Muslims and Buddhists on its long journey out to the North Sea, where Chris cast it into the water as a symbol of peace and hope. Chloe also photographs non-religious rituals: the mudlarkers who take daily pilgrimages out to the shoreline, the ship spotters at Tilbury who sit every day by the passenger ferry, sipping hot chocolate from flasks.

We reached Gravesend Sailing Club and found Helen waiting for us inside. The club is based in a small wooden building overlooking the river; the building was constructed in the 1950s, but the club itself is much older. Helen showed us a faded sepia photograph of the old club room in the Victorian era. 'It is the oldest-established sailing club on the Lower Thames. Of course, women were not allowed in the club back then,' she said. 'In fact, there were no lady members until relatively recently. I do remember being brought into the club-house by my father as a child, but my mother would not have come in on her own. Post-war, there were new motions put forward, but there was always a group of gentlemen who protested. Eventually, we were allowed one lady representative on the general committee, who was shut in the bar once the men had got their drinks until the point on the agenda came to report from the ladies. Then they would open the door and she would say something like, "Well, this year we've made over a hundred cups of tea for members and we are getting short of teaspoons. Could we get six more teaspoons, please?"' Helen proudly told us that she became, in the early 1970s, the first female commodore of the club, which involved preparing annual reports, making speeches 'and ensuring you did a reasonably entertaining job of it'.

Helen started sailing in an EOD at the age of three and has been on the Estuary waters ever since. A lifetime of sailing here has enabled her to create a perfect memory map of the sandbanks and the creeks around the Kent coast: she described the place with knowledge and intimacy, without needing any maps or charts. Her memories stretch

back to the 1930s, when the river traffic outside Gravesend Sailing Club was heavy and she would weave her way through fleets of Thames barges and past an old hulk called HMS *Cornwall* (a reform school for naughty boys), dodging tugs moored four deep. Three or four dozen bawleys would moor up overnight in front of the Clarendon Hotel, the crew boiling the shrimp on board then selling them by the pint, unshelled, straight off the boat.

After leaving Helen and Jane at the club, I made my way back along the promenade, past Bawley Bay, and decided to stop for a quick drink in the Three Daws before heading back to Tilbury. Inside, the panelled walls are covered in sepia versions of what Gravesend and the docks once were. As I examined these framed pictures, I noticed an extremely thin, tall man with a lined face, wearing tattered jeans and an old camouflage-patterned shirt, watching me with interest. After a while, he approached me and introduced himself as River Jim, a local historian and licensed mudlarker of the Thames Estuary.

'Gravesend is what I live and breathe,' he said, staring at me intently. 'My family have lived here for three hundred years.'

Without stopping for breath, he embarked on a potted history of the town, a place on the boundary between London and the wider world. 'We're halfway between the sea and the land. The sea comes in as the tide ebbs and flows; some days you can smell the sea and other days you can smell the fresh water. We're a coastal resort, we're a seaside resort and we're a river resort.'

He spoke with great passion and at speed, wringing his hands then gesticulating wildly. 'We are a rough port town full of smugglers and press gangs and stories. I find a lot of stoneware from the seventeenth century, Delftware from Holland, coins from the Baltic, clay pipes with Virginian tobacco.' Jim's speech raced through local history, some of which I knew already but many new stories, too: the unmarked grave of the Native American princess Pocahontas; James Ogle-thorpe's expedition to settle Georgia in the eighteenth century; the 1840s exodus to colonize Australia. He described the *Northfleet* disaster, a ship that was hit off Dungeness in the nineteenth century: 'nearly three hundred people died: immigrants – women, children and men.' And he recalled memories of the time before the Iron Curtain fell, when East German and Russian communist sailors would sneak off their berths into Gravesend to buy cheap toys for their children. 'We have a high percentage of migrants here; bearded Sikh men wearing brightly coloured turbans sit on benches in the town square with Polish workers. We've always heard accents and voices here, and people have left their mark through objects that wash up on the shore . . . then somebody like me – a scavenger, a rogue, a mudlarker – will find them and try to understand them. It is all history: it has no cut-off point; it continues all the time.'

Jim spent his childhood playing down on the riverside, searching for treasure. Since then, he has received his mudlarking licence from the Port of London Authority, and he still spends a great deal of time exploring the foreshore at Gravesend, 70 per cent of which consists of man-made objects: 'You can find everything there – from a pair of sunglasses lost on a sunny day to the occasional silver coin worn flat by years in the Thames. The plastic looks prehistoric, but is actually from the 1950s; it's a bit like *Planet of the Apes*, when they find the cave with the human items all fossilized. I found a stone head over there – very small, about two inches high – and it was from Mesopotamia, 3,500 years old. Victorian and medieval objects and the occasional piece of Roman pottery, right back to Mesolithic flints from Doggerland. There's an older landscape underlying the present one. The Estuary is not a permanent thing. It's moving, it's changing, it's eroding.'

Jim told me that mudlarking is a solitary sport. 'You can't concentrate with people jabbering in your ear. You just put your head down, and stare and stare and stare. You've got to rely on that eye. It's like putting a floppy disk in your brain – if I decide I am going to look for a coin, I just look for a round disc. I might take a small trowel to prise something out, but a good mudlarker uses their eyeballs and nothing

else. The lads up London who dig five-foot holes and have to use a metal detector – that's not for me. I prefer the challenge of looking – that's part of the pleasure.'

His favourite find of all time was a local tap token from the Three Daws Inn, in which we were sitting. It's a small, round piece of flat tin about an inch across, which once would have entitled the barrow boy to a free pint when he came in to deliver beer. 'It has no monetary value, but for me it was a triumph. I'd rather find that than any gold sovereign or medieval silver coin. It's local, it's something I desired and strained my damn eyeballs to heaven and back for.'

Jim's enthusiasm was tinged with sadness as he admitted that things have been getting harder in recent years. 'There's been a lot of silt build-up on the foreshore. You can't go mudlarking in Gravesend any more.' There's no way for him to know if this is caused by the ferry constantly churning up the mud, or a ferocious storm a few years back, or building works downriver for the super port.

He has started exploring further afield, along the wilder coastline of the nearby Hoo Peninsula. 'It's wonderful to get out on the marsh, to bigger horizons. The desolation, the birds, the semi-wild ponies roaming around . . . You can look back at Gravesend in the distance and sense you're on a marginal land. Give it another 1953 flood, and that place would become the North Sea again. If there's a breach in the sea wall, it floods. The salt marsh has a memory: it wants to go back to what it was.'

But the mud there on the foreshore is also extremely dangerous: Jim will not walk out unless he sees plenty of stone, brick and tile. The ground is soft, sinking and deceptive. 'You can't just go on a ramble out there, 'cos you could end up to your neck in mud. And it's an isolated place and people might not find you. I have nightmares about drowning in mud.'

He described the flotsam and jetsam that washed up on the fore-shore of the Hoo, which included a lot of modern detritus blown off container vessels and rubbish barges coming up the Thames. The

concrete sea wall acts as a buffer for endless bits of plastic, bottle tops, builder's helmets, fast-food containers – all sorts, including human remains sometimes. Jim had never found a body but knew other mud-larkers who had, although he did not expand on these stories. Once, he found a message in a bottle from a boy who had dropped the bottle in Southend about two months earlier. Quite often, he finds little statues and bowls of incense and burnt offerings which have washed ashore from Hindu ceremonies. 'They deposit these objects in the river as part of their religious practices, and they dissolve over time. I don't touch them, because they are sacred.'

Before I left to get back on the ferry, he showed me some extraordinary photographs on his smartphone of watercolour paintings he had done. 'Years of mudlarking have burnt the Thames foreshore into my brain. So when I come to paint a picture I attempt to illustrate every pebble, every stone, every piece of china, coin and tooth. The same eye that enables me to draw in this much detail is the same eye that enables me to spot a fragment of coin sticking out of mud amongst trillions of stones.

'Everyone draws pictures of Thames tugs and boats, but the Estuary is more than that,' he said. 'It's the river wall, it's the foreshore, it's the seaweed, it's what's been left behind by human society; it floods and ebbs, it disappears for five thousand years and comes back as farmland or salt marsh. I never get bored of it. When I come back I can taste the salt on my lips and smell it in my hair. I fall straight to sleep and dream of mud.'

19

The Marsh Country

These wide-open spaces lend the peninsula its particular and unique appeal – the way the sky over the Estuary seems uncommonly deep, the way the drawl of a river boat and the call of curlews arcing overhead is gathered up by the air and held there for longer than usual, so that the sound sifts down, slow as snow. Brought together, these expanses encourage a corresponding openness within; they leave space for weather and light, all the tangible atmospheres of our living, breathing world. To be out there on the peninsula, at the edge of the spangled sea, can be as liberating as it gets in a landscape.

> – Julian Hoffman, excerpt from his talk for
> Shorelines Literary Festival of the Sea, 2013

The waterlogged, muddy edges of the Hoo Peninsula stretch from Gravesend to All Hallows for twenty-five miles along the Kent coast of the Estuary. Tidal waters flow seamlessly in and out of this ever-changing landscape of saltwater wetlands and grazing marshes, home to many rare breeds of birds, including kestrels, buzzards, night-ingales and skylarks, as well as butterflies and amphibians. It all remains under constant threat from both Boris Johnson's planned Thames Estuary Airport and other possible future developments on this expansive wild tract of land just thirty miles outside of London.

Greece-based ornithologist and award-winning nature writer

Julian Hoffman became fascinated with this uniquely distinctive edge-land region after visiting one winter on a research trip to meet the Friends of the North Kent Marshes group in the midst of the No Estuary Airport campaign. After taking a train out of London, he arrived to snow and frigid winds. He went out on the marshes for the first time and, even in those dreadful weather conditions, fell instantaneously in love with the place. He appreciates its historic and literary connections and extraordinary wildlife but what really drove his interest was the threat to conservation. 'Even though the area had been accorded the highest level of protection outside of being designated a National Park, there still seemed to be governments and individuals who had the economic and political power to undo those protective measures.' Since that time, the Hoo has pulled him back repeatedly, 'like a magnet, like a compass'.

In the village of Cooling, we stood in drizzling rain in front of a row of lozenge-shaped stone graves covered in pale green and grey lichen near the side entrance of the thirteenth-century St James's Church. 'This is the place Dickens evokes so beautifully in the first pages of *Great Expectations*,' said Julian. 'Towards the end of his life, he lived in nearby Gad's Hill and walked extensively across this landscape. Beyond the churchyard are the flat, misty wildernesses of the marsh where Pip first encounters Magwitch.'

Inside the church, we entered a dark, narrow alcove beside the altar which housed a nineteenth-century grotto. The walls were covered in thousands of cockleshells, embedded there over the years by fishermen from the marshland communities. Julian was horrified by Norman Foster's plans for the Estuary Airport, which included moving St James's Church and other historic buildings on the Hoo Peninsula brick by brick. 'You could, in theory, physically move this church, but it would lose all its meaning,' he said with passion. 'How would you transplant the story of these men who came ashore and, day by day, added these shells to these walls?'

St Helen's Church in Cliffe is another man-made landmark on the

Hoo, perched on the edge of a chalk ridge with expansive views over the Estuary. In the north-west corner of its cemetery sits a nineteenth-century charnel house built for storing the bones and bodies of the unnamed dead who washed up with the tides at Lower Hope. We went into the tiny stone building, and Julian pointed out the great stone slab in the centre, where bodies pulled from the Estuary were temporarily laid to rest until they could be identified and buried. Above us was the louvred roof, ventilated to allow odours and gases to escape.

We left St Helen's and walked down the hill to the shoreline, reaching the sodden landscape of the marsh, which was veined with creeks and inlets and patches of shining water. The great quay cranes at London Gateway and the chimneys of Shell Haven were shadowy and faint on the horizon through the mist and rain. As we meandered towards the river, hopping over shallow ditches, winding our way amongst old timbers of former piers, around reed-covered chalk pits and remnants of abandoned cement works grown over with weeds,

Julian stopped suddenly. 'Listen,' he said, smiling and raising a finger to the sky. 'That is the rare sound of two male skylarks in territorial aerial battle above.'

As we walked on, hunkering down against the wind and rain whipping across the marsh, Julian told me about the importance of the Hoo for the 300,000 migratory birds which winter there each year. They mainly come from breeding grounds in northern Europe, but some come from as far north as the Arctic. 'Avocets that became extinct in Britain in the nineteenth century now breed here once again: I find it extraordinary that a species that disappeared has returned. Last year, at the Cliffe Pools, black-winged stilts arrived for the first time ever. Herons love to wade in the pools here, and there are little patches of woodland on these marshes where nightingales still thrive. The canals and dykes are fringed with reeds in spring and early summer, alive with the birdsong of reed warblers, cuckoos, green woodpeckers and corn buntings.' Julian was concerned that this unique habitat may yet be under threat from government development plans. The Estuary Airport had been ruled out by the Davies Airport Commission, and independent studies had been scathing on environmental and economic grounds, as well as for reasons of unfeasibility – but in a recent document Boris Johnson has placed the Estuary Airport back on the agenda as part of his future plan for London, so the threat remains.

We crossed some stiles, walked through a gate and moved into a more rural zone. Peculiar grassy mounds stood out amongst the flat saltings, and the place was littered with crumbling farm buildings and abandoned military structures: echoes of former human habitation. 'If you walk along the edge, coming towards Gravesend,' said Julian, 'you see these strange, little, empty villages that were erected for practice bombing and used for war games in the Second World War.'

Grazing cattle and sheep lifted their heads to gaze after us in surprise as we moved through the marsh towards the river. 'In the summer, when these grasses have grown longer and start waving in the wind, the place looks like the English equivalent of a prairie,'

said Julian. As we moved further towards the coastline, we experienced a strange optical illusion: we could not see the Estuary because of the sea wall, and a container ship floating past in the distance appeared to glide on the land. Undoubtedly, there was a dreamlike, eerie quality to the place.

We walked in silence for a while, the rain hammering down ever harder, then stopped near a muddy pathway. 'If the airport plans ever come to fruition, all of this area would be consumed by it,' said Julian, gesturing towards the wild, watery landscape around us. 'There'd be nothing left of this peninsula, the sky above would be filled with planes, the honking and circling of the geese out on the flat land would disappear. This place is lodged deep in the ancient memories of bird species. They've been coming back to the Thames Estuary for thousands of years, so the notion of trying to relocate them is ridiculous.'

The haunting cries of a curlew in flight filled the air temporarily

as we moved ever further through the mesmeric landscape to our destination, Egypt Bay. It was a little inlet, another place Dickens borrowed for *Great Expectations*; the broad sands were riddled with gull prints, the weaves and bends of the birds' imprints. There was a glorious quality to the light; even on such a dismal day, the river looked grey, tinged with blue. The mist had obscured the view of the Essex coast, but I knew we were standing directly opposite Canvey Island and the jetty where members of Dr Feelgood used to sit and dream and watch the big ships drift by. As we stood in the bay, talking, a great clanking noise drifted across the water from the other side: the sound of industry on the river somewhere nearby. It's an ever-present soundscape on the estuarine shoreline: when the gas tanks at Shell Haven were demolished to make way for the London Gateway Port, people in Kent telephoned the police because they thought there had been a huge explosion: the ground shook, the windows in their home shook – the noise reverberated all the way along the coast.

Before we left the Hoo, we went to meet two founding members of the Friends of North Kent Marshes. Local housewives Joan Darwell and Gill Moore have lived in the same village of Cliffe for many years. 'We're not born environmentalists, just ordinary people trying to protect an area that is both globally important for wildlife and also our home,' said Gill. 'We're going to continue to do everything within our power to make sure both our cultural heritage and the beautiful wilderness of this area are not destroyed.'

After the initial campaign to block the airport, they formed a campaign liaison group that eventually became the Friends of North Kent Marshes. They work with the Kent Wildlife Trust, Medway Council and Kent County Council to promote, protect and celebrate the area, organizing walking tours around the marshes, to the bluebell woods and the historic churches. 'How can people fight to protect a place if they don't know what there is here to protect?' said Joan.

Joan and Gill told me that when Boris Johnson first put his

transport plans for the area together and consultations were going on in London shopping centres, they set up camp outside, giving out alternative information about how the plans would destroy globally important wetlands, which were and still are protected under local, national and international law. The low-lying hills of the Hoo Peninsula would have been flattened and the spoil thrown out on top of the marshes, and 27,000 people's homes would have been destroyed, causing the biggest mass movement of people in Britain since the Second World War.

At the height of the campaign, there was tremendous local support, and speakers had to talk outside because the halls were so crammed with people. 'Now, that enthusiasm has died off, and they think, "Oh, that will never happen," but the Mayor of London has included this monstrous and unsustainable idea as a viable option in the London infrastructure plan for 2050.'

Graveyard of Lost Species

The Thames Estuary is an edgeland – not quite river, not quite the open sea. It is an in-between place, a place of transition, a welcoming gateway, a corridor of trade, the front line for the defence of the realm and a gradual opening into the rest of the world. Part industrial heartland, part wild marshland, it teems with nature in acres of lonely, wide-open landscapes that sit in awkward harmony with the visual noise of seaside fronts. Echoes of the sound of early punk mix with Brent geese, cargo ships and foghorns that invade the business of the high street, creating an unmistakable soundscape. It is hard to capture, describe or categorize and has been a source of endless fascination and mystery for writers, artists and thinkers over many years.

                – Colette Bailey, artistic director of Metal

An unknown number of hulks and wrecks exist in the Estuary, including many boats and barges that have been either abandoned at the end of their days or deliberately sunk to save on salvage or mooring costs. The practice of wrecking vessels in this way is centuries old. Many former working boats were deliberately ruined because it was less expensive than scrapping them, and most of these boat graveyards are found in the small creeks and inlets near the Kent and Essex coasts. There is a well-known burial ground of barges at Bedlams Bottom, off the Swale, which includes the remains of champion racing barge

Veronica; at low tide, her ribs can be seen sticking out of the mud. There is another boat graveyard in the upper reaches of Leigh Creek. I took a trip to visit this place late one summer afternoon in a small motorboat, driven by a local character called Brum.

He was standing at the marina entrance when I arrived, with his arms folded and wearing a faded blue fisherman's smock, a woolly hat, jeans and wellingtons with thick socks folded over the top. His ruddy face was framed by a thick ginger beard and lined by a life spent outdoors. He looked like the archetypal fisherman.

Brum lives in Leigh Marina, on a Dutch-built steel gaff cutter called *Sylvia May*, after his mother and his grandmother, who were from one of the oldest Leigh fishing families. His uncle had the vessel built with the gratuity given to him when he left the army after the war. The boat was originally used for fishing and harvesting white weed, a soft coral particular to the Thames Estuary which has been gathered for centuries by fishermen and cocklers on both sides of the river. Brum started on the river at sixteen, trawling for Dover sole in the summer and sprat and herring in the winter. He worked for a

while as the mate on *Thistle* and now works in the boatyard in Leigh, where his father was once employed as a marine engineer. He has many jobs: moving the boats around, dredging the harbour to stop it silting up, manning the Leigh Sailing Club support boats during races and skippering the RIB for the diving team on the *London*. One week, he might be fishing, filling in for someone on holiday; the following week, he might work on a tug, towing crane barges or hoppers full of mud.

Brum led me through the marina, then we climbed down a small ladder on the quayside and stepped on board the skiff. He started up the outboard engine, and we motored away from the cockleboats and sailing boats moored nearby and headed out towards the entrance to the creek. On the way, we passed an old steel lighter near the train station which had originally been used for carrying cargo up the River Lea and had since become the fireworks barge for Southend Council.

It was a warm, bright day and the low water sparkled amongst the reed beds. It felt good to be back out on the Estuary again: the first time for me since my accident. The water was flat and calm in the sheltered creek and we moved slowly amongst the abandoned remains of rotting boats and half-submerged barges, most of which Brum knew by name.

As we passed the empty fibreglass shell of an old trawler, Brum talked further about his own fishing experience on the Estuary; his attitude was very different from that of other fishermen I had spoken to. There was no romance about the job for him, he hated the early mornings and working throughout the night, and told me he never really fell in love with fishing, it was just something he knew. 'I often thought, "Why the hell am I out here?"' he said. 'Especially when you knew you hadn't earned anything, 'cos you were always paid on the share.'

But, like all fishermen, he had great stories. One night, he had been fishing over on the Kent side, near the *Montgomery*, when they trawled up a bomb: 'a great lump of rusty metal with a point on one end'. The skipper told them to put it back where it came from, so they motored inside the exclusion zone, pushed the bomb up the deck with two lumps of wood, then chucked it back over the side, right on top of the shipwreck beneath. 'The skipper was leaning out the window, going, "For fuck's sake, don't hit that bit on the end!"'

He worked for the Gilsons on many occasions; they had a big fleet of boats, including cockleboats and trawlers. Early one morning, Brum fell between two boats in the dark whilst stepping from one to another when waiting to go sprat fishing. He was wearing three-quarter-length, thigh-high waders, with an oilskin bib and brace and another oilskin on top of that. With the weight of all that gear, he immediately started to go under. Paul Gilson reacted instantly, grabbing him under the armpits and pulling him out of the water: 'He saved my life. If he hadn't done that, I would not be here now.'

We reached a grassy lump in the middle of the creek, the resting place of an old Thames barge. 'You can't see much of her when the tide's in, but she's been here since the Second World War. Someone nicked all the gear off her whilst her owners were away at war.' A white egret walked past on the muddy bank between the wreck and the edge of the green salt marsh.

We went as far as we could up the creek, past the remains of the oldest vessel in the graveyard, a sail barge called *Come at Last*, then Brum turned the boat around and steered us towards the bleached-out shell of a forty-foot Thames bawley. *Souvenir* was built in 1933 and used mainly for catching shrimp and whitebait in the Estuary. She became beyond repair many years ago and had been laid out on the marsh to die – a visible remnant of a bygone era.

Bawleys were once a common sight on the Estuary, particularly around Leigh and Gravesend. Brum explained to me that they were predominantly used for shrimping in the summer and stowboating in the winter. Stowboating was a traditional form of stationary fishing particular to the Thames Estuary, which involved a large, conical net

held open by two bolts of timber and lowered down on an anchor chain. The net would be suspended beneath the boat, streaming out into the tide, ready for shoals of whitebait, sprats or flatfish to sweep in. A lot of the sprats were put in barrels, salted down and exported to Russia and Poland. 'Stowboating was a big industry in the Estuary years ago, but the old order passes; very few people do this now,' said Brum mournfully, who went on to tell me that he felt he had been born fifty years too late.

I told him about my conversation with John Cotgrove, whose predecessors had worked as bawley men in Leigh for generations. They sold shrimp to the tourist industry; John remembered shrimping in his Uncle Sid's boat back in the 1940s. They would trawl the Estuary for a few hours before heaving the nets back up and emptying the contents on to the deck. Crabs and shram (bits of seaweed and other organic debris) would be thrown back over the side and the shrimp tipped directly into a copper boiler in the middle of the deck which had a coke fire burning beneath it. The shrimp were cooked on board straight away then laid out on netting on the deck to dry before being packed away in baskets called 'pads', ready to be labelled back on the wharf then loaded into a special compartment on a train bound for London and the customers waiting at Billingsgate.

We returned to the marina and Brum took me on board *Endeavour*, a historic bawley boat moored there. After being wrecked out on the mud for decades, she was eventually rescued and fully restored some years ago. Another of Brum's many estuarine jobs is to look after *Endeavour* as a sort of house boatman: he goes aboard every week, runs the engine up when she's on the mooring – lets the air through her.

She was originally built as a cockler in 1927, when 'they'd anchor over the sandbanks then wait for the tide to go out before climbing over the side. They used jumbos to jump up and down on to make the cockles come higher out of the mud. Then they would scrape them out with a rake. When the tide came in, the boat would float, and then they'd sail it back into Leigh to unload.' Brum used to work on the unloading crew, standing down in the hold, filling buckets with shellfish, which were then carried off by hand, using buckets and yokes. Then the shellfish would be washed and steamed, to be sold directly to the public from the cockle sheds in the old town, often by the women of the families.

Brum stepped up on board *Endeavour* and lifted a couple of boards off the deck to show me the space beneath where the cockles were once stored. An official brass plaque on her side marks the bawley as one of six Leigh cockleboats in the fleet of Little Ships at Dunkirk. Paul Gilson sometimes skippers the boat back to Dunkirk for memorial celebrations. Every time they visit in *Endeavour* they place a wreath of flowers in the water in memory of those Leigh cocklemen who lost their lives on *Renown*.

Wrecked on the Intertidal Zone

Here are the names of the disappeared that haunt the Thames
Estuary. The pitch pine planking of the *Souvenir* is inhabited,
scarred, cut, and incised with that which has been lost at sea,
displaced, dispossessed, evicted, or pushed to extinction.

— Epitaphs of the Common Mud
(bulwarks of the main hull of the *Souvenir*, www.yoha.co.uk)

A few weeks later, I was sitting in the bowels of the *Souvenir*, which
was resting on her side on the beach beside the Belton Way Small
Craft Club in Leigh-on-Sea. She had been towed there by Brum, who
had been looking out of the window of the boat club one day and seen
that the artists had finally managed to refloat the wreck. He raced
over in his motorboat, tied a line to her and pulled her at high speed
straight up on to the shingle shore. 'Cheers went up inside the club,'
said Graham Harwood, who was sitting inside the hold with me. 'All
the local fishermen thought we were completely insane at first, but
they got behind the idea eventually.'

Graham and his wife, Matsuko, are internationally acclaimed artists, part of a collective known as YoHa. They live in Leigh and, over
the years, have become fully embedded in the community of the old
town, particularly after Graham spent five summers on the towpath
near the beach restoring his 1930s gaff-rigged cutter. During that
time, he got to know some local fishermen and sailors, who advised

him on the best way to fix his boat – old techniques like steam bending oak frames and caulking the deck seams with melted pitch. Graham listened to their advice and their stories, as well as their concerns, about the river and he started to think about how he could represent the complex stories, contradictory beliefs and ideas about the Estuary he'd heard from the people who sit every day in the club – the cocklers, the people in the yard, those down on the shoreline in little huts, in containers, in caravans and on boats.

In 2013, an artist-led, socially engaged art and citizen science project, *Wrecked on the Intertidal Zone*, developed from these initial thoughts. YoHa collaborated with Critical Art Ensemble, Arts Catalyst and artists Andy Freeman and Fran Gallardo, as well as with local ecologists, fishermen, ex-industrialists, engineers, interest groups and the general public in Southend and Leigh-on-Sea, to create a series of public artworks.

Fran Gallardo worked on a project called *Talking Dirty: Tongue First*, part of the *Wreck* series, which involved a number of public events based around local foods, where they came from, their preparation and consumption. He started by making vaporizing juices for e-cigarettes from natural ingredients from the Estuary, creating elderflower and grass-marshland flavours, which led to a cookery book containing recipes such as Thames skate cooked over sea coal from old wrecks with samphire, and mud cola, a drink made from Estuary mud which contains *Mycobacterium vaccae*, a non-pathogenic species of mycobacteria that induces neurogenesis (the growth and development of neurons), which stimulates the generation of serotonin and norepinephrine in the brain and thus acts as an antidepressant.

I had been to one of these public tasting events at Chalkwell Hall and sampled this extraordinary menu. The mud cola was delicious, as was the sashimi of freshly caught grey mullet, but I was not keen on the soy sauce made from human hair! I listened with great interest to Fran talk about food sources in the Estuary that had now vanished,

like brown shrimp, which were once caught in great numbers on the bawleys. From the mid to the late twentieth century, shrimp caught in the Estuary were airlifted to Morocco, where they were hand peeled in factories then sent back in jars to the UK. One of the dishes at the tasting consisted of a single brown shrimp, which we were invited to peel, to understand the history of labour involved in the industry.

The disappearance of the brown shrimp is a symptom of a wider shift in the Estuary ecosystem. Paul Gilson had told me that when he started work in the 1960s, the Blyth Sands up to Gravesend were filled with brown shrimp; they are bottom feeders and lived off the raw sewage dumped from the 'Bovril boats' in the Black Deeps. For over a century from the late 1880s onwards, four specially constructed tankers known as 'sludge vessels', 'gravy boats' or, in later years, 'Bovril boats' arrived from East London on every weekday tide, loaded down with 1,500 tons of raw sewage, which was then cast into the Estuary. When the river was cleaned up and altered with chemicals, the shrimp disappeared. I remember going to the beach and trying to swim in the Estuary one summer in the 1980s. Police were walking up and down the shoreline, warning people of the dangers; there were rumours that there was a risk of polio and other infections from the filthy water drifting in on the tide. England was the last country in Europe to stop dumping raw sewage at sea.

The chemical contamination of the Estuary was another theme running through the *Wreck* series of events. From 1936 to the mid-1980s, Two Tree Island had been used for landfill and as a sewage works, leaking PCBs (polychlorinated biphenyls, a group of manufactured chemicals which have been banned since the 1920s), DDT (a chemical pesticide believed to cause cancer and harm wildlife) and other dangerous chemicals into the salt marsh. 'Southend-on-Sea and Castle Point local authorities have little data about what lurks beneath the uneven rubble and plastic bags of dog poo,' said Graham. In 2004, the island's chemical cocktail leached into the genomes of surrounding shellfish. It was a tip, then suddenly it became a nature reserve, because it was so polluted there was nothing else to do with it. Is this what we have to do? Pollute the shit out of a place first before it is allowed to return to nature?' YoHa led a number of citizen science workshops last year, testing the soil and water on Two Tree Island for toxicity. The tests revealed that the soil in parts of the island is badly polluted with arsenic and PCBs. The group concluded that the black-berries were edible, as were most wild foods that grow on the island but are not in direct contact with the soil, but the ground itself is heavily contaminated.

Another public workshop involved walking out on the mud around the island with amateur biologist and gardener Paul Huxster, using geo-locating devices such as smartphone GPS and geo-tagging cameras to document eelgrass and cordgrass spatial fluctuations across Leigh's tidelands in order to create an interactive map. 'Local bio-diversity depends on these two plant species,' said Graham. 'The grasses on the mudflats have become important food sources for migrating

birds, but siltation and rising sea temperatures are causing these grasses to diminish on Essex shorelines.'

Graveyard of Lost Species, the most complex of all the *Wreck* series projects, evolved over many stages, the first being to rescue *Souvenir* temporarily from her watery graveyard by refloating her then towing her up on to the beach. The twelve-ton boat had to be dug out from the marsh by hand, which took weeks. 'She was full of mud, old tyres and bits of iron with sharp, jagged edges. We had to empty her out first, then dig out the keel,' said Graham. 'We were lying half buried in the mud and every time the tide came in the mud would pour back in again. It was incredibly hard physical work. Matsuko got stuck in the mud and we had to dig her out. We fixed batons all the way along the keel then wrapped plastic round one side and pumped *Souvenir* out with massive salvage pumps. Eventually, she popped up out of the mud. I set chains round her and managed to pull the bow round, then Brum saw us and we just rammed her on to the beach.'

The next stage involved inscribing the sides of the boat with fragments of text from local legends and memories before refloating her back out on the marsh to decompose over time. As Graham talked, Brum appeared beside the boat. 'It has been my honour to be involved in this project in some way,' he said, clearly moved. 'These artists are giving her a dignified send-off.'

'It will be an anti-monument – the opposite of the majority of monuments, which normally start with a big chunk of stone and the idea that "this is going to last for ever,"' said Steve Kurtz from Critical Art Ensemble. 'Instead, we have used really precarious materials that will come apart just like our memories do, which are fragile and will change over time and disappear.'

The project made me think of Rachel Whiteread's *House*, a poured-concrete sculpture of the interior of a terraced house in East London, constructed to reveal an absence. It became hugely popular and there was great controversy around the demolition of the work, which had been made to exist purely as a memory trace. I asked Steve what would happen if the same thing occurred with *Souvenir* and the local council decided she should stay on the beach because she became such a great attraction. 'That would ruin the work completely,' he said, 'as an object and as an idea; it would be far better if the young people of Essex went out there and burnt her.'

Sealand

It's quite lawless at sea, you're much nearer death all the time. Even if you are not far from the shore people can't necessarily get to you and the weather changes so quickly, the sea changes constantly, it means you are also in a different place emotionally – super alert, highly charged, all your survival instincts fully tuned in. You do things that maybe you wouldn't do onshore.

— Sue Jones, curator of the *Seafort Project*

I sat in the dark in the car beside Leigh-on-Sea-based photographer Simon Fowler, who had come with me to document the day. Looking across the water, I could see the distant lights of Harwich Port and hear the strange clanking sounds of containers being lifted on and off the quay cranes on big ships drifting across the harbour. Gradually, the stars started to fade from the night sky and a faint dawn light illuminated the sailing yachts and weekend cruisers bobbing around in the marina in front of us. Apart from a single fishing boat motoring out towards the North Sea, the place looked deserted. I sent Michael Bates a text to check we were in the right location. He confirmed – they would be there by 5.30 a.m. and we needed to be ready to get on board as soon as they arrived. Time was going to be tight if we were to catch the first tide out.

Soon after, their silver 4x4 pulled into the car park, towing a large, black, ex-SAS RIB. Michael's son James jumped out and quickly introduced himself before climbing on board the boat and further inflating the rubber sides with a hand pump. Michael saw my look of concern and roared with laughter. 'Don't worry – these things are made to be dropped out of a Chinook straight into the water.' James then reversed the car down the slipway and unhooked the RIB from the road trailer. We were given life jackets and hard hats, then Simon and I hopped on board. 'Make sure you keep your feet up,' said James, 'it can get very wet back there; and hold on tight.'

Michael stood at the wheel, turned on the engine and pushed the throttle into drive. We sped out of the harbour at a speed of thirty-five knots, skating across the water. Every time we hit a wave, the boat would bounce up into the air then smack down hard against the surface of the sea. Tears were streaming down my face from the wind pressure. It was absolutely terrifying and exhilarating in equal measure, and the harder I laughed, the faster Michael went. It was a matter of minutes before we reached the pontoon in Harwich, where we picked up the film crew that was making a TV documentary about Sealand. 'Health-and-safety briefing,' said James as they stepped nervously on board with all their gear. 'If he says, "Jump in the water!"' he said, pointing towards Michael, 'jump.'

The film crew struggled to protect their equipment from the spray coming up over the top of the open boat as we headed out of the harbour, bouncing across the waves towards the sea fort. They had hired a fishing trawler for their producer and drone operator but the RIB soon left it far behind.

It was not long before the distinctive silhouette of Sealand came into view on the horizon. As we moved nearer, I saw the yellow arm of the crane sticking out over one side of the platform and, closer still, the dreaded bosun's chair became visible, dangling from the end of a cable. It was even worse than I had anticipated. It looked like a homemade swing for a child: a single, narrow plank of wood with two bits of rope attached either side and no safety chain at all.

As we approached, I expressed my fears about going up in it to Michael. 'For God's sake,' he said, 'you've pestered me non-stop for over two years to get out here – you've got to do it now!' The tide swirled ominously around the great circular, concrete legs of the fort as we pulled alongside, the motor still running. 'This chair is nothing,' said Michael. 'When I was about fifteen, there was only a rope ladder. I fell off it once, straight into the sea. It was November, I was wearing waders – it could have been fatal, but I managed to swim back and climb up.' If he was trying to make me feel better, it was not working.

Simon and I needed to get off the boat quickly because the documentary team wanted to film Michael and James motoring around the sea fort in the RIB alone. Simon offered to go up first, which made my anxiety even worse, as he missed the swing when it came down, then it flew back round and nearly knocked him out. On a second attempt, Michael grabbed hold of it and just shoved Simon on. He was immediately winched up and, before I had time to think about

it, the bosun's chair was back down in the boat. I quickly hauled myself up on to the seat, wrapped my arms around the ropes, held on tightly and did not look down.

As the swing reached the level of the platform, I saw a man in blue overalls operating the noisy, diesel-powered winch. Great plumes of black smoke were coming out of the machine beside him, which, ironically, was called Plummet; it had originally been used to lug the Southend lifeboat up on to the pier from the water. Simon was standing behind the man holding a rope, which he pulled on hard, and the arm of the crane swung around on to the platform. I quickly jumped off on to solid ground, elated to have made it safely on to the fort.

The man in overalls threw down another line for James below, and he attached a large cockle bag to the end. As I stood there and started to take in my surroundings, the man came over and introduced himself as Mike Barrington, Head of Homeland Security: 'I'm basically the engineer, the gardener and God knows what else as well.' He told us that the cockle bag was filled with his supplies for the next two weeks. He pulled out a bottle of whisky from the top. 'The important stuff is here,' he said, looking pleased.

We were standing on a wide, rusty, metal platform covered in bags of cement and aggregate, an old cement mixer, piles of rope, car batteries, gas canisters, rusting generators, petrol cans, hosepipes, stacks of wood, tools, and other bits and pieces you might find in a garden shed. 'Before you start walking about, I better give you a health-and-safety briefing,' said Mike. 'Don't go over there,' he said, pointing towards the southern end of the platform. 'There was a big fire there a few years ago, after one of the generators blew up. If you walk on that side, you will just fall into the sea. Apart from that, there are no health-and-safety rules on Sealand.'

Looking down over the edge, we could see Michael and James in the water below, speeding around the fort in great wide circles in the RIB with the fishing trawler following behind, filming the action. They were going to be a while, so we had an hour or two to explore.

Mike proudly showed us his nursery on the deck, where he was growing potatoes in bags of compost, beside a pile of lobster pots. 'You have to be pretty self-sufficient here,' he said. 'You never know if the support boat will be able to get here with fresh supplies.'

He took us up another level, to the helipad above. The views across to Harwich and out to the North Sea were breathtaking. Two Sealand black-, red-and-white-striped flags were flying in the wind on tall flagpoles at either end, next to wind turbines which Mike had built and erected himself. He told us he hates taking the flagpoles down when the helicopter comes. They were put there deliberately to prevent another air assault like the one that had resulted in Michael being imprisoned on the fort in 1978. 'There were Molotov cocktails flying about here and hand-gun battles on top of the fort back then,' he said. 'This place has a colourful history.' I asked Mike about the other guards who work on Sealand, and he said nobody had lasted as long

as him. 'There was Matt the Prat,' he said. 'But he sliced half his ear off after walking into the wind turbine.'

Mike initially came out to Sealand twenty-five years ago to fix one of the generators, after getting to know Roy Bates and his wife, Joan, through the pirate radio scene. The idea of spending time out on the sea fort appealed to him, and he offered the couple his services. 'I like not being nagged and told what time to get up, and I like my own company, big time. I also like designing things and building things.' At one point, Mike stayed solo on Sealand for over six months: 'We

ran out of money, there was no point in sending boats backwards and forwards, so I stayed to keep it going.'

When we arrived, he had not seen anyone for a couple of weeks and seemed keen to talk. He spoke about his ex-girlfriend. 'Never go out with an Italian,' he warned, 'they are unpredictable and crazy.' Back on the lower platform, he led us inside the building and showed us around the kitchen, which he had built himself. There were many homely touches in the room: a flowery enamel wall clock, paintings hanging on the walls and a candelabra on the table.

We sat around the table, drinking mugs of sugary tea. Mike described Roy as a wicked old bugger whom he thought the world of. 'He was the father I never had. I don't handle land so well sometimes,' he confided. 'Roy understood me.' Sea-steading has become the norm for Mike now, but he occasionally goes through a phase where he does not want to come back out: 'I get these funny ideas something's going to go wrong.' Fortunately, he has a good support force around him: a boatman who brings him back and forth and the

radio communication system in the corner of the kitchen so he can always get in touch with someone if need be.

As we sat talking, the film crew's drone appeared outside the kitchen window, hovering for a while and buzzing loudly. We could see the camera lens focusing in on us. 'If I had a shotgun, I'd shoot the bloody thing down,' Mike said.

We went into the narrow, steel-lined and riveted hallway, which had a number of rooms coming off it. The naval officers once lived here; the anti-aircraft guns were on the roof above. When Mike first arrived on the fort, one of the big guns was still in place. 'I went outside to have a pee at night and used to walk into the counterbalance weight on the way back – it wasn't very forgiving. I gather they cut that up and chucked it over the side at some point.'

He led us into the lounge next door, a cosy room with large, comfortable sofas, framed prints on the walls, chintzy curtains and a log-burning stove in one corner. Whilst we were there, James called on the satellite phone: the film crew wanted to come up. Mike went back out on to the deck to winch them in. After a very exciting morning and an early start, I fell asleep on the sofa.

James popped his head round the door around the time I woke up. Michael was being filmed up on the helipad, Simon was taking photographs and Mike was trying to find a way to take the drone out. James, whose official title is Prince Royal of Sealand, sat on the sofa with me and unspooled his memories. 'From an early age, it was just normal that my family had a sea fort in the middle of the Estuary,' he said. 'My brother and I used to get lifted up in a little crate. I remember peering over the edge at the sea – I must have been a toddler.' As a young boy, he was on occasion stranded on the fort with his dad: 'We'd come out for three days, then get stuck for three weeks – the weather would turn and there would be no way of getting back. So I'd be sitting there, feeling homesick, waiting to see my mum. But we kept ourselves busy, doing things all boys enjoy. Dad used to teach us how to use shotguns and make bombs with gunpowder.'

More recently, James came and lived on Sealand for a couple of weeks after he got engaged. 'It's nice to get away from everything. At night, it is so dark you can just see stars. But it's not really a safe environment for a young family . . . My wife wanted to come out today but she's blimmin' six months pregnant – I'm not having that. She's the same as me, she likes a bit of adventure.'

James splits his working life between skippering his dad's cockleboat and running Sealand. He gets about thirty emails a day from different people, wanting citizenship, residency, passports: 'This week, we've got someone giving us banks of solar panels. People really get behind the Sealand idea – it captures their imagination. The whole concept is barmy. I don't know how my grandpa even had the thought.' Like Mike, James feels very strongly the sense of freedom at the heart of Sealand: 'It's all about independence. We set our own laws, we do our own thing, we don't worry about what the mainland has to say – this is our territory. We protect our freedom fiercely.'

We went out on to the deck to see where everyone else was. Michael was standing on the helipad in full flow, re-enacting the armed siege for the film crew. 'Oy, Lichtenstein!' he said with a wink. 'You've got a German name – you could be one of the German terrorists. Come and stand over here.'

After they finished filming on the helipad, Mike offered to take us all on a tour inside one of the concrete legs. We followed him down the steep, steel stairway. Each of the seven floors contained a single, circular, white-painted wood-panelled room. The first few floors were filled with generators and other equipment, then came a series of comfortable-looking bedrooms and even a chapel. When Mike first arrived, there were still traces of naval occupation in these rooms: an armoury on one level and a fuel dump at the bottom; the metal bunks stood in one tower and the walls had hooks, where hammocks would have hung. 'There was a hundred-odd men out here on duty – confined

twelve to a room. A young lad of eighteen just folded up his kit one day and jumped over the side, committed suicide.'

We carried on down the rickety ladder. One floor was jam-packed with huge, defunct computer servers: a business enterprise that had been shut down. Another served as a workshop for Mike, where he 'tinkers about' with electronics, old generators and car parts.

At last, we reached the seventh floor. We could hear the sea sloshing around the edges of the tower outside. Just as Mike was showing us the steel-grilled door of the small prison where the German raiders had been locked up in the 1970s, the lights went out and we were plunged into pitch blackness. 'Bloody generator,' he said. After much hilarity, we made our way back up to the kitchen in the dark.

The film crew went off to get some wide shots, and I sat in the kitchen with James and Michael, who told me more about their cockling business. After decades away from the trade, the Bates family have recently returned to cockling: Michael was fishing in the outside area years ago and managed to get a cockling licence before the rules changed. There was resentment: his first boat was deliberately sunk in the Estuary, and it was not insured so he temporarily lost his livelihood.

Despite these setbacks, he persisted with cockling and now owns two modern boats. The *Charlotte Joan* (named after his daughter and late mother) was specially built seven years ago, but he worked on her for only one season before his sons took over. 'They went out on her and did well: they didn't run aground, they got back, they unloaded the boat and did it again the next day. The next season, they just stepped straight into the breach, and they've hardly let me near it since.'

Cockling runs in the family. James's great-grandfather worked in the trade and warned his son not to get involved, 'because cocklers don't ever make any money, they've all got the arse hanging out of their trousers and they're always skint'. He was talking about a time when cocklers worked with hand rakes on the mud: back-breaking work with little financial reward. But the industry changed in the 1950s, when new, mechanized boats were introduced using a system of pushing water down a venturi dredge at high pressure, which then fires the cockles back up into the boat. (However, it often damaged them in the process.) Michael Bates worked on these boats in the 1960s and described the conditions as dreadful. 'Back then, cockling was an awful environment to work in but, nowadays, it's almost a pleasure.' Modern cockleboats today are also highly efficient: they can dredge more cockles in one hour than twelve men could collect by hand in a day, making cockling a multimillion-pound business.

The family now feels like an accepted part of the tight-knit community. They are even involved in a group of cockle licensees taking DP World to court for loss of earnings due to the dredgings in 2010. 'The yield on the cockles went through the floor; it cost us hundreds of thousands each. Cockles are filter fish, so if the water is full of sand they are affected. We believe they were also affected by the noise, the crashing and banging, all that commotion. The cockles were very thin that year; we weren't getting the amount of meat out of them we should do. And since they started dredging, the size has been down, which means the price in general has been down. We've had surveys done to take samples all around the fishing area for six or seven years now, because we could see this coming – we've sent them down to a team of scientists in Devon.'

23

Cockling

When I was fifteen, I worked at the cockle sheds, starting at 3 a.m. The cocklers would come off the cockleboats, bouncing along the planks, with a yoke and two baskets full of cockles. There'd be a mountain of cockles that needed to be steamed. I put them into a steamer – it was like working in a sauna. I can remember working in a vest in the middle of winter because it was so hot. Once I'd steamed the cockles, I'd put them on to a machine that shook the cockle out of the shell, which made an incredible noise. Big piles of empty shells would be dumped outside. Then I had to put my hands in big bags of salt and salt the cockles down.

– Mark Bradford

Simon and I met Barto on Cockle Beach in the late afternoon. Soon after, James Bates pulled up behind the wooden sheds with the RIB attached to the back of his truck. He told us to jump in quickly; it was a race against time to catch the ebb tide out. Within a few minutes, we had reached the slipway on Two Tree and James reversed down to the water's edge and unhooked the RIB whilst Barto loaded up the many bags. James expected the trip to last twenty-four hours but told us to bring lots to eat and drink, 'just in case we get stuck out on the mud for an extra day'. Soon Simon and I were gripping on hard to the back of the driver's seat as James sped along the Ray Gut, skimming across the shallow water to reach the mooring before the tide disappeared beneath us. Ten minutes later, we pulled up alongside the *Charlotte Joan*, which was moored on a buoy just west of Southend Pier, about a mile away from the shore.

We climbed off the RIB and up on to the deck of the cockleboat and helped Barto offload. James went straight into the wheelhouse and turned on the diesel engine, which vibrated through the steel-lined deck. We began motoring out towards the pier, past the familiar landscape of Southend seafront. It was a very low state of tide by then; exposed mud sat just a few feet away, shoals of grey mullet swam around in the clear water nearby.

Once we passed over the ridge of the Ray Gut, we were safely in deep water. James put the autopilot on and showed us around the working boat. An ex-military hydraulic crane used for lifting one-ton bags of cockles out of the hold sat near the back of the deck. Pipes, cans of diesel, old rope, folded, empty cocklebags, rubber tyres and plastic chutes were neatly stacked around the crane. Heavy dredging equipment ran along the starboard side. The dredge head, which looked like a giant vacuum cleaner, with steel blades attached beneath, hung off derricks at the back of the boat. Barto told us that he is responsible for setting up the blades of the dredge, a precision job: if he gets it wrong, he will damage the cockles. After three seasons of working on the boat as a deck hand, he can now feel in the darkness when he has the blades at the right place, which is just below the mud line.

Two thick pipes led to the dredge head, one for blowing water to liquefy the mud, the other for sucking up the cockles; both pass along the length of the boat, up into an open barrel, a riddle, made from steel bars. James explained that, during dredging, the riddle spins to separate out small cockles from large; shells, debris and mud are then pumped back into the water via a waste chute. The mature cockles travel along another chute, straight into the open, steel-lined hold, which can be accessed via a vertical ladder near the wheelhouse. Barto

spends most of his working life down in the hold sorting the cockles, even though this often makes him seasick.

The vessel was also equipped with mussel, clam, shrimp and white-weeding gear so the crew can continue to make a profit from the boat when the short cockling season ends. James's great-great-grandfather was an accomplished sailor who started fishing commercially for white weed when he was a young man. It used to be gathered by towing small rakes along the sea floor on a rope, then hauling them up by hand. Then it was washed and dried out and sent to home-workers, who made it into little sprays for flower arrangements, as decoration in aquariums and for lining coffins for funerals. In Victorian times, a sizeable cottage industry developed around cleaning, bunching and dying white weed various colours. 'We used to export thousands of bunches to America, Canada, Australia, Holland and all round the world.'

Until fairly recently, most cocklers in Leigh used to top up their salaries by white-weeding when the cockling season ended, but there are very few people left in the Estuary who do this now. The *Charlotte Joan* has trawled for white weed before, using large rakes of about thirty feet long which are winched off each side of the boat on derricks. When the rakes are hauled up, the white weed is shaken off the teeth and any shell, shram and starfish are cleaned from it. But white weed has been supplanted by modern plastics and artificial flowers. A couple of years ago, when the dredging was underway for the new super port, white weed failed to grow in the Estuary for the first time in living memory. It is also a habitat for crabs, worms and crustaceans, so its demise had a knock-on effect for the fishermen.

Climbing down a narrow, vertical ladder, we entered the low-ceilinged engine room. It was so noisy we had to wear ear protectors; it was also incredibly hot and claustrophobic. We didn't stay long. When we got back up on deck, I asked James where the toilet was, and he handed me a bucket. I thought he was joking.

James went into the wheelhouse to check on our progress whilst I sat on the bucket, hidden from view by the steep rake of the wheelhouse. We passed Mulberry Harbour close up as the sun started to set behind us. There was still quite a lot of activity out in the shipping lanes towards Kent. Spray was coming up over the foredeck. I moved away as quickly as possible, following careful instructions not to empty the bucket over the side near the bow unless I wanted the wind to blow its contents back all over me.

I joined the others in the wheelhouse. In the corner above the doorframe was a small box installed by the Marine Management Organization. The movements of the boat are strictly regulated to ensure the crew does not over-fish. The boat is not allowed to leave dock until this GPS tracker is turned on. Every year, the Association of Inshore Fisheries and Conservation Authorities (IFCA) surveys the cockle beds to assess the stock before the cockling season starts; the cocklers are allowed to take a third of the stock, one third is left for procreation and the final third is for gulls, waders and other seabirds. This policy ensures that stocks are replenished, but it can be frustrating for the cocklers. The hold of the *Charlotte Joan* can carry up to thirty tons of cockles, but regulations allow a maximum of twelve tons twice a week in the short cockling season.

A long wooden dashboard covered in multiple instrument panels, including depth sounders and fish finders, ran the length of the wheel-house. A CCTV monitor showed a live feed from inside the riddle: there was a single piece of white weed stuck in the bars. When the riddle is moving, James watches the screen constantly to observe the cockles coming up from the sea floor. If he notices that there is not enough water, it means that something is blocking the dredge; if there are no cockles coming up, the boat is in the wrong place and needs to move. Another CCTV monitor revealed a live image of the engine room, so our skipper could check for any burst pipes or other problems.

James told me one of the most important instruments was the plotter, an electronic navigational chart of the Estuary combined with GPS data indicating the boat's current position, heading and speed; it also functions as a contemporary memory map. Years ago,

cocklers would have used a daily diary for the same thing. 'The old boys used to say, "Well, where did we go this time last year?" They'd look back in the diary to see if they'd had a good haul. If the weather and tides were roughly the same, they'd try the same spot.'

Now, plotters save the location of every fruitful cockling haul. A red cross on this chart marked a successful fishing spot in the area by Buxey Sand near Dengie Peninsula, where James had been cockling a few seasons ago 'in horrendous rough weather: there were thirty-eight boats all working the same sandbank at once – we were lucky there wasn't a collision.' He explained that only licensed cocklers can work in the inside areas, whereas any boat with a fishing licence can cockle in the outside areas.

Another symbol on the chart indicated the place where the towing arm from the front of a cockleboat had been ripped clean off by something below a few years back, probably an anchor or a hidden wreck. A blue arrow marked the place where the wreck of a fishing boat called *Pisces* lay in the mud. 'It can be a dangerous business working with such heavy gear with so many obstacles in low water. When a crew finds good grounds, everyone wants in and, by the afternoon, the word will be out. Boats sneak out without any lights in the dark to get to their secret spot without anyone finding out, but they always do,' said James, laughing. He spoke for a while about the old Leigh boys and the old ways: 'Drinking hard and working hard was the cockling way of life. On Sunday night, Dad would pick up deck hands directly from the pub, stinking of booze and fags. Once, he had to chuck a bucket of water over one to wake him up from a drunken stupor.'

We passed Blacktail Beacon, opposite the Maplin Sands. I watched the light fade and the sky turn pink as we entered West Swin and made our way through the choppy, grey-green water out towards the fishing grounds. We were heading to East Barrow Spit, which is further out in the Estuary than most of the Leigh cockleboats venture. 'The majority work from the boom on the Maplin Sands to the

Blacktail Spit, but it's deeper water at Barrow,' said James. 'Every crewman hates the Barrows: you are so exposed out there. It takes a long time and the weather can be rough, but the cockles are bigger than those on the sands.' The first time he came to these grounds, a few years ago, he could fill the boat with twelve tons in forty-five minutes, but the patch of ground had thinned out dramatically since then.

James suggested we take a seasickness tablet, as he was expecting a turbulent night. As the sun disappeared from the sky, we were opposite Foulness, just outside the main shipping lane, four nautical miles away from the cockling grounds. We were travelling at a speed of seven knots, with a north-easterly wind. As we moved further away from the coastline in the dark night, the boat began to pitch more violently back and forth in the deep water. Apart from the distant lights of container ships in the nearby shipping channel, it was completely black outside. The sky was clear and filled with stars. It was cold and noisy out on deck, so I stayed in the relative warmth of the wheelhouse.

As we headed out in increasingly rough waters towards the Gunfleet wind farm, James talked about the near-misses he has had whilst cutting through the rows of turbines there when travelling from Leigh out to Sealand on the bigger RIB. He told me a story about a yacht whose sails got caught in one of the turbines. The boat was lifted out of the water a few feet and the sail was shredded but, luckily, no one on board was badly injured.

Conversation continued into the night. We spoke about Colin Dolby, the sadness of his loss and how deeply affected by the tragedy the whole fishing community were. James said he had seen Jane's youngest son at a party recently, and that he looked so much like Colin it took his breath away. He felt it was so unfair that fishermen are forced out in all weathers to provide for their families; it was easier for cocklers, who work only in the summer months and always have two people on board.

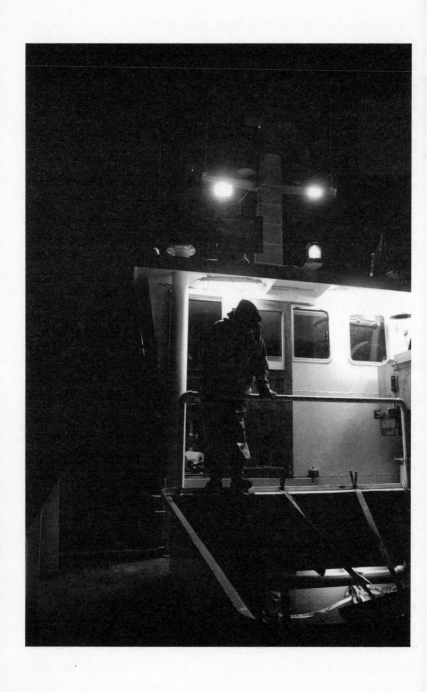

An hour or so later, we reached the fishing grounds of East Barrow, an exposed sandbank in between the shipping lanes of Barrow and Middle Deep – a desolate place in the middle of the Estuary. No other cockleboats were there. Regulations stipulated that we would not be able to start cockling until 9 p.m., so we circled around slowly in the dark. It was rough out in the open water, and James was concerned that the tide might be too high to cockle; if the water is too deep, the dredge head can't reach the sea floor. The boat rolled back and forth, and I was temporarily lulled into sleep.

When it was time to start cockling, Barto put his wellies, waterproof trousers and jacket on, and went out on deck. Whilst he was fixing the chutes into the hold in preparation, James turned on the pump engine, lowered the dredge and began trawling. The heavy equipment made the boat tip over starboard, and the noise was deafening. The sea churned wildly behind the boat, lit up by the bright lights on deck.

As the dredge head travelled along the sea floor, cockles started to come up into the riddle then pour down into the hold. Barto leapt about energetically, adjusting the chutes, filling up the bags with cockles, checking the position of the dredge head. Simon was excited by the action and keen to catch it on film, which made me anxious. In a working environment, surrounded by powerful, heavy machinery, I knew too well the potential dangers of cameras and boats. Barto stayed out on deck throughout the night. He must have eaten about ten Mars bars, and a mountain of ham sandwiches, just to keep going.

Whilst we were dredging, the boat was pitching and yawing, as well as rolling wildly from side to side and spinning round and round in circles. I found it nearly impossible to stand up on deck and hung on to the sides of my seat in the wheelhouse, watching the distant lights of a wind farm on the horizon appear briefly then disappear as the bow rose up steeply and then came down again. When we spun full circle, I would get a brief glimpse of the wind farm, which was the only thing I could see to orientate myself; it was like being on a

bucking bronco or the most intense fairground ride imaginable. 'Never mind – only another eight hours of this,' said James, grinning.

Simon came back into the wheelhouse and tried to make a cup of tea: the water went everywhere. James took over, never taking his eyes off the screens. He was highly alert the whole time, listening to the sound of the engine and the pump, watching the riddle to check the boat was always in the right spot, and the radar screen for other vessels or obstacles in the water. I looked at the red line on the tracker, which showed the tightness of the repeated circle tracks we were making on top of the sandbank.

After a while I got used to the violent movements of the boat and the incredible noise but, later in the night, as I sat pissing into the bucket on the freezing-cold deck, looking down into the dark steel hold below, which now contained tons of wet, stinking cockles, and flicking bits of seaweed and broken cockleshell out of my hair, I thought for a moment that I would quite like to go home. That was not an option, so I decided to try to have a sleep instead.

James looked surprised at the suggestion but opened up a hatch in the floor of the wheelhouse which led down to a cabin below. Somehow, I managed to climb down into the pitch-black space and lie on one of the bunks. It was quite claustrophobic and astonishingly noisy. I held on tight to the edges of the bed, curling my fingers around the sides to stop myself being thrown on to the floor: it was like being inside a tumble drier.

I slept deeply for five hours, waking at 3.30 a.m. Whilst I was sleeping, the weather had turned for the worse, with a wind speed of force six, occasionally force seven. The waters in East Barrow had been so rough our skipper had been seasick, which had never happened before. After this, James had decided he'd had enough and moved the boat to the more sheltered waters off the Maplin Sands. There were about seven other cockleboats working throughout the night in the area, and they circled the sandbanks together, a ballet of boats and lights.

As the night wore on, the water beneath us disappeared and, soon enough, we were stuck on Maplin Sands. This is a common occurrence in the tidal waters of the Estuary, an expected part of any cockling trip. The dredge was brought back into the boat and the engines were turned off; my ears rang from the noise for hours afterwards. We had about six tons of cockles in the hold by then. 'I would have liked to have had more, but it hasn't been our night,' said James. He tried for a while to get us off the sandbank manually, using the throttle and the bow thruster, but we didn't have enough power.

He was frustrated to see that some of the other cockleboats were still fishing, for another half an hour or so, orbiting us in the low water. The *Charlotte Joan* has a deeper keel, which means she gets stuck in shallower water; on the other hand, she is steadier in bad weather and one of the fastest boats in the fleet. We listened to the VHF radio for a while, hearing voices from the other boats still spinning around us: 'Ain't a lot out there, mate'; 'Pretty scratchy, man'; 'Itchy and scratchy'; 'Had enough shit today, just need to get something down the hold would be nice'; 'Had one good hour on the flood'; 'You've been all over them, mate, you scoffed them all up!' James responded but did not tell them there was a woman on board: 'otherwise, it will get really crude.' But it was too late; they spotted me standing beside him in the wheelhouse, 'Oy oy, fuckin' 'ell, that'll keep you warm at . . .' He turned the radio off quickly, apologizing.

By 4.30 a.m., all the other cockling boats were also grounded. Slowly, the engines were turned off, and the lights on deck. Simon, James and Barto went down into the cabin to sleep. I sat alone in the wheelhouse, in the silence, surrounded by darkness and mud.

24

Foulness

The way goes curving eastward for a mile from the Wakering
Stairs in the parish of Great Wakering until it is nearly half that
distance from the shore, and then turns north-eastward to keep
almost straight ahead for the next five miles, fording Havengore,
New England and Shelford Creeks in the early part of its course
and turning suddenly into Fishermen's Head on the island. Seven
branch tracks leave the mainway, one proceeding to Havengore
Island, one to New England. The other five all end in Foulness.
Between three and four hundred broom-like plants are now
maintained as guiding marks on the seaward side of the main
track, and give it the local title of the broomway.

                               – *Essex Review*, Edgar Brown, October 1927

As the dawn light filtered through the darkness, the misty coastline
of the mysterious Foulness Island became visible across the great
expanse of mud. The land was purchased by the MOD over 160 years
ago as a firing range and weapons-testing site for heavy gunnery.
Most local people have never visited the island; access is severely
restricted. This enforced isolation has ensured that Foulness has been
protected from major development. The land is predominantly pas-
toral and sparsely populated, and the foreshore is a wild place. Rare
plants such as sea kale, golden samphire and sea purslane thrive on
the shingle, and turnstones, oystercatchers and sandlings run along

the water's edge, but Maplin Sands is also a forbidden military zone, an ever-shifting, dynamic landscape of multiple hazards.

Apart from the many unexploded bombs that lie hidden beneath the mud, there are also deadly pockets of quicksand known as coffins, formed by munitions landing heavily on the sands and creating craters which then fill up with liquefied sand. Many people have been swallowed by these quicksands or drowned after losing their way and being engulfed by the incoming tide.

Running parallel to the Foulness coastline is the Broomway, recently dubbed 'Britain's most dangerous path'. This very old tidal sea road starts at Wakering Stairs then curves eastward across the mud before running north-eastward for five miles and finishing at Fishermen's Head. The causeway was named after the hundreds of plants which were once used as guiding marks on the seaward side of the main track. The Broomway was the quickest way to get from one side of Foulness to the other and was used for centuries by locals who travelled across it by horse and cart, pony and trap, bicycle and even by car. After a few too many pints in the local pub, many have lost their bearings on the way home and never been seen again. When the military first occupied the place in the mid-nineteenth century, they used the sea road to bring heavy equipment across in steam lorries but later constructed bridges across the many creeks which infiltrate the island, creating a continuous coast road and leaving the Broomway to fall into disuse.

Few people know the way along this ancient route today, although more have visited in recent years after reading about the place in Robert Macfarlane's *The Old Ways*. Macfarlane is fascinated by this high road in the sea, which he traversed on foot after receiving detailed instructions from a local guide who told him that 'it is foolish, if not suicidal, to attempt the Broomway on a flood tide.'

Last summer, I walked the Broomway with local guide Brian Dawson, soon after the tide had started to ebb. As we went, he told me stories from the mud. Once, a boy fell over the side of his Thames barge whilst sailing at low tide in the fog across these sands; he was wading along in four feet of water, shouting at his skipper to wait for him, but they never found each other again. A squaddie from Shoeburyness barracks was out on the mudflats exercising his horse one day when a sudden fog bank blanked everything out. Nearby, a Thames barge was sitting on the mud, and the crew heard the horse neighing. The skipper later found the squaddie out on the sands; together, they managed to find the horse and get it safely up on to the barge, where they waited for the incoming tide.

Without an expert guide like Brian, it is nearly impossible to distinguish the pathway today from the great, flat, featureless expanse of mud and silt all around. The broom and brush markers disappeared decades ago. We walked on late into the afternoon, squelching across the rippling sands in the shimmering light, the water lapping at our ankles. We could see Southend in the distance to the west most of the time, but little else, then all of a sudden the wind turbines appeared

on the horizon as the light sea mist around us cleared in the afternoon breeze. Just as quickly, they disappeared again as the wind dropped. It was easy to imagine how you could become disorientated out in this 'mirror world', where sky becomes sea and the landscape constantly loses its edges.

Brian said he had seen significant changes in the foreshore in recent years, which he put down to the dredging. 'I walk along the mud all the time,' he said. 'I have noticed the mud here is lower than usual; bricks and bombs are being exposed. At the moment, Shoeburyness beach is closed because bombs have come out of the mud.'

Wildfowlers, fishermen and cocklers have made their living on this unstable and dangerous terrain for centuries. John Cotgrove used to go wildfowling for widgeon on the mudflats in the 1940s, when they were still covered in barbed wire, munitions and mines. He was aware of the dangers and always took a compass with him. One time, he was out there with his yellow Labrador in thick fog: 'I could hear all these hot dinners flying around but could not see a damn thing. Eventually, I put my gun up and just went bang. When I started

plucking the bird later, I was surprised to see there were no shot marks on it. It had been hit in the guts by the wad on top of the cartridge, so it must have flown right above me.'

Peter Lily, Paul Gilson's engineer, is one of the last remaining islanders still fishing with kettle nets staked out on Foulness Sands, not far from the shore. Kettle fishing has been practised on Foulness since Saxon times. The ebb tide comes through the V-shaped nets and flatfish such as Dover sole, turbot and flounder are herded through the long wings. Just inside the sea walls of Foulness, you can still find shallow pits filled with seawater which were once used for keeping fish caught in kettles before they were taken to market.

Gathering shellfish from the shore is the oldest industry in the Thames Estuary region, and cockling has taken place on these sands since the Romans occupied this shoreline, or possibly earlier. I spoke to Barry Meddle from Leigh, who is in his eighties now but has been cockling on the Maplin Sands since he was a boy of ten, as did his father, grandfather and great-grandfather before him. 'It was a much more romantic job – it was all skill; now it's all machinery and gadgets,' he said.

'We took the boats to the sands then anchored up. Whilst we were waiting for the tide to go out we used to fry a breakfast, and if we had any spare time we used to play cards or fish with a rod and line. As soon as the tide went down, we went overboard to get the cockles from the mud. We used to have a rake on a short handle: you bent over and raked them out of the mud into a net on a frame and then into the baskets. When you'd filled up the baskets, you carried them to the boat and just kept repeating that all day. Sometimes, if we filled up before the tide came back in, we would play football or cricket. We even took some old golf clubs and balls out one time.'

Back on the *Charlotte Joan*, I watched the sun rise and the tide slowly start to creep back over the Maplin Sands. She floated off the mud, and James and Barto came into the wheelhouse from the cabin below. Soon enough, we were underway once more, circling the sands

with the dredge to fill up our load before returning. I watched Barto in the hold, jumping up and down on a full bag of cockles. Then he reached into one of the bags and handed me a small, green, cone-shaped piece of metal – the head of a bomb. 'Careful it's not radioactive,' said James, who told me to throw it back just in case, before showing me a picture on his phone of a two-foot-long bomb they had accidentally dredged up the week before and wisely put back overboard. 'We are working near the firing range: lots of shrapnel and ammunition are sucked up in the dredger,' said James.

Large parts of the island, including the Broomway and Maplin and Foulness Sands, are closed to the public when the artillery range is in use. Strict guidelines are set by the MOD about when it is safe to fish. If a working boat becomes grounded on the sand during man-oeuvres, it could be deadly. James showed me a chart with named, graded areas marked on it. He checks it each time he goes out so he knows exactly when and where the MOD will be firing.

By one thirty in the afternoon, all twelve bags were full of cockles. We stayed on Maplin Sands for another forty minutes before heading back to the Shoebury Boom to catch the flood tide back into Leigh. James phoned through to the fisheries to tell them we would be landing in a couple of hours' time, and Michael called soon after to tell us he would meet us at Bell Wharf. It was their last run of the season. 'It will be nice to have my Sundays back,' said James as we motored towards the pier.

PART III

The Outer Reaches

25

Jacomina

The broad inlet of the shallow North Sea passes gradually into the contracted shape of the river; but for a long time the feeling of the open water remains with the ship steering to the westward through one of the lighted and buoyed passage-ways of the Thames, such as Queen's Channel, Prince's Channel, Four-Fathom Channel; or else coming down the Swin from the north. The rush of the yellow flood-tide hurries her up as if into the unknown between the two fading lines of the coast. There are no features to this land, no conspicuous, far-famed landmarks for the eye; there is nothing so far down to tell you of the greatest agglomeration of mankind on earth dwelling no more than five and twenty miles away . . .

— *The Mirror of the Sea*, Joseph Conrad, 1906

Some years had passed since our trip on *Ideeal* when I received an invitation from the musician John Eacott to take part in another five-day expedition on the Estuary. The idea was to explore the outer reaches, then travel upriver towards London from the North Sea in an ocean-going cruising yacht called *Jacomina* belonging to John and his wife, Lena. The boat was on her way home after a five-month-long sea voyage around Europe and the British Isles, where John had been performing *Floodtide* at various locations with different local musicians and picking up passengers en route. He wanted the original members of the *Ideeal* residency to be the last crew on *Jacomina*'s epic journey, but only the filmmaker James Price and myself were available to come. We were joined by photographer Simon Fowler.

Simon and I got on the boat at Brighton Marina; John and James met us at the gates of the West Pier. It was great to see them both again but, as we walked along the pontoon, the nerves I had tried to suppress all day about getting back on a sailing boat resurfaced. My anxiety increased when I realized that the crew consisted of just John, myself, James and Simon. Lena had gone home; John was the only experienced sailor amongst us.

We made our way towards *Jacomina*, which was moored up in the marina, bobbing up and down gently in the water. John explained that she is a Swan 46, one of the best-designed racing cruisers ever produced. She has a standard fin keel, a tall rig and a white fibreglass hull with blue stripes. We climbed on to her beautifully crafted teak deck, which was covered in a complex-looking array of ropes and

winches. Her aluminium mast with the mainsail furled up under its cover stood some way in front of the cockpit, which housed a single stainless-steel wheel wrapped in a material that looked like soft green suede but was in fact elk hide. John showed us the many cabinets built into the seating around the cockpit housing ropes, fenders, winches, torches and buckets, as well as the small hatch at the bow where the anchor lay hidden.

We followed him down the companionway and entered the spacious interior, which included a full galley with a gas oven on a gimbal, a working fridge and freezer, two separate cabins (both with bathrooms) and teak-faced cabinets, tables and seats. Being the only woman on the crew, I was offered the guest cabin in the fo'c'sle. Our skipper's cabin was aft and the two others would sleep in berths in the main quarters. John led us over to the multifunctional navigation station beside the companionway and explained the purposes of the different displays on the screen before running through the drill for a mayday situation. He lifted up the floorboards to show us how to operate the main bilge pump before taking us back up on deck to learn how to use the life raft. We ran through what to do in a man-overboard situation and the main hazards on the boat, including getting caught in the ropes or hit on the head with the boom – a common and sometimes lethal sailing accident that occurs particularly whilst gybing. I felt like leaving there and then but managed to control my rising panic and focus on the rest of the evening's training, which involved being taught to trim the main sheet and the genoa, to make fast the mooring ropes, rig the boat and tie up the fenders.

As darkness fell, we went back below deck. Together, we plotted a route which would take us from Brighton, along the south coast past Dover to North Foreland, then across the mouth of the Estuary to Harwich via Kentish Knock and Sealand before heading upriver to London.

John examined the nautical almanac to work out how to use favourable tides, and planned our route on the charts with straight pencil lines, a plotter and dividers, making corrections for tidal flow and allowing for variation differences between magnetic and true north. He told us that sailors have used these techniques for thousands of years to establish the legs of the route. He enjoys working with paper charts and practising traditional navigational methods, which he was taught by his father, who was a pilot and a sailor.

The sextant on board was a gift from John's father: an antique brass instrument made for the American navy in 1943, it still worked perfectly. John explained how to take a sight by looking at the horizon through one of the two mirrors. Light from the sun reflects off the mirror and can be seen through the eyepiece, creating the illusion of the sun being superimposed on the horizon; then the angle between the sun and the horizon can be measured. John used this sextant to sail across Biscay recently. He bemoaned the fact that these techniques were now being lost to GPS.

I slept fitfully that night, anxious about the coming days. After an early start next morning, we slipped our mooring and motored towards the marina entrance. There was a moderate breeze and an uncomfortable chop near the harbour mouth, caused by the waves bouncing off the large concrete caissons there, which made the boat pitch violently back and forth. Because we were such an inexperienced crew, it took us a long time to hoist the mainsail. In the meantime the boom banged wildly across the deck, which I found extremely alarming, but when the sail was up the boat steadied herself somewhat and, slowly, I began to calm down and find my footing. Straight away, John put me on the helm, which helped me focus, and I surprised myself by managing to steer us out of the marina into the English Channel.

We sailed for sixty-five nautical miles that day, along the south coast, past Newhaven, Eastbourne and Hastings, with a good tide behind us and a north-westerly breeze. It took me some time to get used to the movements of the boat; I was constantly afraid at first that she would tip right into the water when she heeled over, but as the afternoon wore on I began to enjoy the experience immensely.

The tide set against us as we reached Dungeness, so we went inshore to catch a favourable counter-current and watched the fishermen on the shingle beach casting their lines into the water against the backdrop of the nuclear power station; Derek Jarman's weatherboard house and garden lay in the far distance.

We saw the White Cliffs of Dover long before we entered the marina. John radioed ahead to get permission to enter and we berthed in the tidal basin for the night. I slept well. By the time we sailed out of the harbour to a glorious day the following morning, I was really starting to find my sea legs.

I took over from John and helmed the boat for a while as we sailed close-hauled, heeling on port tack, along the Dover Straits, past Deal and Sandwich towards North Foreland, the officially recognized south-eastern entrance point to the Thames Estuary. The coast there is formed of nearly perpendicular chalk cliffs, which look spectacular from the water. A single lighthouse stands on rising ground close to

the headland, warning shipping away from the rocky shoreline. An orange-and-blue pilot cutter sped past close to shore to intercept a big ship. A fishing boat passed on our starboard side, followed by a flock of seagulls.

The traffic on the water increased as we sailed with a fair tide past the headland of North Foreland and out into the wide-open mouth of the Estuary: the place on the nautical map where the tidal waters of the North Sea flow into the mouth of England's longest river. Goods and people from all over the world have arrived in Britain via this well-used sea route, from as far back as Roman times, when vast quantities of luxury commodities, including pottery, marble, wine, olive oil and silver, would travel upriver to Londinium from the furthest reaches of the Roman empire. In the Anglo-Saxon era Viking longboats swept across the North Sea and into the Estuary to invade Sheppey, then Benfleet, before moving further along the riverside towards the monasteries of London.

The water was a light olive-green. I could see a wind farm in the distance, tankers and other big ships on the horizon far out in the North Sea, along with four cargo ships waiting at a designated anchorage to the side of the main shipping routes. John told me there were two zones: one for hazardous, and another for non-hazardous cargoes.

Spray from a rogue wave splashed over the bow as we picked up speed, sailing on our bearing towards Kentish Knock buoy – the central point of the outer reaches of the Estuary. The yacht cut easily through the water, which turned a lead-grey colour towards the Kent coast, where heavy, dark clouds hung above the cliffs near Margate. Flickers of bright white light glinted along the coastline as the sun reflected off the windows of buildings near the shore.

We sailed north, then north-west, towards Harwich, pitching forward and rocking aft. Ahead of us, we saw the London Array wind farm and a vast expanse of grey-green water. The coastline of Margate became a thick line in the distance. As we moved further offshore through a slight sea state, the water turned a deep jade-green, threaded through with flashes of silver when the sun managed to break through the gloomy sky above. There was not another vessel in sight. A line of cumulus clouds hung over the Suffolk coast, which was not visible at that point, being hidden behind the curvature of the Earth. We were sailing along an arc where the edges of the North Sea and the outer reaches of the Estuary merge, being careful to avoid the many sandbanks in the area on our way.

By the time we sailed past London Array on our port side, the sun was shining brightly. The great turbines turned slowly in the wind. Kent became a fine black slither then gradually disappeared altogether. The sea was a perfect mirror, reflecting the sky above. It was incredibly peaceful out there on the edge. We sailed in silence for some time, listening to the hypnotic sounds of the boat gently parting the waves, the halyards tapping against the mast in the wind and water sloshing in and out of the cockpit drains, bubbling up rhythmically before dropping down again.

I found the constant rocking movement of the boat and the ever-changing sea- and sky-scape all around us, with its constantly shifting colours and patterns, extremely meditative and recuperative. Sailing across the great breadth of the Estuary during that long, elastic afternoon, I felt a sense of peace I had not experienced for a long time.

I helmed again for a while, close-hauled on starboard tack, following the wind as it changed, constantly adjusting the wheel to try to achieve an apparent wind angle of forty-five degrees, watching with glee as the telltales on the genoa flew horizontally in the wind. We were heeling gently in a light breeze, travelling at five and a half knots. A container ship headed towards *Jacomina*, then altered its course, possibly to give way to us. John was standing beside me at the wheel; James and Simon were both positioned near the bow, cameras permanently attached to one eye, shooting the magnificent scene all around us.

We tacked out towards the east, away from the wind farm, laying towards Kentish Knock. There was a clear horizon and good visibility. The sea temporarily turned white-gold ahead, reflecting the bright sky above. Another wind farm loomed in front of us. The radio briefly crackled into life, a French voice came on air for a few seconds then disappeared. A large oil tanker headed south-east into the North Sea, probably going to Rotterdam.

We had been sailing for some hours across the Estuary, over a watery expanse featureless apart from the wind farms, which were ever present. Our skipper checked the charts constantly, relying on them for accurate locations of the long sandbanks stretching out like fingers in all directions. The wind picked up, and we increased our speed to six and a half knots.

In the early evening, just as the sun was beginning to set, we reached a large buoy bobbing on the waves, striped in black and yellow and with a diamond-shaped head topped by a triangular hat with the words 'Kentish Knock' in white-and-black letters on the side. John told us that each buoy has its own unique characteristics – some of them have bells, whilst others emit low, mournful sounds created by air being driven through a horn by the waves.

The Kentish Knock buoy was silent as we came alongside, giving no audible warning of the dangers lying beneath: the buoy marks the site of an extremely shallow area of the North Sea bed, where multiple vessels have met their fate over time. During the First Anglo-Dutch War, the English launched a surprise attack on a Dutch fleet of over

sixty warships moored there, with devastating consequences. Remnants of this great sea battle probably still lie buried in the Kentish Knock mud, along with the remains of many other vessels, including a German U-boat and a 400-ton nineteenth-century merchant ship called *Juliana East Indiaman*.

Many merchant ships – hulls creaking, sails billowing – came into the Estuary at this point from the Mediterranean, carrying exotic goods from Europe and beyond. They helped establish sea power in the East Indies, which eventually led to the foundation of the East India Company and the beginning of Britain's colonization of India. The seventeenth and eighteenth centuries were the Golden Age of the Thames Estuary, when this stretch of water was the major highway of the British Empire. Tea, silks, opium, salt, cotton and indigo dye flooded into the Port of London via the Estuary from all over the world.

On Christmas Eve 1822, *Juliana East Indiaman* was travelling back to London from Bengal filled with cargo when she ran aground on Kentish Knock and lost her rudder. She immediately began to take on water. The crew worked desperately throughout the night, under the command of Captain Ogilvie, who gave the order to abandon ship on Christmas Day. They 'hoisted out the longboat', and all thirty-seven crew members and passengers got safely on board, but Ogilvie then ordered his exhausted crew to return to the sinking ship to attempt to recover her precious cargo. During that dreadful night, 'the sea ran mountains high' and, as they stood on the deck hauling boxes out of the hold, 'a most violent sea broke upon them, and shivered the boat into pieces'. Shortly after, the longboat sank as well. There were only two survivors, picked up by a fishing boat the following morning.

After this disaster, a buoy was placed on the Kentish Knock shoal to warn approaching shipping of the low water there. A light vessel replaced this buoy in 1840, followed by numerous lightships for the next 170 years. John remembered seeing the Trinity House light vessel, which was painted red to make it visible in the day. It used to be manned by a small crew. Lightships do not have engines; they have to be towed out to their locations. As we sailed past, I imagined what a dangerous and lonely job it must have been for those crews, stranded out there on the edge of the North Sea and the outer reaches of the Thames Estuary with no means of escape if they ran into difficulty.

We continued sailing north-west towards Harwich. There was no land visible at this point. The sea seemed to fall away from the horizon in every direction, creating the illusion that we were in the middle of a giant, circular infinity pool constantly overflowing with water.

We were sailing over Doggerland, a sunken, lost landscape which was once a vast land mass connecting Britain to mainland Europe during and after the last Ice Age. The outer edges of Dogger Bank sit somewhere near the southern part of Harwich, off the Essex coast, and Norfolk, and stretch further north into the North Sea. This prehistoric landscape was gradually flooded by rising sea levels and has now completely disappeared far beneath the sea. Fishermen trawling in the area have recovered remnants of this submerged world,

dredging up fossil bones, rhino teeth, mammoth tusks and flint, evidence of great beasts which once roamed that forgotten place.

A single plume of black diesel smoke rose from a tanker in the distance on our starboard quarter. A line of deep crimson sat above the horizon, with great, grey, painterly clouds hanging above. John pointed out a squall to port, a solid, dark streak in the sky stretching down to the sea which indicated rain. He could read the landscape around us in ways we could not. He constantly made calculations and adjustments to our route, depending on sea state, water depth, weather, tide and wind.

As the light began to fade from the sky, he prepared us for the night sail ahead, showing us where the torches and the harnesses were and how to tether ourselves to the jack stays that ran along the length of the boat if we needed to move to the bow. I had imagined we would be enveloped in total darkness when the sun finally set, but it happened gently; it was a gradual process. The seascape around us slowly darkened, then faded to black.

A small white light on the mast illuminated the boat just enough for us to be able to see on deck. When the clouds parted, the sky was filled with stars, which were reflected in the water. In the darkness of the night I became acutely aware of the sound of the sea and the continuous rolling of the boat. Sound seemed to take on a different texture; it was sharper, richer and more intense somehow. I stood beside John at the helm, watching the wake of *Jacomina* in the murky sea behind, which occasionally became luminescent in the water. In the far distance, out in the North Sea, the water merged with the horizon, and there was only blackness. The space we were in lost its edges and became indefinable. Lights flickered in the water all around us. John told me that the red lights behind us denoted the tops of wind turbines on a wind farm; non-flashing lights indicated other vessels – green on starboard, red on port, white on stern; flashing lights were marks or buoys; pillars of light were lighthouses or lightships.

A vessel passed by on our starboard side as we entered the Long Sand Head two-way route. As we passed the mark in the darkness, a deep, low moan escaped from the horn of the buoy – the sound of the North Sea at night.

John went below deck for a while to prepare the pilotage plan for our night entry to Harwich, leaving me at the helm. Simon and James were sitting near the bow, watching out for any debris, obstacles or vessels in the water.

In the far distance, I thought I saw the distinctive table-shaped outline of Sealand. Faint lights glittered on the horizon from the port of Felixstowe as we headed towards the Suffolk coast. A dredger moved into the shipping channel, her stern lights gradually fading into the blackness as she motored out into the North Sea.

As we moved further towards the coast, Sealand came into sharp focus, even though the fort was unlit, just a large black silhouette against the dark night. Simultaneous firework displays onshore at Walton-on-the-Naze and Harwich temporarily lit up the sky. Another big ship passed on our starboard side; the swell rocked the boat. The clouds lifted and the sky looked full of stars.

As we eventually came alongside the former naval fort, a single light went on in one of the rooms on the platform, causing the deck of the boat to be momentarily illuminated. I wondered if Prince Michael was at home but expected it was the guard, Mike Barrington. The dreaded winch and that tiny swing seat on the end was barely visible as we drifted past in the darkness, but I knew it was there and shuddered at the thought – or it might have been the cold. I pushed my hands deeper into the fleecy, lined pockets of the sailing jacket Jonny had lent me before I left as we sailed on into the night.

John switched the radio to Harwich VTS as we entered the deep-water channel into Harwich. We headed towards Cliff Foot, a red buoy which had been strategically placed there to help navigate shipping into the busy port. As we sailed into the mouth of the port, we heard the cranking noise of the quay cranes, six in total, all in action, loading into or offloading from giant container ships moored alongside. The port was brightly lit and full of activity, in sharp contrast to the empty black seascape behind. A ferry passed by on our port side in front of one of the container ships; its dark silhouette was partly illuminated by lights from the cabin portholes. Steam poured out of a funnel on deck, merging with the smoke from the heavy industrial dockside.

Simon got the halyard ready to run by taking it off the winch. We headed up into the wind hard right, then dropped the mainsail, which fell heavily on to the boom. James and I managed to tie up the sail loosely as we motored leisurely into the middle of the circular harbour.

After a few moments trying to get our bearings, we made our way in the darkness towards a pontoon on our starboard side. A large banner on a building behind the pontoon read 'Welcome to historic Harwich'. We tied the fenders on to moor up alongside another boat and made fast. It was midnight by then, and we were all exhausted. After ensuring the boat was secure for the night, we went straight to sleep, to the sounds of the screeching and banging of the working port on the other side of the harbour.

26

Barrow Deep

And in the great silence the deep, faint booming of the big guns being tested at Shoeburyness hangs about the Nore – a historical spot in the keeping of one of England's appointed guardians.
— *The Mirror of the Sea*, Joseph Conrad, 1906

The plan was to travel south-east, following the natural channels between the sandbanks from Harwich to the Gunfleet, then south-west into East Swin and Barrow Deep, before traversing over the sandbar into the Knock John and Knob channels, then on to Shivering and Red Sands and, finally, into the River Swale, where we would moor for the night. The passage of approximately forty nautical miles would take us into the heart of the Outer Estuary, through the seascape we had wanted to explore over four years before on *Ideeal*.

Blinding white light reflected off the water in the harbour as we sailed out of Harwich in the early morning. The sky above was a clear, bright blue. In front of us, the Harwich–Hook of Holland ferry cut a swathe through the sea as it headed out of the deep-water channel towards Rotterdam. My maternal grandmother, Molly, worked on these ships in the early 1970s, collecting data for a small government department called the Office of Information. She would ask the passengers a series of questions about where they were from and how long they were staying in the country. She loved the work, meeting all these new people, and she was never seasick, even when the crossings were rough. My mother said it was considered to be quite a glamorous occupation at the time. She would stay overnight in a hotel in Holland and bring back exotic treats such as chocolate liqueurs, which were hard to come by in England at that time. She worked before this in Tilbury, at the cruise terminal, conducting these surveys as passengers disembarked on to the large wooden pontoon there. At the time of our sailing trip on *Jacomina*, I was involved in curating a multidisciplinary festival of the Thames Estuary for arts organization Metal, which would take place at the cruise terminal in Tilbury the following year. I had invited John Eacott to perform *Floodtide* there, and he had chosen the pontoon where my grandmother would have stood all those years ago as the location for his performance.

As we sailed past the busy industrial port again, I saw the huge container ship from the night before, now fully loaded and about to depart. On the opposite side of the harbour stood the old town of Harwich, the most northern coastal place in Essex, with its distinctive church spire and Regency-style houses along the shoreline.

As we left the noise and chaos of the harbour behind, there was a great bang as the boom flipped over port side. We were sailing goose-winged on a dead run with the wind right behind us and a high risk of an accidental gybe. We altered course, James winched in the main sheet and the boat began to heel more dramatically. In the narrow channel out, there were many big ships and lots of activity, and then we entered the silent Estuary.

Sealand slowly came into focus on the horizon out towards the North Sea. From that distance, the shape of the distant fort looked much like the Hebrew letter *chai* (which means 'life'), standing alone on the edge of the sea. We passed Armada buoy and the water changed colour to a rich pea-green mixed with streaks of orange. Dark shadows flitted across the surface of the sea as wispy high-altitude clouds passed quickly overhead. The deep water of the shipping channel further north was a dark aquamarine.

Even though we were on a rising tide, from the moment we entered Estuary waters, there was a constant risk of touching the bottom with the deep keel of the yacht. Standing at the helm, I looked for signs of breaking water – indicators of sandbanks. John instructed me to check the depth reading constantly. As we tacked towards North Cardinal, the echo sounder in front of me showed the distance between the boat and the seabed had gone down to thirteen feet. I saw waves breaking on a sandbank on our starboard side and realized we might run aground.

Before buoyage, the Estuary would have been a deadly place to navigate through because of these submerged sandbanks. They are particular to estuaries and deltas, where wind and tide, exacerbated by shallow water, creates huge sandbars which can eventually become land. This is seen in exaggerated ways in delta landscapes like the Mississippi and the Nile, but also in the Thames Estuary (which is sometimes referred to as the Thames Delta) in places such as Canvey Island, which were created by tidal deposits of silt and sand over time.

We soon reached Gunfleet wind farm. Apart from a fishing boat moving along the edge of a row of turbines, there were no other visible vessels. We gybed, turning ninety degrees bearing south-west, leaving Gunfleet to our port side and sailing leisurely on a broad reach. The Essex shoreline soon faded into the distance until only the tips of the quay cranes of the port could be seen, rising up above the horizon behind the curvature of the Earth.

The wind dropped. We put the engine on for a while and motored along East Swin, which is a well-used shipping channel flanked by sandbanks. Looking at the chart, I noticed we were sailing over a disused explosives dumping ground. As we reached Barrow number three deep anchorage, Jaywick and Clacton became visible in the distance and the chimney on Sheppey also came into view. From that point onwards, we never lost sight of land again.

By the early afternoon, we had reached the deep-water channel of Barrow Deep, which runs parallel to Black Deep. The two age-old shipping lanes are separated by the Middle Sunk Sandbank. Deep-draught vessels and bulk carriers use these channels to enter or exit the Medway and the Estuary. In the sixteenth century, Richard III was believed to have disposed of the murdered bodies of Edward V and the Duke of York in the Black Deep, 'whereby they should never rise up, or be any more seen', but these places have also been used as dumping grounds for thousands of tons of untreated raw sewage that would arrive daily on the 'gravy boats'. William Sangster, a Methodist preacher of the early twentieth century, described the process with surprising poetry: 'When the vessel reaches the Black Deep, the valves are opened and the complete cargo runs out in about twenty minutes. Down it goes, down into the salt aseptic sea. A dark stain spreads over the wake of the ship.'

As we motored along Barrow Deep, flotsam drifted past – mainly seaweed, but the occasional piece of wood. Flags denoting lobster pots bobbed up and down all around, attached to plastic cartons or small buoys. The only rubbish I saw in the sea during our entire trip was a still-inflated pink helium balloon.

The Knock John Fort soon came into view: identical in size and shape to Sealand, it is the first place that Roy Bates set up his pirate radio station. On the horizon, we could see the Shivering Sands Sea Forts, alien structures rising out of the water on stilts. I thought instantly of H. G. Wells's description of the Martians in *The War of the Worlds*: 'so far out to sea that their tripod supports were almost entirely submerged'. The Essex coast and the Estuary feature in the novel as Wells describes the stampede of millions of people trying to escape the Martian invasion, which 'spread itself slowly through the home counties . . . and along the roads eastward to Southend and Shoeburyness'. Thousands arrived in Essex to try to escape by boat. As the crowds waited on the shoreline, a Martian appeared, 'advancing along the muddy coast from the direction of Foulness', then another and another, 'all stalking seaward, as if to intercept the escape of the multitudinous vessels that were crowded between Foulness and the Naze'.

The dark shape of the former naval fort, with its gun batteries still in place, looked forbidding as we approached. Knock John Tower sits on a sandbank of the same name. The water depth dropped progressively as we drew nearer. John chose the deepest route by looking thoroughly at the state of the water. He could see where the sandbanks were situated because the water was flat and calm over them, as they take the energy out of the waves and slow the current down. As we got closer, we saw the distinctive fin of a dolphin rise and fall beside the fort. A number of fishermen and sailors I had spoken to had mentioned seeing various new species in the Estuary in the last decade, including octopi, turtles, thresher sharks, dolphins and anchovies.

Knock John is a rusty, riveted, offshore defence platform standing on top of two circular concrete legs. On top of the gun platform is a small upper deck with a radar platform above it. The armaments had long since been removed. The entrances into the tower were welded shut and the place looked completely abandoned. The words 'Radio Essex 222' are still scratched into one side of the structure.

We turned the engine off for a while and circled the fort in silence, listening to the gentle sound of the boat cutting through the water, the creaking of the shrouds, the ensign flapping at the stern, the rattle of the boom and the occasional lonely call of a seagull, and then, in the distance, the great boom of guns being tested on Foulness Island. Mist engulfed the marshy shore, adding to the eeriness of the scene. Time slipped: naval personnel hunkered down on the roof, manning great guns, checking the skies for German aircraft. Now, fish jumped around in the dark shadows beneath the tower. Terns dived in and out of the water around the tower's concrete legs, which contain rooms where over a hundred men would have slept during the war.

We moved reluctantly away, heading straight for Shivering Sands. We had just enough rise of tide to cover the Knock John sandbank. Once we were safely in the channel, the Estuary waters were green and clear; the sky was purple-grey. A coastguard border-control ship came towards us, moving quickly through the water. Seawater splashed up over the bow; the wash made us lurch violently from side to side. There was another big explosion over at Foulness: a great cloud of black smoke rose over the Essex coastline. We were quiet up on deck, feeling a mixture of excited expectation at seeing the forts up close for the first time and a little anxiety about the ever-present possibility of running aground.

The sky and the sea resembled molten lead as we approached the sea forts in the late afternoon. I could see the tip of the collapsed fort at Shivering Sands poking out of the water as we got nearer; it had been knocked into the sea by a passing ship many years before. The remaining six forts, covered in rust, standing on their tripod legs, looked dark, menacing, precarious and strangely beautiful. The thought of staying out there alone for six weeks, as Stephen Turner had, was unimaginable. Then I thought about all those young men trapped out there for over a month at a time during the war, with little to do but wait and listen for the sound of enemy aircraft, and how terrifying it must have been, with such a real threat of being killed by bombs or aircraft fire at any point.

We circled the forts in complete silence, as before; the sound of a nearby bell on a buoy rang out as it rocked in the sea. We caught glimpses of stairwells through open doorways; broken windows, rusting rooftops covered in plants. The words 'Radio City' had been painted on the side of one of the structures. The searchlight tower in which Stephen had stayed stood alone from the rest.

I remembered John Cotgrove's tales of visiting the Shivering Sands Sea Forts in September 1946 as a young teenager after taking a sailing trip from Thorpe Bay with some friends on their EODs. The forts were still occupied by the army then and had gangways, anti-aircraft guns and searchlights. 'As we approached, we saw some pongoes hanging out of a window, they were keen for us to visit, anything to alleviate the boredom. So we climbed up some rickety ladders on to one of the forts. It was horrible inside, very spartan. They were having a party for one of the soldiers' nineteenth birthday. The army

cook made a wretched cake, which looked as though it was covered in ball bearings. We had a sing-song, ate the cake, drank some tea, then the wind got up so we stayed the night in the soldiers' quarters on pipe-cots, which were like shelves with mattresses on – they were pretty rudimentary. We had no way of contacting our parents. My father went out on the mud in the middle of the night, looking for the body of his son. We got hell off our parents when we got home the next day.'

As we sailed away from Shivering Sands towards Red Sands, a distance of just four nautical miles, a container ship passed by, closely followed by a ro-ro cargo vessel. These two sets of army forts had been specifically placed to protect the main shipping channels into London by attacking any German mine-laying ships that tried to enter into these passageways, as well as any Nazi aircraft and doodlebugs. The army and naval forts were just part of the defences employed in the Estuary during the war: an anti-submarine boom was laid off Canvey Island; controlled mines were placed in the channel and four torpedoes fixed at Shell Haven. The old Dutch wall of Canvey Island was fringed with barbed wire, and forts, batteries and a fleet of minesweepers dotted the length of the Thames from Kew to the Nore.

We passed the yellow Princes Inner buoy, which marks the site of a wreck, as we entered the most treacherous area of the Estuary: the Nore – a great swathe of sandbanks which stretch out from the Kent coast right up to the main shipping channels. This is the area where so many vessels, including the *Montgomery*, have met their fate over the years.

There was a foul tide against us when we reached Red Sands. A strong current swirled around the legs of the forts; our skipper looked worried and told us we would not linger there unduly but we were all transfixed by the sight of them. Five intact turrets circle a central command at Red Sands. KEEP OFF! is painted in giant white letters on the side of one of the structures. One of the forts has been partly refurbished by Project Redsand, a group of committed enthusiasts who have been actively involved in conserving these forts for decades, and has new windows, a good access ladder, a landing gantry and a large aerial on the roof. The group now plans to work with business partners to convert the decaying forts into a futuristic-looking luxury hotel complex, with penthouse and executive apartments, a spa and over four hundred rooms. Guests would fly in by helicopter or arrive by hovercraft from Whitstable or Harwich. But, for now, the Red Sands and Shivering Sands Sea Forts stand abandoned in the Estuary, havens for wildlife and poignant reminders of the efforts by the British military to protect London during the Second World War.

Artist Chloe Dewe Mathews recently gained access to these forts, going out there with volunteers from Project Redsand. On her first trip, the fog was so thick they could not see the structures at all until the boat was bang up against them. She started filming from the restored tower, recording details of the atmospheric forts in the sea and the odd sailing or container ship passing by in the white mist. She plans to mix this eerie footage with crackly archive sound recordings she found online – 1960s broadcasts from Radio 390, one of many offshore pirate radio stations that once operated from the sea forts. The station was originally named Radio Eve: it was conceived as an easy-listening station aimed at housewives: 'the women's magazine of the air'.

We headed towards the mouth of the Swale, past Middle Sand to port. The sea was calm and glassy, a deep metal grey. The still water became a mirror, reflecting the sky above; we were immersed in a seascape of quicksilver. Dead ahead we passed the remote hamlet of Shell Ness, a small, sparsely populated coastal town on the most easterly tip of Sheppey. Some of the houses were boarded up. There were a few ramshackle wooden huts on the shore, and nobody on the nudist beach on the foreshore.

With a knot of tide pushing against the boat, we struggled to get into the mouth of the river. The water was falling fast; it was a race against time to reach our mooring. To starboard, the beach turned quickly into marsh, intersected by muddy creeks teeming with bird-life. Black-headed gulls and avocets waded along the water's edge. Terns flew low over the mudflats and the landscape was filled with the sound of birdsong. We narrowly avoided a spit of sand as the water beneath us shallowed rapidly. We reached Sand End intact and watched a single balloonist flying high over the Kent hills.

Basking in the early-evening sun on the Horse Sands lay an entire colony of common and grey seals. As we passed by, they lifted up their tails and turned their heads towards us. One of the younger-looking seals, the colour of rust, slipped into the river and swam towards us for a while before disappearing back under the surface of the water.

Horse Sands had been a popular place for gun-punting – shooting wildfowl from a boat. This is something else John Cotgrove remembered from his youth: hunting in a handmade, single-handed, plywood

gunning punt in the 1940s, towing the punt over from Leigh to the Swale and lying down to sneak along the edge of the creeks in the shallow water. The punts were roughly twenty feet long, shaped like a canoe, with a large, old-fashioned hammer gun mounted on the front; they acted like a mobile bird hide, letting hunters get right up to the birds. John told me a story about his friend David Wallace, who was gun-punting at the Horse sandbank one day: 'He shot some ducks and rode up to the mudbank to collect them, but he didn't anchor his boat. Before he knew it, the punt was away. There he was in February, on a mudbank, in the middle of the river, with the tide coming in. Luckily, a fishing boat came by and picked him up.' A small group of dedicated Kent wildfowlers continue this practice today in the Swale, the only legal place in the Estuary to gun-punt. Most gave up the sport decades ago, due to the danger involved and the protection of wild birds in conservation zones.

We moored *Jacomina* up to a buoy in the middle of the river at

Harty Ferry, a remote spot opposite a small island. We contemplated taking the inflatable dinghy out to the pub on the island, but there was a high chance of getting stuck on the sandbank on the way back, so we sat up on deck instead, drank schnapps and sang some songs whilst listening to the cries of curlews and oystercatchers as the sun went down.

27

Kentish Flats

The water shone pacifically; the sky, without a speck, was a
benign immensity of unstained light; the very mist on the Essex
marsh was like a gauzy and radiant fabric hung from the
wooded rises inland, and draping the low shores in diaphanous
folds. Only the gloom to the west, brooding over the upper
reaches, became more sombre every minute, as if angered by the
approach of the sun.

– *Heart of Darkness*, Joseph Conrad, 1899

John uncleated the mooring buoy alone in the early hours to allow us
the timeless experience of waking up under sail. The rhythmic rocking movement of the boat kept me sleeping until late morning. I finally
awoke to the sound of the keel gently scraping against the soft mud
of the riverbed. Rain was falling hard on the hatch above. I quickly
pulled on my waterproofs and poked my head up out of the companionway: it was a white-out: the edges of the riverbank had disappeared
in the mist and the water was an angry dark green.

The keel temporarily touched the bottom again as we left the
Swale, heading for Four Fathoms Channel. There was a moderate
breeze with a fair tide, but then the weather turned dramatically,
the winds reaching up to force seven. It was hard to see ahead but, as
we sailed back out into the mouth of the Estuary, travelling at a good
rate of knots, I saw the great wind turbines turning at the Kentish

Flats wind farm – the first offshore wind farm in the Thames Estuary. It was originally constructed as a thirty-turbine farm but fifteen new turbines will be installed there over the next few years. When fully operational, they will generate enough power for 42,000 homes in Kent. During the construction of these first few turbines, the noise created by piling the giant legs into the seabed was so loud that residents in Whitstable were kept awake at night as the sound echoed around the bay.

We kept skating across the riverbed on our way out of the Swale, not an uncommon experience, sailing on such a low tide, but rather frightening to me. Our skipper decided the best course of action was to take a short cut to get into deep water quickly, although he was aware there was still a chance of touching bottom. He was trying to find the Overland Passage, which extends from the west end of Horse Channel in a west-north-west direction across Kentish Flats to Four Fathoms Channel. The passage leads between sandbars on its north side and shoals extending from the Isle of Sheppey on its south. Numerous wrecks and obstructions lying in the vicinity of the Overland Passage

were visible on the chart. We hoped the charts were accurate, as we were reliant on them to find safe passage through the sandbanks.

John thought the incoming flood tide would help us along. We were travelling at a speed of five knots, trying to reach deep water on the last ebb of the Thames. There was a light chop at sea and a strong wind of twenty knots from the west, edging up to force six. The boat was pitching hard into the dark water. I could see white-capped waves further out in the Estuary. The sky was flat and white, with a band of deep grey along the horizon. Suddenly, the water depth on the guage dropped to below twelve feet. I was worried and told John the reading, and he nodded solemnly but did not look overly concerned, just told me to keep him closely informed.

Heeling to starboard, the depth reading went up to fifteen feet as we passed the Red Sands Sea Forts. As we sailed speedily along in the pouring rain, I stood beside John at the helm. I asked him if touching the bottom of the riverbed earlier that morning could have harmed *Jacomina* in any way. He explained that the soft mud of the riverbank

would not hurt the boat; however, if we ran aground on the shingle of the estuarine sandbanks, the damage could be serious.

Fingers of high, hard sand stretched out in all directions on either side. We were travelling at a speed of five and a half knots, close to the wind farm, when we came to a sudden halt: we were stuck on a small sandbar called East Spaniard. It was quite a moderate grounding but still forceful for a nineteen-ton boat and the vessel hobby-horsed forward and aft alarmingly.

Simon and John worked for some time, furling and unfurling the genoa before putting the engine in reverse to try to break free from the sandbank. Eventually, their efforts paid off and we were sailing once more, but within a few minutes we ran aground again, heavily this time and dangerously close to the wind turbines. The boat pitched dramatically, then began to heel right over. The echo sound read six feet and the keel was embedded two and a half feet in the sand, causing a great amount of strain. The rain was coming down in sheets, there was a strong wind and the sea was a menacing black-green and choppy. I gripped on to the side of the boat as electric fear coursed through my whole body. The violence of the crash brought back all the memories of my previous sailing accident as the boat began to heel over further to starboard. I tried to calm my rising panic and looked to John for reassurance, watching him closely to try to assess the danger of the situation we were in. I could see the anxiety in his face, although he remained cool and composed at all times. I knew I had to get out of his way: he had enough to deal with without worrying about me. With great difficulty, I managed to crawl along the steeply angled deck before sliding down the companionway. James was lying below deck, suffering with sea-sickness. It was hard to stand up, as the boat was heeling so much, and the sound of the waves battering against the sides of the boat was dreadful. I made my way into my cabin. My hands were shaking as I reached for my mobile phone. I was not really expecting to be able to get a signal out there, but somehow I got through to Jonny, who calmed me down a little and reassured me that this was quite a normal sailing experience out in the Estuary. At worst, he expected we might be stuck out there until the tide turned.

Simon came below deck to put the bilge pump on. I imagined the boat filling with water and felt physically sick. He gave my arm a quick squeeze before leaping back up the ladder to help John. I stood at the foot of the companionway, holding on to the handrail for support, staying in the shadows so that I could see what was going on above deck but they could not see me. I was afraid. During the course of researching this book I had learnt too much about the dangers of running aground on a sandbank out in the Thames Estuary. I knew that the *Montgomery*, *Juliana* and hundreds of others vessels over time had all either broken their backs or been smashed to pieces by waves after grounding on sandbanks, and we had the added danger of being extremely close to the wind turbines. If our rudder broke, we would not be able to sail away and could collide with the great metal legs of the turbines; it would be like throwing a matchstick model against a concrete wall. And even if we managed to get off the sandbank, there was a great risk of grounding again – we had no idea how to locate the deep water.

I watched from below as John radioed through on V HF Channel 16 for help. He got through to two support-and-maintenance vessels which were on site at the wind farm, but the first was unable to get a visual on our position and seemed reluctant to advise us. Luckily, someone on the second, *Valkyrie Whitstable*, jumped into the conversation and came to our aid. 'We can see you. If you sail near to the wind farm, there is deeper water there.' They warned us to be extremely careful; there was another working vessel laying cables with four anchors on the wind farm on our way out.

Finally, John and Simon managed to release *Jacomina* from the sandbank. I came back up on deck as they put up both sails. We turned north-west along the perimeter of the farm and immediately the depth started to shoal dramatically again. It was even more dangerous to ground out there in open water with a wave height of six feet, and John took to the radio once again. *Valkyrie* advised us to sail directly through the wind farm, where there was guaranteed deep water.

Travelling at a speed of six and a half knots, with the boat heeling right over to ensure the keel was angled away from the seabed as much as possible, we sailed right through the middle of the wind farm. Rows of giant turbines spun in the strong wind either side of us. It was still raining hard, with a good breeze, in excess of twenty-five knots, the wind at force six. John asked us to sit on the leeward side to help tip the boat further and reduce the draught. We were inches away from the water, spray was coming up over the deck of the boat – it was absolutely exhilarating. *Valkyrie* escorted us out, making sure we had safe passage to the edge of the farm, then the crew on board waved and turned back. For centuries, vessels at sea have assisted each other in all levels of difficulty like this. 'There is an unspoken code,' said John as he waved goodbye to our rescuers.

We sailed past the sea forts again. The millpond of the day before had been transformed into an entirely different landscape: wild, aggressive and dangerous. A mist had descended, obscuring the coastline on either side. It was a relief to be in the safer waters of the Knob Channel, but we were travelling at a dismal speed, there was a strong wind against us and a steep chop. We were all exhausted, the weather was dreadful and we were having difficulties finding a good berth in London, so a decision was made to cut the trip short and head for Chatham instead.

We tacked towards the Medway. With the wind and rain beating over us, I felt extremely cold. As I helmed us into the mouth of the river, a large container ship passed on our port side. We sailed past the three visible masts of the SS *Richard Montgomery* starboard,

which were covered in seabirds. The prohibited area around the stranded wreck was clearly marked by lighted buoys, which formed a circle around the site.

Two tugs came out of the Medway. I steered to starboard towards a green buoy, showing our intended course to the vessels. The wash of the container ship rocked the boat as the tugs chugged past. As we sailed along the Medway, past the circular forts where Stephen Turner had lived all those weeks, I could feel the adrenaline from earlier leave my body. I started to shake uncontrollably. I went below deck and lay on a sofa, wrapped in a blanket, shivering violently, but I just could not get warm.

We moored up in Chatham dock and debriefed below deck before going our separate ways. John was visibly upset, and I was so sorry that his long journey on *Jacomina* had ended this way. He is such an experienced sailor, he had read the charts thoroughly and calculated the tide height to plan our route, but even with all this, and the added support of depth readings and GPS, we had run aground.

Sandbanks move all the time and buoys are continually adjusted; nautical charts become little more than a record of a moment in time – abstractions of the actual landscape beneath the waves. Unlike most places out at sea, the contours of the Estuary shape-shift constantly with the wind and tides, sandbanks rise up and disappear again, safe channels can become danger zones overnight. I was reminded of the many fishermen and sailors I had spoken to who suspect this process has happened at a much greater rate since the DP World dredging began.

EPILOGUE

As you head west from the mouth of the Estuary into London, the distinctive shape of the giant quay cranes at the London Gateway Port dominates the horizon. They are situated close to Stanford-le-Hope, the village where Joseph Conrad began writing *Heart of Darkness*. The novel opens with a description of the Thames Estuary as the launching place of England's great ships, where Sir Francis Drake sailed past on the *Golden Hind*, which was full of treasure, capturing the imperial ambitions of the nation of the time: 'What greatness had not floated on the ebb of that river into the mystery of an unknown earth! . . . The dreams of men, the seed of commonwealths, the germs of empires.'

Over a century later, this language sounds eerily close to the marketing copy used for the new DP World super port, which aims to become the new gateway for globalization to the UK, with deep-sea access for the 'largest container ships the world has ever seen'. Within the next few years, the London Gateway Port will be completed: it will be the most automated deep-water super port in the world.

I visited the place myself. It looks completely different from anywhere else along the Estuary foreshore, with acres of desert-like sand fields, new roads, surveillance systems, mirrored office buildings and an extremely clean, clinical, almost silent, high-functioning quayside dominated by colossal quay cranes. Few workers were visible on site. Containers were lifted from the ships by automated cranes, then moved around by automated electric trucks operated by people in an office building sitting in front of computer screens. The equipment at the port is hybrid – part diesel, part electric – which means that when a crane goes down it generates power for the next one to go up. Outside, 'the boxes are everywhere, mobile and anonymous, their contents hidden from view' (*The Forgotten Space*, 2010, Noël Burch and Alan Sekula).

DP World have clearly worked hard to keep the construction process as sustainable as possible, in terms of materials, water and energy management. Their environmental and ecological programme is also impressive: they have created new natural habitats for over 320,000 animals; they have cut ditches, scrapes and fleets for birdlife, dug out new ponds and enhanced old bodies of water to create the right depth for rare great-crested newts. Contaminated soil from the decommissioned oil refinery has been cleaned up and recycled. They have built a public bridleway around the site and another nature reserve, working with local schools, the Essex Wildlife Trust and the Royal Society for the Preservation of Birds.

Thousands of jobs will eventually be created for local people at the London Gateway Port and in the surrounding logistics park. The discovery of the Roman salt works, along with the

rediscovery of the *London* and the examination and preservation of many other significant shipwrecks and archaeological finds in the Estuary have all been made possible because of funding by DP World.

'The chaps from Tilbury Docks, the stevedores and the lashers, wanted to come and have a look at this place,' said the environment officer who showed me around. 'They were absolutely astounded. The working environment, the gym facilities, the canteen – they could not believe it.' Many people locally are positive about the new port. Keith Toms, the retired river tugman, said: 'It won't be the same as the docks in my day, but it's better than the void that was left after the docks shut down. I remember, we went into the Royal Docks when it was finishing . . . The desolation still makes me feel emotional. It was just empty. Now you can look at the new port and say, "Maybe life is coming back to the river."'

Globally, sea trade is booming. Ninety per cent of the world's cargo is now transported by sea, on the biggest ships ever constructed. The largest of these deep-hulled container ships are over five storeys high, more than 1,300 feet long, and with a capacity to hold 18,000 containers. They consume up to 380 tons of fuel per day and emit as much pollution as 50 million cars in one year. These giant vessels are the biggest single polluters of the environment on our planet – yet they are a much more eco-friendly method of transporting freight than by road or air, more fuel-efficient per volume shipped than either of the alternatives.

The majority of the cargo on the behemoths travelling up the Thames Estuary to the new port will have been manufactured in China and the Far East. Burch and Sekula's epic documentary *The Forgotten Space* (2010) explores the modern story of globalization and the sea by tracking contemporary maritime trade through the 'life history' of containers. The filmmakers traversed the globe, shooting footage on container ships, in factories, dockyards and freight warehouses, focusing on the testimony of the (often) marginalized people found working in the industry today, often under deplorable working conditions.

The Forgotten Space looks inside the contemporary sea economy of the container ship, revealing the true price that people all over the world are paying for the West's insatiable desire for cheap goods. The majority of such goods will now enter Britain via the Estuary and the London Gateway Port, exerting their toll on the environment and the local ecology.

The impact of the dredging on the fragile ecosystem of the Thames Estuary may have already been extremely damaging, as many people I spoke to whilst researching this book seem to believe. Even the young environment officer who showed me around said, 'I can't look you in the eye and say that the dredging work has not had an impact on the river, but it will recover. It is a strong environment. It will come back.' I expect he is right. In the 1950s, the Thames Estuary was declared biologically dead. Now, seals and other wildlife are thriving and the water is cleaner than ever – but the long-term impact of hundreds of thousands of container ships moving along the

Estuary, polluting the atmosphere and the water of this unique environment, may yet prove to be catastrophic and irreversible.

The new port has already begun to shape and define the future use and character of this historic waterway. When I walked along the coastline with Iain Sinclair, we visited Tilbury Fort and spoke to a man at the reception desk. He talked dolefully about the bright lights of the container port's twenty-four-hour city, the lorries coming and going all the time, the sirens and hooters creating a throbbing, electronic zone that now dominates all the former places of melancholic memory along that coast.

The development of the new port and the big ships that travel there from around the globe are part of the continual battle over the space of the Estuary. In the late nineteenth century, steam and sail were in direct conflict over the same territory. Laws were being challenged about the rights of way on the Estuary of sail-powered vessels, and the courts were not able to control the behaviour of steam-powered ships around the wind-powered ships; it was left to the discretion of the captains of the steamships. The Victorian author Richard Jefferies's essay 'The Modern Thames' discusses the newly untouchable steamship and tugboat pilots: 'They were above the law by virtue of the technological power they were in command of, everything had to get out of their way.'

'Big ships have obviously been coming into this stretch of water since before the Armada,' said poet Justin Hopper, 'but during the Victorian era it happened too quickly. The fishing community had no time to make any adjustments; the steamships were literally slicing through these little fishing smacks. Throughout history, in this location, someone is a victim of the sea grab going on in the Estuary.'

As I disembarked on my final journey for this project, I thought back to that first boat trip on *Ideeal* over five years before and realized that, since that time, I had achieved little more than to capture some moments, to document an interactive encounter with these locations, to gather personal testimonies and recollections that hopefully resonate within a wider experience of this place. In the end, I feel I have created a kind of collective memory map, attempting to highlight what lies under the watermark, what has been obliterated, what is being obliterated and what is still under threat in this indefinable and beautiful place where past flows into present into past in its eternal rhythm.

ACKNOWLEDGEMENTS

This book has taken over five years to research and write and would not have been possible without the help of countless individuals. I would like to thank, above all, my sons, David and Daniel, and my parents, Tony and Nancy, for their considerable support to me whilst I was writing this book. A very special thanks to Kirstie Imber, my intern, whose excellent work on this project transcribing many of the oral history interviews and providing support and advice has been absolutely invaluable. I am also very grateful to my editor, Simon Prosser, at Hamish Hamilton for his continued support of my work and for his patience; the boat trips were particularly hard to organize and, subsequently, the manuscript was delivered much later than originally anticipated. Thanks also to Hermione Thompson for her careful edits, to Anna Ridley and to the rest of the team at Hamish Hamilton, and a special thanks also to my agent, Laura Longrigg, at MBA. Special thanks also to Brian and Jo Wells for being my readers and for all their encouragement and help, and a very special thanks to Jonny Wells, whose editorial help and support throughout has been exceptional. A very special thanks also to John Dickens for his great advice on nautical terminology and support. It was my great pleasure to meet John as an interviewee whilst writing this book; he became a really good friend over the following years, someone I very much admired and had lots of good times with. Tragically, John died of a short and aggressive illness the day I finished writing this book, which has been dedicated to him in his memory. He will be sorely missed by me and by many others in the small fishing community of Leigh-on-Sea.

Much thanks to the Arts Council, who funded both the residency on *Ideeal* and a later Estuary project, *Hadleigh: Experience of Place*, both of which informed this book. Thanks to Colette Bailey and the Metal team, for giving me the time and space to write this book during a residency at Chalkwell Hall in 2015 and for allowing me to curate the *Salon* series of events and the Shorelines Literary Festival of the Sea, which led to a new way of thinking about Essex and the Thames Estuary, as did the winter weekends at Snape Maltings curated by Gareth Evans.

A very special thanks to Simon Callery, who had the original idea to take the cruise along the Estuary back in 2010, and to Ben Eastop for allowing us to use *Ideeal*, his boat and his home, to make that journey. Thanks to crewmates Luke Eastop, Sefryn Penrose, James Price and, particularly, John Eacott, who generously took me out again in *Jacomina* to the outer reaches in 2015. And thank you, Lena Eacott, for letting us use your beautiful boat! Many thanks also to James and Michael Bates, for taking me cockling and to Sealand, and to the many other people who took me out on boats and generously shared their stories with me for this book, often taking time out of their busy work schedules to do so. For this, I am extremely grateful to: Mike Barrington, Barto, Mark Bradford, Vanessa Bradford, Basil Brambleby, Tim Browne, Clive Brummage (Brum), John Cotgrove, Ken Crow, Joan Darwell, Brian Dawson, John Dickens, Jane Dolby, James Elford (River Jim), Carol Ellis, Steve Ellis, Chris Fenwick, Jack Fenwick, Andrew Francis, Fran Gallardo, Paul Gilson, Luisa Hagele, Malcolm Hall, Graham Harwood, Julian Hoffman, Justin Hopper, Peter Lily, Paul Jeffries, Lynn Jones, Sue Jones, Pauline Judd, Tom King, Steve Kurtz, Robert Macfarlane, Chloe Dewe Mathews, Barry Meddle, Alan Mills, Gill Moore, Syd Moore, Ian Ruffles, Rob Sargent, Nastassja Simensky, Dave Simmons, Iain Sinclair, Helen Skellorn, Rob Smith, Germander Speedwell, Keith Toms, Jane Trowell, Stephen Turner, Brian Wells, Jonny Wells, Ken Worpole, Professor Patrick Wright and Matsuko Yokokoji. Special thanks also to Sorcha Daly, who generously allowed me to use excerpts from recordings of fishermen's wives she originally made for her project *The Seagull That Lived in the Shower*: Lara Hurley, Heather Gilson, Linda Spurgeon, Nola Baker and Rosemarie Godbold.

Many institutions have helped tremendously during this project, including: *Aeon* Magazine, Artevents, Arts Catalyst, Arts Council England and Arts Council East, the Bay Museum and Research Centre, Benfleet Yacht Club, the British Library, the *Cambria* Trust, Canvey Yacht Club, Chatham Historic Dockyard, Critical Art Ensemble, DP World, English Heritage, English Nature, the Environment Agency, Essex Record Office, Essex Wildlife Trust, Essex Yacht Club, Focal Point Gallery, Friends of the North Kent Marshes, Gravesend Sailing Club, Kent and Essex Inshore Fisheries Conservation, Leigh Heritage Centre, London Gateway Port, London Tilbury Cruise Terminal, Lower Thames Rowing Club, the Maritime Coastguard Agency, Medway Port Authority, Metal, the National Maritime Museum, the Natural History Museum, the Nautical Archaeology Society, Oxford Archaeology, Platform, Project Redsand, Prouts, the Port of London Authority, the principality of Sealand, the RSPB, the Seafort Project, Shell Haven Project Environmental Action Committee, South Eastern Tug Society, Southend Library, Southend Museum, Thurrock Friends of the Earth, Tilbury Docks, Topsail Charters, Wessex Archaeology, Whitstable Biennale and YoHa. I am extremely grateful to them all.

And a huge thank you to those who have given me permission to use their wonderful images in this book, particularly James Price and Simon Fowler who accompanied me on many of my estuarine journeys. Simon Fowler's photographs can be found on pages: 28, 35, 49, 54, 87, 96, 97, 98, 99, 111, 128, 129, 173, 179, 199, 200, 202, 217, 230, 238, 245, 246, 249, 250, 252, 254, 259, 261, 264, 266, 267, 277, 285, 287, 289, 291, 297, 300, 302, 305, 306, 308, 309, 312, 313 and 316; James Price's on pages: 38, 64, 67, 130, 137, 161, 189, 198 and 276. Thanks also to the Bishopsgate Institute archives for allowing me to use the

ACKNOWLEDGEMENTS

images on pages 5 and 93, to Michael Bates pages 168, 170 and 171, Tim Browne 118, John Cotgrove 113, Jane Dolby 163, Gary Fisher 110, Chris Fenwick 144, 146, Graham Harwood 240, Julian Hoffman 223, Leigh Heritage Centre 155, 157, 273 and 275, David Hasan Lichtenstein 224, Nigel Luckhurst 107, National Maritime Museum, 134, Chloe Dewe Matthews pages 213 and 219, The Seafort Project, 181 and 177, Southend Museum, 125, 138, Nastassja Simensky, 140, Jonny Wells, 120. Images on pages 8, 73, 125, 233 are from private collections. The author has been unable to find the copyright holder for images of the Montgomery on pages 30 and 82. Unless otherwise mentioned above, the rest of the photographs were taken by Rachel Lichtenstein.

Certain books and films have been particularly influential and inspirational. Rather than listing them in a separate bibliography, I have tried wherever possible to mention them within the text. However, I would also like to thank the authors of the following works for paving the way for me. William Addison, *Thames Estuary* (1954), is the only other book I could find on the subject. Many works by local historians and authors have been invaluable to my research, including: Michael Bates, *Holding Down the Fort* (2015), Jane Dolby, *Song of the Sea* (2015), Carol Edwards, *The Life and Times of the Houseboats of Leigh-on-Sea* (2009), Paul Gilson, *Sole Searching* (2011), Robert Hallmann, *Canvey Island* (2006), and Tony Moon, *Down by the Jetty: The Dr Feelgood Story* (2010). I'm also very grateful to Patrick Wright for his excellent book *The River: The Thames in Our Time* (1999) and for introducing me to Uwe Johnson's essay 'An Unfathomable Ship' (*Granta*, 1979). Many thanks also to William Raban; his *Thames Film* (1986) had a huge impact on my way of thinking about the Estuary, as did Joseph Conrad's great work of non-fiction and memoir, *The Mirror of the Sea* (1906), which informs this text throughout.

Websites

www.cambriabargecharter.co.uk
www.chloedewemathews.com
www.drfeelgood.org
www.essexyachtclub.co.uk
www.fishermensmission.org.uk
www.fishwiveschoir.co.uk
www.metalculture.com/projects/estuary-festival
www.nigelluckhurst.co.uk
www.northkentmarshes.org.uk
www.platformlondon.org
www.project-redsand.com
www.rachellichtenstein.com
www.sdoralhistory.blogspot.co.uk
www.seafort.org
www.sealandgov.org
www.simon-fowler.co.uk
www.thelondonwreckproject.co.uk
www.yoha.co.uk/wrecked

GLOSSARY

Astern Manoeuvring a vessel backwards; to the rear of the vessel

Barge A towed or self-propelled flat-bottomed boat, built mainly for river, canal and coastal transport of heavy goods

Bawley A broad-beamed, shallow-draught, cutter-rigged fishing boat used for shrimping in the Thames Estuary. The name derives from the 'boiler' fitted on the boats by shrimpers to cook the catch on the way back to port

Bilge Lower point of the inner hull of a ship

Boom A spar attached to the foot of a sail

Bow The front of a boat

Bow line A mooring line tied to the bow (a bowline is a knot)

Bowsprit A spar that extends at the bows of a ship

Brail To furl a sail by pulling it in towards the mast, or the ropes used to do so

Catamaran A twin-hulled boat

Close-hauled Sailing to windward with the sails sheeted in

Coaster A shallow-hulled ship used for trade

Cutter A small, single-masted boat with two or more headsails and often a bowsprit

Derrick A lifting device composed of one mast or pole and a boom or jib

Ensign A red, white or blue flag with a Union Jack at the top corner next to the flag staff flown by British-registered ships and boats

Estuary One Design (EOD) Originally made as a wooden clinker racing dinghy, designed by Morgan Giles in 1919

Fin keel A boat's single keel, shaped like an inverted dorsal fin

Fo'c'sle /forecastle The forward part of a ship below the deck, traditionally used as the crew's living quarters

Foredeck The deck at the forward part of a boat or ship

Foresail A triangular sail set at the bow of a boat

Gaff A spar on a traditionally rigged vessel such as a Thames barge

Gaff-rigged A boat rigged with a four-cornered sail supported by a spar or gaff which extends aft from the mast

Genoa A large, triangular foresail that overlaps the mainsail

Gybe A sailing manoeuvre that involves swinging a sail or boom across the boat in a following wind

Halyard A rope or tackle for hoisting and lowering sails

Horse Attachment of sheets to the deck of the vessel (mainsheet horse)

Hull The shell and framework of a boat

ISO A fourteen-foot, two-man trapeze boat with an asymmetrical spinnaker

Jack stays Safety lines that run along a boat's deck to enable sailors to attach themselves to the boat via a harness

Jib A small, triangular foresail

Keel The central structural basis of the hull

Kent and Essex IFCA Kent and Essex Inshore Fisheries Conservation

Ketch A two-masted sailboat

Knot A unit of speed: 1 nautical mile (1.852 km; 1.1508 mile) per hour

Leeboard Wood or metal attachments to the hull to prevent leeway

Leeward On or towards the side sheltered from the wind (opposite to windward)

Lighter An unpowered, flat-bottomed barge used to transfer goods and passengers to and from moored ships

Mainsail Principal sail on a ship's main mast

Mast A vertical pole on a ship, which supports sails or rigging

Mate The person on a boat who is second in charge after the captain

Mizzen – The small mast at the rear of a two-masted ketch or yawl

MMO Marine Monitoring Organisation

Pongoes A British slang term for soldiers, dating from the nineteenth century

Port When facing forward, the left-hand side of a ship

Ratline A small rope forming a rung of a rope ladder on a ship

RIB A rigid inflatable boat

Rigging The system of masts and lines on ships and other sailing vessels

Ro-ro Vessel with 'roll-on/roll-off' facilities

Rudder A steering device

Schooner A type of sailing vessel with two or more masts, typically with the foremast being smaller than the main mast

Skiff A small boat, traditionally a coastal or river craft, for leisure or fishing, which can be crewed by one person

Skipper The ship's captain

Smack A traditional fishing boat used in England and the Atlantic coast of America for most of the nineteenth century

Spar A ship's mast, boom, yard or gaff

Spinnaker A large, three-cornered, lightweight sail carried in front of the mast when the wind is astern

Sprit A spar crossing a four-cornered sail diagonally

Spritsail rig A four-cornered sail extended by a sprit

Starboard When facing forward, the right-hand side of a ship

Stern The back part of a ship

Stevedore A person employed at a dock to load and unload ships

Telegraph A heavy brass instrument used as a communicating device between the bridge and the engine room

Telltales Small lengths of cloth or wool on either side of a sail to indicate airflow

Tender A boat used to service or support other, larger boats

Third hand A licensed crew member of a merchant ship; fourth, or on some ocean liners, fifth in command

Topsail A ship's sail above the mainsail

Trawler Either a fishing boat that uses a trawl net to catch fish or a fisherman who uses a trawl net

Tug A boat that manoeuvres other vessels by pushing or towing them

Wayfarer A wooden- or fibreglass-hulled, Bermuda-rigged sailing dinghy

Wheelhouse A shelter where the ship's steering wheel is kept

Winch A mechanical device used to adjust the tension of a rope

Windlass A winch used to raise a ship's anchor

Yawing To twist or oscillate about a vertical axis